CORNELIUS RYAN

The Longest Day

JUNE 6, 1944

SIMON AND SCHUSTER · NEW YORK · 1959

*Lines from the song "I Double Dare You" copyright
MCMXXXVII by Shapiro, Bernstein & Co., Inc.,
New York. By permission of the publisher.*

Portions of this book appeared originally in
Reader's Digest

W

LIBRARY OF CONGRESS CATALOG CARD NUMBER: 59-9499
MANUFACTURED IN THE UNITED STATES OF AMERICA
BY H. WOLFF BOOK MFG. CO., INC., NEW YORK

FOR ALL THE MEN OF D DAY

CONTENTS

"Believe me, Lang, the first twenty-four hours of the invasion will be decisive . . . the fate of Germany depends on the outcome . . . for the Allies, as well as Germany, it will be the longest day."

—*Field Marshal Erwin Rommel*
to his aide, April 22, 1944

FOREWORD

D Day, Tuesday, June 6, 1944

OPERATION OVERLORD, *the Allied invasion of Europe, began at precisely fifteen minutes after midnight on June 6, 1944—in the first hour of a day that would be forever known as D Day. At that moment a few specially chosen men of the American 101st and 82nd airborne divisions stepped out of their planes into the moonlit night over Normandy. Five minutes later and fifty miles away a small group of men from the British 6th Airborne Division plunged out of their planes. These were the pathfinders, the men who were to light the dropping zones for the paratroopers and glider-borne infantry that were soon to follow.*

The Allied airborne armies clearly marked the extreme limits of the Normandy battlefield. Between them and along the French coastline lay five invasion beaches: Utah, Omaha, Gold, Juno and Sword. Through the predawn hours as paratroopers fought in the dark hedgerows of Normandy, the greatest armada the world had ever known began to assemble off those beaches—almost five thousand ships carrying more than two hundred thousand soldiers, sailors and coastguardmen. Beginning at 6:30 A.M. and preceded by a massive naval and air bombardment, a few thousand of these men waded ashore in the first wave of the invasion.

What follows is not a military history. It is the story of people: the men of the Allied forces, the enemy they fought and the civilians who were caught up in the bloody confusion of D Day— the day the battle began that ended Hitler's insane gamble to dominate the world.

PART ONE

The Wait

★ 1 ★

THE VILLAGE was silent in the damp June morning. Its name was La Roche-Guyon and it had sat undisturbed for nearly twelve centuries in a great lazy loop of the Seine roughly midway between Paris and Normandy. For years it had been just a place that people passed through on their way to somewhere else. Its only distinction was its castle, the seat of the Dukes de La Roche-foucauld. It was this castle jutting out from the backdrop of hills behind the village that had brought an end to the peace of La Roche-Guyon.

On this gray morning the castle loomed up over everything, its massive stones glistening with dampness. It was almost 6 A.M., but nothing stirred in the two great cobbled courtyards. Outside the gates the main road stretched broad and empty, and in the village the windows of the red-roofed houses were still shuttered. La Roche-Guyon was very quiet—so quiet that it appeared to be deserted. But the silence was deceptive. Behind the shuttered windows people waited for a bell to ring.

At 6 A.M. the bell in the fifteenth-century Church of St. Samson next to the castle would sound the Angelus. In more peaceful days it had had a simple meaning—in La Roche-Guyon the villagers would cross themselves and pause for a moment of prayer. But now the Angelus meant much more than a moment of meditation. This morning when the bell rang it would mark the end of the night's curfew and the beginning of the 1,451st day of German occupation.

Everywhere in La Roche-Guyon there were sentries. Huddled in their camouflage capes, they stood inside both gates of the castle, at road blocks at each end of the village, in pillboxes built flush into the chalk outcroppings of the foothills and in the crumbling ruins of an old tower on the highest hill above the castle. From up there machine gunners could see everything that moved in this, the most occupied village in all of occupied France.

Behind its pastoral front La Roche-Guyon was really a prison; for every one of the 543 villagers, in and around the area there were more than three German soldiers. One of these soldiers was Field Marshal Erwin Rommel, commander in chief of Army Group B, the most powerful force in the German west. His headquarters was in the castle of La Roche-Guyon.

From here in this crucial fifth year of World War II, a tense, determined Rommel prepared to fight the most desperate battle of his career. Under his command more than half a million men manned defenses along a tremendous length of coastline—stretching almost eight hundred miles, from the dikes of Holland to the Atlantic-washed shores of the Brittany peninsula. His main strength, the Fifteenth Army, was concentrated about the Pas-de-Calais, at the narrowest point of the Channel between France and England.

Night after night, Allied bombers hit this area. Bomb-weary veterans of the Fifteenth Army bitterly joked that the place for a rest cure was in the zone of the Seventh Army in Normandy. Hardly a bomb had fallen there.

For months, behind a fantastic jungle of beach obstacles and mine fields, Rommel's troops had waited in their concrete coastal fortifications. But the blue-gray English Channel had remained empty of ships. Nothing had happened. From La Roche-Guyon, on this gloomy and peaceful Sunday morning, there was still no sign of the Allied invasion. It was June 4, 1944.

14

★ 2 ★

IN THE ground-floor room he used as an office, Rommel was alone. He sat behind a massive Renaissance desk, working by the light of a single desk lamp. The room was large and high-ceilinged. Along one wall stretched a faded Gobelin tapestry. On another the haughty face of Duke François de La Rochefoucauld —a seventeenth-century writer of maxims and an ancestor of the present Duke—looked down out of a heavy gold frame. There were a few chairs casually placed on the highly polished parquet floor and thick draperies at the windows, but little else.

In particular, there was nothing of Rommel in this room but himself. There were no photographs of his wife Lucie-Maria or his fifteen-year-old son Manfred. There were no mementos of his great victories in the North African deserts in the early days of the war—not even the garish field marshal's baton which Hitler had so exuberantly bestowed upon him in 1942. (Only once had Rommel carried the eighteen-inch, three-pound gold baton with its red velvet covering studded with gold eagles and black swastikas: that was the day he got it.) There wasn't even a map showing the dispositions of his troops. The legendary "Desert Fox" remained as elusive and shadowy as ever; he could have walked out of that room without leaving a trace.

Although the fifty-one-year-old Rommel looked older than his years, he remained as tireless as ever. Nobody at Army Group B could remember a single night when he had slept longer than five hours. This morning, as usual, he had been up since before four. Now he too waited impatiently for six o'clock. At that time he would breakfast with his staff—and then depart for Germany.

This would be Rommel's first leave at home in months. He would go by car; Hitler had made it almost impossible for senior officers to fly by insisting that they use "three-engined aircraft . . . and always with a fighter escort." Rommel disliked flying anyway; he would make the eight-hour journey home, to Herrlingen, Ulm, in his big black convertible Horch.

He was looking forward to the trip, but the decision to go had not been an easy one to make. On Rommel's shoulders lay the enormous responsibility of repulsing the Allied assault the moment it began. Hitler's Third Reich was reeling from one disaster after another; day and night thousands of Allied bombers pounded Germany, Russia's massive forces had driven into Poland, Allied troops were at the gates of Rome—everywhere the great armies of the Wehrmacht were being driven back and destroyed. Germany was still far from beaten, but the Allied invasion would be the decisive battle. Nothing less than the future of Germany was at stake, and no one knew it better than Rommel.

Yet this morning Rommel was going home. For months he had hoped to spend a few days in Germany the first part of June. There were many reasons why he now believed he could leave, and although he would never have admitted it, he desperately needed rest. Just a few days earlier he had telephoned his superior, the aged Field Marshal Gerd von Rundstedt, Commander in Chief West, requesting permission to make the trip; the request had been immediately granted. Next he had made a courtesy call to Von Rundstedt's headquarters at St.-Germain-en-Laye, outside of Paris, to take his leave formally. Both Von Rundstedt and his chief of staff, Major General Günther Blumentritt, had been shocked at Rommel's haggard appearance. Blumentritt would always remember that Rommel looked "tired and tense . . . a man who needed to be home for a few days with his family."

Rommel *was* tense and edgy. From the very day he arrived in France toward the end of 1943, the problems of where and how to meet the Allied attack had imposed on him an almost intolerable burden. Like everybody else along the invasion front, he had been living through a nightmare of suspense. Hanging over him always was the need to outthink the Allies as to their probable intentions—how they would launch the attack, where they would attempt to land and, above all, when.

Only one person really knew the strain that Rommel was under. To his wife, Lucie-Maria, he confided everything. In less than four months he had written her more than forty letters and in almost every other letter he had made a new prediction about the Allied assault.

On March 30 he wrote: "Now that March is nearing its end and without the Anglo-Americans having started their attack . . . I'm beginning to believe they have lost confidence in their cause."

On April 6: "Here the tension is growing from day to day . . . It will probably be only weeks that separate us from the decisive events . . ."

On April 26: "In England morale is bad . . . there is one strike after another and the cries of 'Down with Churchill and the Jews' and for peace are getting louder . . . these are bad omens for such a risky offensive."

On April 27: "It appears now that the British and Americans are not going to be so accommodating as to come in the immediate future."

On May 6: "Still no signs of the British and Americans . . . Every day, every week . . . we get stronger. . . . I am looking forward to the battle with confidence . . . perhaps it will come on May 15, perhaps at the end of the month."

On May 15: "I can't take many more big [inspection] trips . . .

17

because one never knows when the invasion will begin. I believe only a few more weeks remain until things begin here in the west."

On May 19: "I hope I can get ahead with my plans faster than before . . . [but] I am wondering if I can spare a few days in June to get away from here. Right now there isn't a chance."

But there was a chance after all. One of the reasons for Rommel's decision to leave at this time was his own estimate of the Allies' intentions. Before him now on the desk was Army Group B's weekly report. This meticulously compiled evaluation was due to be sent by noon of the following day to Field Marshal von Rundstedt's headquarters, or, as it was generally known in military jargon, OB West (*Oberbefehlshaber West*). From there after further embroidery it would become part of the over-all theater report and then it would be forwarded to Hitler's headquarters, OKW (*Oberkommando der Wehrmacht**).

Rommel's estimate read in part that the Allies had reached a "high degree of readiness" and that there was an "increased volume of messages going to the French resistance." But, it went on, "according to past experience this is not indicative that an invasion is imminent . . ."

This time Rommel had guessed wrong.

I**N THE OFFICE** of the chief of staff, down the corridor from the Field Marshal's study, Captain Hellmuth Lang, Rommel's thirty-six-year-old aide, picked up the morning report. It was always his

* Armed Forces High Command.

first chore for the commander in chief. Rommel liked to get the report early so that he could discuss it with his staff at breakfast. But there was nothing much in it this morning; the invasion front remained quiet except for the continuing nightly bombing of the Pas-de-Calais. There seemed no doubt about it: Besides all the other indications, this marathon bombing pointed to the Pas-de-Calais as the place the Allies had chosen for their attack. If they were going to invade at all it would be there. Nearly everybody seemed to think so.

Lang looked at his watch; it was a few minutes of 6 A.M. They would leave at seven sharp and they should make good time. There was no escort, just two cars, Rommel's and one belonging to Colonel Hans George von Tempelhof, Army Group B's operations officer, who was going along with them. As usual, the various military commanders in the areas through which they would pass had not been informed of the Field Marshal's plans. Rommel liked it that way; he hated to be delayed by the fuss and protocol of heel-clicking commanders and motorcycle escorts awaiting him at the entrance to each city. So with a bit of luck they should reach Ulm about three.

There was the usual problem: what to take along for the Field Marshal's lunch. Rommel did not smoke, rarely drank, and cared so little for food that he sometimes forgot to eat. Often when going over the arrangements for a long journey with Lang, Rommel would run a pencil through the proposed luncheon and write in big black letters "Simple field kitchen meal." Sometimes he would confuse Lang even more by saying, "Of course, if you want to throw in a chop or two that won't bother me." The attentive Lang never quite knew what to order from the kitchen. This morning, besides a vacuum jug of consommé, he had ordered an assortment of sandwiches. His guess was that Rommel, as usual, would forget about lunch anyway.

Lang left the office and walked down the oak-paneled corridor. From the rooms on either side of him came the hum of conversation and the clacking of typewriters; Army Group B headquarters was an extremely busy place now. Lang had often wondered how the Duke and the Duchess, who occupied the floors above, could possibly sleep through all the noise.

At the end of the corridor Lang stopped before a massive door. He knocked gently, turned the handle and walked in. Rommel did not look up. He was so engrossed in the papers before him that he seemed quite unaware that his aide had entered the room, but Lang knew better than to interrupt. He stood waiting.

Rommel glanced up from his desk. "Good morning, Lang," he said.

"Good morning, Field Marshal. The report." Lang handed it over. Then he left the room and waited outside the door to escort Rommel down to breakfast. The Field Marshal seemed extremely busy this morning. Lang, who knew how impulsive and changeable Rommel could be, wondered if they were really leaving after all.

Rommel had no intention of canceling the trip. Although no definite appointment had yet been made, he hoped to see Hitler. All field marshals had access to the Führer, and Rommel had telephoned his old friend, Major General Rudolf Schmundt, Hitler's adjutant, requesting an appointment. Schmundt thought the meeting could be arranged sometime between the sixth and the ninth. It was typical of Rommel that nobody outside of his own staff knew that he intended to see Hitler. In the official diaries at Rundstedt's headquarters, it was simply noted that Rommel was spending a few days' leave at home.

Rommel was quite confident that he could leave his headquarters at this time. Now that May had passed—and it had been a month of perfect weather for the Allied attack—he had reached the conclusion that the invasion would not come for several more weeks. He was so confident of this that he had even set a deadline for the completion of all anti-invasion obstacle programs. On his desk was an order to the Seventh and Fifteenth armies. "Every possible effort," it read, "must be made to complete obstacles so as to make a low-tide landing possible only at extreme cost to the enemy . . . work must be pushed forward . . . completion is to be reported to my headquarters by June 20."

He now reasoned—as did Hitler and the German High Command—that the invasion would take place either simultaneously with the Red Army's summer offensive, or shortly after. The Russian attack, they knew, could not begin until the late thaw in Poland, and therefore they did not think the offensive could be mounted until the latter part of June.

In the west the weather had been bad for several days, and it promised to be even worse. The 5 A.M. report, prepared by Colonel Professor Walter Stöbe, the Luftwaffe's chief meteorologist in Paris, predicted increasing cloudiness, high winds and rain. Even now a twenty- to thirty-mile-an-hour wind was blowing in the Channel. To Rommel, it seemed hardly likely that the Allies would dare launch their attack during the next few days.

Even at La Roche-Guyon, during the night, the weather had changed. Almost opposite Rommel's desk two tall French windows opened out onto a terraced rose garden. It was not much of a rose garden this morning—rose petals, broken branches and twigs were strewn all over. Shortly before dawn a brief summer storm had come out of the English Channel, swept along part of the French coast and then passed on.

Rommel opened the door of his office and stepped out. "Good morning, Lang," he said, as though he had not seen his aide until that moment. "Are we ready to go?" Together they went down to breakfast.

Outside in the village of La Roche-Guyon the bell in the Church of St. Samson sounded the Angelus. Each note fought for its existence against the wind. It was 6 A.M.

B<small>ETWEEN</small> Rommel and Lang an easy, informal relationship existed. They had been constantly together for months. Lang had joined Rommel in February and hardly a day had passed since without a long inspection trip somewhere. Usually they were on the road by 4:30 A.M., driving at top speed to some distant part of Rommel's command. One day it would be Holland, another day Belgium, the next day Normandy or Brittany. The determined Field Marshal had taken advantage of every moment. "I have only one real enemy now," he had told Lang, "and that is time." To conquer time Rommel spared neither himself nor his men; it had been that way from the moment he had been sent to France in November 1943.

That fall Von Rundstedt, responsible for the defense of all Western Europe, had asked Hitler for reinforcements. Instead, he had got the hardheaded, daring and ambitious Rommel. To the humiliation of the aristocratic sixty-eight-year-old Commander in Chief West, Rommel arrived with a *Gummibefehl,* an "elastic directive," ordering him to inspect the coastal fortifications—Hitler's much-publicized "Atlantic Wall"—and then to report directly back to the Führer's headquarters, OKW. The embarrassed and disappointed Von Rundstedt was so upset by the arrival of the younger Rommel—he referred to him as the *"Marschall Bubi"* (roughly, the "Marshal Laddie")—that he asked Field Marshal Wilhelm Keitel, Chief of OKW, if Rommel was being considered as his successor. He was told "not to draw any false conclusions," that with all "Rommel's capabilities he is not up to that job."

Shortly after his arrival, Rommel had made a whirlwind inspection of the Atlantic Wall—and what he saw appalled him. In only a few places were the massive concrete and steel fortifications along the coast completed: at the principal ports and river mouths and overlooking the straits, roughly from above Le Havre to Holland. Elsewhere the defenses were in various stages of completion. In some places work had not even begun. True, the Atlantic Wall was a formidable barrier even in its present state. Where it was finished, it fairly bristled with heavy guns. But there were not enough of them to suit Rommel. There was not enough of anything to stop the sort of onslaught that Rommel— always remembering his crushing defeat at the hands of Montgomery in North Africa the year before—knew must surely come. To his critical eye the Atlantic Wall was a farce. Using one of the most descriptive words in any language, he had denounced it as a "figment of Hitler's *Wolkenkuckucksheim* [cloud cuckoo land]."

Just two years before, the wall had hardly existed at all.

Up to 1942 victory had seemed so certain to the Führer and his strutting Nazis that there was no need for coastal fortifications. The swastika flew everywhere. Austria and Czechoslovakia had been picked off before the war even started. Poland had been carved up between Germany and Russia as long ago as 1939. The war was not even a year old when the countries of Western Europe began falling like so many rotten apples. Denmark fell in a day. Norway, infiltrated from within, took a little longer: six weeks. Then that May and June, in just twenty-seven days and without overture of any sort, Hitler's blitzkrieging troops had plunged into Holland, Belgium, Luxembourg, France, and, as an incredulous world watched, had driven the British into the sea at Dunkirk. After the collapse of France all that remained was England—standing alone. What need had Hitler for a "wall"?

But Hitler didn't invade England. His generals wanted him to,

23

but Hitler waited, thinking the British would sue for peace. As time passed the situation rapidly changed. With U.S. aid, Britain began staging a slow but sure recovery. Hitler, by now deeply involved in Russia—he attacked the Soviet Union in June 1941— saw that the coast of France was no longer an offensive springboard. It was now a soft spot in his defenses. By the fall of 1941 he began talking to his generals about making Europe an "impregnable fortress." And in December, after the U.S. had entered the war, the Führer ranted to the world that "a belt of strongpoints and gigantic fortifications runs from Kirkenes [on the Norwegian-Finnish frontier] . . . to the Pyrenees [on the Franco-Spanish border] . . . and it is my unshakable decision to make this front impregnable against every enemy."

It was a wild, impossible boast. Discounting the indentations, this coastline running from the Arctic Ocean in the north to the Bay of Biscay in the south stretched almost three thousand miles.

Even directly across from Britain at the narrowest part of the Channel, the fortifications didn't exist. But Hitler had become obsessed with the fortress concept. Colonel General Franz Halder, then Chief of the German General Staff, well remembers the first time Hitler outlined his fantastic scheme. Halder, who would never forgive Hitler for refusing to invade England, was cool to the whole idea. He ventured the opinion that fortifications "if they were needed" should be constructed "behind the coastline out of range of naval guns," otherwise troops might be pinned down. Hitler dashed across the room to a table on which there was a large map and for a full five minutes threw an unforgettable tantrum. Pounding the map with his clenched fist he screamed, "Bombs and shells will fall here . . . here . . . here . . . and here . . . in front of the wall, behind it and on it . . . but the troops will be safe in the wall! Then they'll come out and fight!"

Halder said nothing, but he knew, as did the other generals in the High Command, that despite all the Reich's intoxicating victories the Führer already feared a second front—an invasion.

24

Still, little work was done on the fortifications. In 1942, as the tide of war began to swing against Hitler, British commandos began raiding the "impregnable" fortress of Europe. Then came the bloodiest commando raid of the war, when more than five thousand heroic Canadians landed at Dieppe. It was a bloody curtain-raiser to the invasion. Allied planners learned just how strongly the Germans had fortified the ports. The Canadians had 3,369 casualties, of which 900 were dead. The raid was disastrous, but it shocked Hitler. The Atlantic Wall, he thundered at his generals, must be completed at top speed. Construction was to be rushed "fanatically."

It was. Thousands of slave laborers worked night and day to build the fortifications. Millions of tons of concrete were poured; so much was used that all over Hitler's Europe it became impossible to get concrete for anything else. Staggering quantities of steel were ordered, but this commodity was in such short supply that the engineers were forced to do without it. As a result few of the bunkers or blockhouses had swiveling cupolas, which required steel for the turrets, and the arc of fire from the guns was thereby restricted. So great was the demand for materials and equipment that parts of the old French Maginot Line and Germany's frontier fortifications (the Siegfried Line) were cannibalized for the Atlantic Wall. By the end of 1943, although the wall was far from finished, over half a million men were working on it and the fortifications had become a menacing reality.

Hitler knew that invasion was inevitable, and now he was faced with another great problem: finding the divisions to man his growing defenses. In Russia division after division was being chewed up as the Wehrmacht tried to hold a 2,000-mile front against relentless Soviet attacks. In Italy, knocked out of the war after the invasion of Sicily, thousands of troops were still pinned down. So, by 1944, Hitler was forced to bolster his garrisons in the west with a strange conglomeration of replacements—old men and young boys, the remnants of divisions shattered on the

Russian front, impressed "volunteers" from occupied countries (there were units of Poles, Hungarians, Czechs, Roumanians and Yugoslavs, to mention just a few) and even two Russian divisions composed of men who preferred fighting for the Nazis to remaining in prison camps. Questionable as these troops might prove to be in combat, they filled out the gaps. He still had a hard core of battle-hardened troops and panzers. By D Day Hitler's strength in the west would total a formidable sixty divisions.

Not all these divisions would be up to full strength, but Hitler was still relying on his Atlantic Wall; that would make the difference. Yet men like Rommel who had been fighting—and losing— on other fronts were shocked when they saw the fortifications. Rommel had not been in France since 1941. And he, like many other German generals, believing in Hitler's propaganda, had thought that the defenses were almost completed.

His scathing denunciation of the "wall" came as no surprise to Von Rundstedt at OB West. He heartily concurred; indeed, it was probably the only time that he completely agreed with Rommel on anything. The wise old Von Rundstedt had never believed in fixed defenses. He had masterminded the successful outflanking of the Maginot Line in 1940 that had led to the collapse of France. To him Hitler's Atlantic Wall was nothing more than an "enormous bluff . . . more for the German people than for the enemy . . . and the enemy, through his agents, knows more about it than we do." It would "temporarily obstruct" the Allied attack, but it would not stop it. Nothing, Von Rundstedt was convinced, could prevent the initial landings from being successful. His plan to defeat the invasion was to hold the great mass of his troops back from the coast and to attack *after* the Allied troops had landed. That would be the moment to strike, he believed— when the enemy was still weak, without adequate supply lines and struggling to organize in isolated bridgeheads.

With this theory Rommel disagreed completely. He was positive that there was only one way to smash the attack: meet it head on. There would be no time to bring up reinforcements from the rear; he was certain that they would be destroyed by incessant air attacks or the massive weight of naval or artillery bombardment. Everything, in his view, from troops to panzer divisions, had to be held ready at the coast or just behind it. His aide well remembered a day when Rommel had summed up his strategy. They had stood on a deserted beach, and Rommel, a short, stocky figure in a heavy greatcoat with an old muffler around his throat, had stalked up and down waving his "informal" marshal's baton, a two-foot-long silver-topped black stick with a red, black and white tassel. He had pointed to the sands with his baton and said, "The war will be won or lost on the beaches. We'll have only one chance to stop the enemy and that's while he's in the water . . . struggling to get ashore. Reserves will never get up to the point of attack and it's foolish even to consider them. The *Hauptkampflinie* [main line of resistance] will be here . . . everything we have must be on the coast. Believe me, Lang, the first twenty-four hours of the invasion will be decisive . . . for the Allies, as well as Germany, it will be the longest day."

Hitler had approved Rommel's plan in general, and from then on Von Rundstedt had become merely a figurehead. Rommel executed Von Rundstedt's orders only if they agreed with his own ideas. To get his way he would frequently use a single but powerful argument. "The Führer," Rommel would remark, "gave quite explicit orders to me." He never said this directly to the dignified Von Rundstedt, but rather to OB West's chief of staff, Major General Blumentritt.

With Hitler's backing and Von Rundstedt's reluctant acceptance ("That Bohemian corporal, Hitler," snapped the Commander in Chief West, "usually decides against himself") the determined Rommel had set out completely to overhaul the existing anti-invasion plans.

In a few short months Rommel's ruthless drive had changed

the whole picture. On every beach where he considered a landing possible he had ordered his soldiers, working with local conscripted labor battalions, to erect barriers of crude anti-invasion obstacles. These obstacles—jagged triangles of steel, saw-toothed gatelike structures of iron, metal-tipped wooden stakes and concrete cones—were planted just below high- and low-tide water marks. Strapped to them were deadly mines. Where there were not enough mines, shells had been used, their noses pointing ominously out to sea. A touch would cause them to explode instantly.

Rommel's strange inventions (he had designed most of them himself) were both simple and deadly. Their object was to impale and destroy troop-filled landing craft or to obstruct them long enough for shore batteries to zero in. Either way, he reasoned, the enemy soldiers would be decimated long before they reached the beaches. More than half a million of these lethal underwater obstacles now stretched along the coastline.

Still Rommel, the perfectionist, was not satisfied. In the sands, in bluffs, in gullies and pathways leading off the beaches, he ordered mines laid—all varieties, from the large pancake type, capable of blowing off a tank's tracks, to the small S mine which when stepped on bounded into the air and exploded level with a man's midriff. Over five million of these mines now infested the coast. Before the attack came, Rommel hoped to have another six million planted. Eventually he hoped to girdle the invasion coast with sixty million mines.*

* Rommel was fascinated by mines as a defensive weapon. On one inspection trip with the Field Marshal, Major General Alfred Gause (Rommel's chief of staff before Major General Dr. Hans Speidel) pointed to several acres of wild spring flowers and said, "Isn't that a wonderful sight?" Rommel nodded and said, "You might make a note, Gause—that area will take about one thousand mines." And on yet another occasion when they were en route to Paris, Gause suggested that they visit the famous porcelain china works at Sèvres. Gause was surprised when Rommel agreed. But Rommel was not interested in the works of art he was shown. He walked quickly through the display rooms and, turning to Gause, said, "Find out if they can make waterproof casings for my sea mines."

The Wait

Overlooking the coastline, back of this jungle of mines and obstacles, Rommel's troops waited in pillboxes, concrete bunkers and communication trenches, all surrounded by layers of barbed wire. From these positions every piece of artillery that the Field Marshal had been able to lay hands on looked down on sands and sea, already sighted in to give overlapping fields of fire. Some guns were actually in positions on the seashore itself. These were hidden in concrete emplacements beneath innocent-looking seaside homes, their barrels aimed not toward the sea but directly down the beaches, so as to fire at point-blank range along the waves of assaulting troops.

Rommel took advantage of every new technique or development. Where he was short of guns, he positioned batteries of rocket launchers or multiple mortar throwers. At one place he even had miniature robot tanks called "Goliaths." These devices, capable of carrying more than half a ton of explosives, could be guided by remote control from the fortifications down onto the beaches and detonated among troops or landing craft.

About all that was missing from Rommel's medieval arsenal of weapons were crucibles of molten lead to pour down on the attackers—and in a way he had the modern equivalent: automatic flame throwers. At some places along the front, webs of piping ran out from concealed kerosene tanks to the grassy approaches leading off the beaches. At the press of a button, advancing troops would be instantly swallowed by flame.

Nor had Rommel forgotten the threat of parachutists or glider-borne infantry. Behind the fortifications low-lying areas had been flooded, and into every open field within seven or eight miles of the coast heavy stakes had been driven and booby-trapped. Trip wires were strung between these posts. When touched, they would immediately set off mines or shells.

Rommel had organized a bloody welcome for the Allied troops. Never in the history of modern warfare had a more powerful or deadly array of defenses been prepared for an invading force.

Yet Rommel was not content. He wanted more pillboxes, more beach obstacles, more mines, more guns and troops. Most of all he wanted the massive panzer divisions which were lying in reserve far from the coast. He had won memorable battles with panzers in the North African deserts. Now, at this crucial moment, neither he nor Rundstedt could move these armored formations without Hitler's consent. The Führer insisted on holding them under his personal authority. Rommel needed at least five panzer divisions at the coast, ready to counterattack within the first few hours of the Allied assault. There was only one way to get them—he would see Hitler. Rommel had often told Lang, "The last man who sees Hitler wins the game." On this leaden morning in La Roche-Guyon, as he prepared to leave for Germany and the long drive home, Rommel was more determined than ever to win the game.

★ 5 ★

At Fifteenth Army headquarters near the Belgian border, 125 miles away, one man was glad to see the morning of June 4 arrive. Lieutenant Colonel Hellmuth Meyer sat in his office, haggard and bleary-eyed. He had not really had a good night's sleep since June 1. But the night that had just passed had been the worst yet; he would never forget it.

Meyer had a frustrating, nerve-racking job. Besides being the Fifteenth Army's intelligence officer, he also headed up the only counterintelligence team on the invasion front. The heart of his setup was a thirty-man radio interception crew who worked in shifts around the clock in a concrete bunker crammed full of the most delicate radio equipment. Their job was to listen, nothing more. But each man was an expert who spoke three languages fluently, and there was hardly a word, hardly a single stutter of Morse code whispering through the ether from Allied sources that they did not hear.

Meyer's men were so experienced and their equipment was so sensitive that they were even able to pick up calls from radio transmitters in military-police jeeps in England more than a hundred miles away. This had been a great help to Meyer. American and British MPs, chatting with one another by radio as they directed troop convoys, had helped him no end in compiling a list of the various divisions stationed in England. But for some time now Meyer's operators had been unable to pick up any more of these calls. This was also significant to Meyer; it meant that a strict radio silence had been imposed. It was just one more clue to add to the many he already had that the invasion was close at hand.

With all the other intelligence reports available to him, items like this helped Meyer develop a picture of Allied planning. And he was good at his job. Several times a day he sifted through sheaves of monitored reports, always searching for the suspicious, the unusual—and even the unbelievable.

During the night his men had picked up the unbelievable. The message, a high-speed press cable, had been monitored just after dark. It read: "URGENT PRESS ASSOCIATED NYK FLASH EISENHOWER'S HQ ANNOUNCES ALLIED LANDINGS IN FRANCE."

Meyer was dumfounded. His first impulse was to alert the headquarters staff. But he had paused and calmed down, because Meyer knew the message had to be wrong.

There were two reasons why. First, there was the complete

31

absence of any activity along the invasion front—he would have known immediately if there had been an attack. Second, in January Admiral Wilhelm Canaris, then chief of German intelligence, had given Meyer the details of a fantastic two-part signal which he said the Allies would use to alert the underground prior to the invasion.

Canaris had warned that the Allies would broadcast hundreds of messages to the underground in the months preceding the attack. Only a few of these would actually relate to D Day; the remainder would be fake, deliberately designed to mislead and confuse. Canaris had been explicit: Meyer was to monitor all these messages in order not to miss the all-important one.

At first Meyer had been skeptical. It had seemed madness to him to depend entirely on only one message. Besides, he knew from past experience that Berlin's sources of information were inaccurate ninety per cent of the time. He had a whole file of false reports to prove his point; the Allies seemed to have fed every German agent from Stockholm to Ankara with the "exact" place and date of the invasion—and no two of the reports agreed.

But this time Meyer knew Berlin was right. On the night of June 1, Meyer's men, after months of monitoring, had intercepted the first part of the Allied message—exactly as described by Canaris. It was not unlike the hundreds of other coded sentences that Meyer's men had picked up during the previous months. Daily, after the regular BBC news broadcasts, coded instructions in French, Dutch, Danish and Norwegian were read out to the underground. Most of the messages were meaningless to Meyer, and it was exasperating not to be able to decode such cryptic fragments as "The Trojan War will not be held," "Molasses tomorrow will spurt forth cognac," "John has a long mustache," or "Sabine has just had mumps and jaundice." But the message that followed the 9 P.M. BBC news on the night of June 1 was one that Meyer understood only too well.

"Kindly listen now to a few personal messages," said the voice in French. Instantly Sergeant Walter Reichling switched on a wire recorder. There was a pause, and then: *"Les sanglots longs des violons de l'automne* [The long sobs of the violins of autumn].*"*

Reichling suddenly clapped his hands over his earphones. Then he tore them off and rushed out of the bunker for Meyer's quarters. The sergeant burst into Meyer's office and excitedly said, "Sir, the first part of the message—it's here."

Together they returned to the radio bunker, where Meyer listened to the recording. There it was—the message that Canaris had warned them to expect. It was the first line of "Chanson d'Automne [Song of Autumn]" by the nineteenth-century French poet Paul Verlaine. According to Canaris' information, this line from Verlaine was to be transmitted on the "first or fifteenth of a month . . . and will represent the first half of a message announcing the Anglo-American invasion."

The last half of the message would be the second line of the Verlaine poem, *"Blessent mon coeur d'une langueur monotone* [Wound my heart with a monotonous languor]." When this was broadcast it would mean, according to Canaris, that "the invasion will begin within forty-eight hours . . . the count starting at 0000 hours of the day following the transmission."

Immediately on hearing the recording of the first line from Verlaine, Meyer informed the Fifteenth Army's chief of staff, Major General Rudolf Hofmann. "The first message has come," he told Hofmann. "Now something is going to happen."

"Are you absolutely sure?" Hofmann asked.

"We recorded it," Meyer replied.

Hofmann immediately gave the alarm to alert the whole of the Fifteenth Army.

Meyer meanwhile sent the message by teletype to OKW. Next he telephoned Rundstedt's headquarters (OB West) and Rommel's headquarters (Army Group B).

At OKW the message was delivered to Colonel General Alfred

33

Jodl, Chief of Operations. The message remained on Jodl's desk. He did not order an alert. He assumed Rundstedt had done so; but Rundstedt thought Rommel's headquarters had issued the order.*

Along the invasion coast only one army was placed on readiness: the Fifteenth. The Seventh Army, holding the coast of Normandy, heard nothing about the message and was not alerted.

On the nights of the second and third of June the first part of the message was again broadcast. This worried Meyer; according to his information it should have been broadcast only once. He could only assume that the Allies were repeating the alert in order to make sure it was received by the underground.

Within the hour after the message was repeated on the night of June 3, the AP flash regarding the Allied landings in France had been picked up. If the Canaris warning was right, the AP report must be wrong. After his first moment of panic, Meyer had bet on Canaris. Now he was weary, but elated. The coming of the dawn and the continued peacefulness along the front had more than proved him right.

Now there was nothing to do but wait for the last half of the vital alert, which might come at any moment. Its awesome significance overwhelmed Meyer. The defeat of the Allied invasion, the lives of hundreds of thousands of his countrymen, the very existence of his country would depend on the speed with which he and his men monitored the broadcast and alerted the front. Meyer and his men would be ready as never before. He could only hope that his superiors also realized the importance of the message.

As Meyer settled down to wait, 125 miles away the commander of Army Group B was preparing to leave for Germany.

* Rommel must have known about the message; but from his own estimate of Allied intentions it is obvious that he must have discounted it.

★ 6 ★

Field Marshal Rommel carefully spread a little honey on a slice of buttered bread. At the breakfast table sat his brilliant chief of staff, Major General Dr. Hans Speidel, and several members of his staff. There was no formality. The table talk was easy and uninhibited; it was almost like a family gathering with the father sitting at the head of the table. In a way it was a kind of close-knit family. Each of the officers had been hand-picked by Rommel and they were devoted to him. All of them this morning had briefed Rommel on various questions which they hoped he would raise with Hitler. Rommel had said little. He had simply listened. Now he was impatient to leave. He looked at his watch. "Gentlemen," he said abruptly, "I must go."

Outside the main entrance Rommel's chauffeur, Daniel, stood by the Field Marshal's car with the door open. Rommel invited Colonel von Tempelhof, besides Lang the only other staff officer going with them, to ride with him in the Horch. Tempelhof's car could follow behind. Rommel shook hands with each member of his official family, spoke briefly to his chief of staff and then took his usual seat next to the chauffeur. Lang and Colonel von Tempelhof sat in the back. "We can go now, Daniel," said Rommel.

Slowly the car circled the courtyard and drove out through the main gate, passing the sixteen square-cut linden trees along the driveway. In the village it turned left onto the main Paris road.

It was 7 A.M. Leaving La Roche-Guyon on this particular dis-

35

mal Sunday morning, June 4, suited Rommel fine. The timing of the trip could not have been better. Beside him on the seat was a cardboard box containing a pair of handmade gray suède shoes, size five and a half, for his wife. There was a particular and very human reason why he wanted to be with her on Tuesday, June 6. It was her birthday.*

In England it was 8 A.M. (There was one hour's difference between British Double Summer Time and German Central Time.) In a house trailer in a wood near Portsmouth, General Dwight D. Eisenhower, the Allied Supreme Commander, was sound asleep after having been up nearly all night. For several hours now coded messages had been going out by telephone, by messenger and by radio from his headquarters nearby. Eisenhower, at about the time Rommel got up, had made a fateful decision: Because of unfavorable weather conditions he had postponed the Allied invasion by twenty-four hours. If conditions were right, D Day would be Tuesday, June 6.

* Since World War II, many of Rommel's senior officers have stood shoulder to shoulder in an effort to alibi the circumstances surrounding Rommel's absence from the front on June 4 and 5 and for the best part of D Day itself. In books, articles and interviews they have stated that Rommel left for Germany on June 5. This is not true. They also claim that Hitler ordered him to Germany. This is not true. The only person at Hitler's headquarters who knew of Rommel's intended visit was the Führer's adjutant, Major General Rudolf Schmundt. General Walter Warlimont, then Deputy Chief of Operations at OKW, has told me that neither Jodl, Keitel nor himself was even aware that Rommel was in Germany. Even on D Day Warlimont thought that Rommel was at his headquarters conducting the battle. As to the date of Rommel's departure from Normandy, it was June 4; the incontrovertible proof lies in the meticulously recorded Army Group B War Diary, which gives the exact time.

LIEUTENANT COMMANDER GEORGE D. HOFFMAN, thirty-three-year-old skipper of the destroyer U.S.S. *Corry,* looked through his binoculars at the long column of ships plowing steadily across the English Channel behind him. It seemed incredible to him that they had got this far without an attack of some sort. They were on course and exactly on time. The crawling convoy, following a circuitous route and moving less than four miles an hour, had sailed more than eighty miles since leaving Plymouth the night before. But at any moment now Hoffman expected to meet trouble—U-boat or aircraft attack or both. At the very least he expected to encounter mine fields, for as every minute passed they were sailing farther into enemy waters. France lay ahead, now only forty miles away.

The young commander—he had "fleeted up" on the *Corry* from a lieutenant to skipper in less than three years—was immensely proud to be leading this magnificent convoy. But as he looked at it through his glasses he knew that it was a sitting duck for the enemy.

Ahead were the mine sweepers, six small ships spread out in a diagonal formation, like one side of an inverted V, each one trailing in the water, off to its right, a long saw-toothed wire sweep to cut through the moorings and detonate floating mines. Behind the mine sweepers came the lean, sleek shapes of the "shepherds," the escorting destroyers. And behind them, stretching back as far as the eye could see, came the convoy, a great procession of lumbering, unwieldy landing ships carrying thousands of troops, tanks, guns, vehicles and ammunition. Each of the heavily laden ships flew an antiaircraft barrage balloon at the end of a stout cable. And because these protective balloons, all flying at the same altitude, swung out in the face of the brisk wind, the entire convoy appeared to be listing drunkenly to one side.

To Hoffman it was quite a sight. Estimating the distance separating one ship from the next and knowing the total number of vessels, he figured that the tail end of this fantastic parade must still be back in England, in Plymouth Harbor.

And this was only one convoy. Hoffman knew that dozens of others had been due to sail when he did, or would leave England during the day. That night all of them would converge on the Bay of the Seine. By morning an immense fleet of five thousand ships would stand off the invasion beaches of Normandy.

Hoffman could hardly wait to see it. The convoy that he led had left England early because it had the farthest to go. It was part of a massive American force, the 4th Division, destined for a place that Hoffman, like millions of other Americans, had never heard of before—a stretch of wind-blown sand on the eastern side of the Cherbourg peninsula that had been given the code name "Utah." Twelve miles to the southeast, in front of the seaside villages of Vierville and Colleville, lay the other American beach, "Omaha," a crescent-shaped strip of silvery strand where the men of the 1st and 29th divisions would land.

The *Corry*'s captain had expected to see other convoys near him this morning, but he seemed to have the Channel all to himself. He wasn't disturbed. Somewhere in the vicinity, he knew, other convoys attached to either "Force U" or "Force O" were sailing for Normandy. Hoffman did not know that because of the uncertain weather conditions a worried Eisenhower had permitted fewer than a score of slow-moving convoys to set sail during the night.

Suddenly the bridge telephone buzzed. One of the deck officers reached for it but Hoffman, who was closer, picked up the phone. "Bridge," he said. "This is the captain." He listened for a moment. "Are you quite sure?" he asked. "Has the message been repeated?" Hoffman listened a moment longer, then he replaced the receiver on its cradle. It was unbelievable: the whole convoy had been ordered back to England—no reason given. What could have happened? Had the invasion been postponed?

Hoffman looked through his glasses at the mine sweepers ahead; they hadn't changed course. Neither had the destroyers behind them. Had they received the message? Before doing anything else he decided to see the turnabout message for himself—he had to be sure. Quickly he climbed down to the radio shack one deck below.

Radioman Third Class Bennie Glisson had made no mistake. Showing his skipper the radio logbook, he said, "I checked it twice just to be certain." Hoffman hurried back to the bridge.

His job and that of the other destroyers now was to wheel this monstrous convoy around, and quickly. Because he was in the lead his immediate concern was the flotilla of mine sweepers several miles ahead. He could not contact them by radio because a strict radio silence had been imposed. "All engines ahead full speed," Hoffman ordered. "Close up on the mine sweepers. Signalman on the light."

As the *Corry* raced forward Hoffman looked back and saw the destroyers behind him wheel and swing around the flanks of the convoy. Now, with signal lights blinking, they began the huge job of turning the convoy around. A worried Hoffman realized that they were dangerously close to France—just thirty-eight miles. Had they been spotted yet? It would be a miracle if they got away with the turnabout undetected.

Down in the radio shack Bennie Glisson continued to pick up the coded postponement message every fifteen minutes. To him it was the worst news he had received in a long time, for it seemed to confirm a nagging suspicion: that the Germans knew all about the invasion. Had D Day been called off because the Germans had found out? Like thousands of other men Bennie did not see how the invasion preparations—the convoys, the ships, men and supplies that filled every port, inlet and harbor from Land's End to Portsmouth—could possibly have gone unnoticed by Luftwaffe reconnaissance planes. And if the message simply meant that the invasion had been postponed for some other reason, then it followed that the Germans had still more time to spot the Allied armada.

The twenty-three-year-old radio operator turned the dial of another set and tuned in Radio Paris, the German propaganda station. He wanted to hear sexy-voiced "Axis Sally." Her taunting broadcasts were amusing because they were so inaccurate, but you never could tell. There was another reason: The "Berlin Bitch," as she was often irreverently called, seemed to have an inexhaustible supply of the latest hit tunes.

Bennie didn't get a chance to listen because just then a long string of coded weather reports began coming in. But as he finished typing up these messages "Axis Sally" put on her first record of the day. Bennie instantly recognized the opening bars of the popular wartime tune "I Double Dare You." But new lyrics had been written for the song. As he listened, they confirmed his worst fears. That morning a little before eight Bennie and many thousands of Allied troops who had steeled themselves for the invasion of Normandy on June 5, and who now had another agonizing twenty-four hours to wait, heard "I Double Dare You" with these pertinent, if chilling, lines:

> *"I double dare you to come over here.*
> *I double dare you to venture too near.*

Take off your high hat and quit that bragging.
Cut out that claptrap and keep your hair on.
Can't you take a dare on?

I double dare you to venture a raid.
I double dare you to try and invade.
And if your loud propaganda means half of what it
  says,
I double dare you to come over here.
I double dare you."

★ 8 ★

IN THE HUGE Operations Center at Allied naval headquarters in Southwick House outside Portsmouth, they waited for the ships to come back.

The long, high room with its white-and-gold wallpaper was the scene of intense activity. One entire wall was covered by a gigantic chart of the English Channel. Every few minutes two Wrens, working from a traveling stepladder, moved colored markers over the face of the chart as they plotted the new positions of each returning convoy. Clustered in groups of two and three, staff officers from the various Allied services watched in silence as each new report came in. Outwardly they appeared calm, but there was no disguising the strain that everybody felt. Not only must the convoys wheel about, almost under the very

41

noses of the enemy, and return to England along specific, mine-swept tracks; they were now faced with the threat of another enemy—a storm at sea. For the slow-moving landing craft, heavily loaded with troops and supplies, a storm could be disastrous. Already the wind in the Channel was blowing up to thirty miles an hour, with waves up to five feet, and the weather was due to get worse.

As the minutes passed, the face of the chart reflected the orderly pattern of the recall. There were streams of markers back-tracking up the Irish Sea, clustered in the vicinity of the Isle of Wight and huddled together in various ports and anchorages along the southwest coast of England. It would take some of the convoys nearly all day to put back to port.

The location of each convoy and that of nearly every other ship of the Allied fleet could be seen at a glance on the board. But two vessels were not shown—a pair of midget submarines. They seemed to have disappeared completely off the chart.

In an office nearby, a pretty twenty-four-year-old Wren lieutenant wondered how soon her husband would make it back to his home port. Naomi Coles Honour was a bit anxious but not unduly worried yet, even though her friends in "Ops" seemed to know nothing about the whereabouts of her husband, Lieutenant George Honour, and his 57-foot-long midget submarine, the X23.

One mile off the coast of France a periscope broke the surface of the water. Thirty feet below, crouching in the cramped control room of the X23, Lieutenant George Honour pushed his cap back. "Well, gentlemen," he recalls saying, "let's take a look-see."

Cushioning one eye against the rubber-cupped eyepiece, he slowly pivoted the periscope around, and as the distorting shimmer of water disappeared from the lens the blurred image before him straightened out and became the sleepy resort town of Ouistreham near the mouth of the Orne. They were so close in and his view was so magnified that Honour could see smoke rising from chimneys and, in the far distance, a plane that had just taken off from Carpiquet Airport near Caen. He could also see the enemy. Fascinated, he watched German troops calmly working among the anti-invasion obstacles on the sandy beaches that stretched away on either side.

It was a great moment for the twenty-six-year-old Royal Navy Reserve lieutenant. Standing back from the periscope, he said to Lieutenant Lionel G. Lyne, the navigational expert in charge of the operation, "Take a look, Thin—we're almost bang on the target."

In a way the invasion had already begun. The first craft and the first men of the Allied forces were in position off the beaches of Normandy. Directly ahead of the X23 lay the British-Canadian assault sector. Lieutenant Honour and his crew were not unaware of the significance of this particular date. On another June 4, four years earlier, at a place less than two hundred miles away, the last of 338,000 British troops had been evacuated from a blazing port called Dunkirk. On the X23 it was a tense, proud moment for the five specially chosen Englishmen. They were the British vanguard; the men of the X23 were leading the way back to France for the thousands of their countrymen who would soon follow.

These five men crouching in the tiny all-purpose cabin of the X23 wore rubber frogmen's suits, and they carried ingeniously falsified papers that would have passed the scrutiny of the most suspicious German sentry. Each had a false French identity card complete with photograph, plus work permits and ration cards bearing official-looking German rubber-stamped impressions, and other letters and documents. In case anything went wrong and the X23 was sunk or had to be abandoned, her crew members were to swim ashore and, armed with new identities, try to escape capture and make contact with the French underground.

The X23's mission was a particularly hazardous one. Twenty

minutes before H Hour, the midget sub and her sister ship, the X20—some twenty miles farther down the coast, opposite the little village of Le Hamel—would boldly come to the surface to act as navigational markers, clearly defining the extreme limits of the British-Canadian assault zone: three beaches that had been given the code names Sword, Juno and Gold.

The plan they were to follow was involved and elaborate. An automatic radio beacon capable of sending out a continuous signal was to be switched on the moment they surfaced. At the same time sonar apparatus would automatically broadcast sound waves through the water which could be picked up by underwater listening devices. The fleet carrying British and Canadian troops would home in on either one or both of the signals.

Each midget also carried an 18-foot telescopic mast to which was attached a small but powerful searchlight that could send out a flashing beam capable of being seen more than five miles away. If the light showed green, it would mean that the subs were on target; if not, the light would be red.

As additional navigation aids, the plan called for each midget to launch a moored rubber dinghy with a man in it and allow it to drift a certain distance toward shore. The dinghies had been outfitted with searchlights which would be operated by their crewmen. By taking bearings on the lights of the midgets and their drifting dinghies, approaching ships would be able to pinpoint the exact positions of the three assault beaches.

Nothing had been forgotten, not even the danger that the little sub might be run over by some lumbering landing craft. As protection the X23 would be clearly marked by a large yellow flag. The point had not escaped Honour that the flag would also make them a fine target for the Germans. Notwithstanding, he planned to fly a second flag, a large white Navy "battle duster." Honour and his crew were prepared to risk enemy shellfire, but they were taking no chances on being rammed and sunk.

All this paraphernalia and more had been packed into the already cramped innards of the X23. Two extra crewmen, both navigation experts, had also been added to the sub's normal complement of three men. There was scarcely room now to stand up or sit down in the X23's single all-purpose cabin, which was only five feet eight inches high, five feet wide and barely eight feet long. Already it was hot and stuffy, and the atmosphere would get much worse before they dared surface, which would not be until after dark.

Even in daylight in these shallow coastal waters, Honour knew that there was always the possibility of being spotted by low-flying reconnaissance planes or patrol boats—and the longer they stayed at periscope depth the greater was the risk.

At the periscope Lieutenant Lyne took a series of bearings. He quickly identified several landmarks: the Ouistreham lighthouse, the town church and the spires of two others in the villages of Langrune and St.-Aubin-sur-Mer a few miles away. Honour had been right. They were almost "bang on the target," barely three quarters of a mile from their plotted position.

Honour was relieved to be this close. It had been a long, harrowing trip. They had covered the ninety miles from Portsmouth in a little under two days, and much of that time they had traveled through mine fields. Now they would get into position and then drop to the bottom. "Operation Gambit" was off to a good start. Secretly he wished that some other code word had been chosen. Although he was not superstitious, on looking up the meaning of the word the young skipper had been shocked to discover that "gambit" meant "throwing away the opening pawns."

Honour took one last look through the periscope at the Germans working on the beaches. All hell would break loose on those beaches by this time tomorrow, he thought. "Down periscope," he ordered. Submerged, and out of radio communication with their base, Honour and the crew of the X23 did not know that the invasion had been postponed.

45

★ 9 ★

By 11 A.M. the gale in the Channel was blowing hard. In the restricted coastal areas of Britain, sealed off from the remainder of the country, the invasion forces sweated it out. Their world now was the assembly areas, the airfields and the ships. It was almost as though they were physically severed from the mainland —caught up strangely between the familiar world of England and the unknown world of Normandy. Separating them from the world they knew was a tight curtain of security.

On the other side of that curtain life went on as usual. People went about their accustomed routines unaware that hundreds of thousands of men waited out an order that would mark the beginning of the end of World War II.

In the town of Leatherhead, Surrey, a slight, fifty-four-year-old physics teacher was walking his dog. Leonard Sidney Dawe was a quiet, unassuming sort of man and outside of a small circle of friends he was unknown. Yet the retiring Dawe enjoyed a public following far exceeding that of a film star. Every day upwards of a million people struggled over the crossword puzzle that he and his friend Melville Jones, another schoolteacher, prepared for each morning's London *Daily Telegraph*.

For more than twenty years Dawe had been the *Telegraph's*

senior crossword compiler and in that time his tough, intricate puzzles had both exasperated and satisfied countless millions. Some addicts claimed that the *Times*'s puzzle was tougher, but Dawe's fans were quick to point out that the *Telegraph*'s crossword had never repeated the same clue twice. That was a matter of considerable pride to the reserved Dawe.

Dawe would have been astonished to know that ever since May 2 he had been the subject of a most discreet inquiry by a certain department in Scotland Yard charged with counter-espionage, M.I.5. For over a month his puzzles had thrown one scare after another into many sections of the Allied High Command.

On this particular Sunday morning M.I.5 had decided to talk to Dawe. When he returned home he found two men waiting for him. Dawe, like everybody else, had heard of M.I.5, but what could they possibly want with him?

"Mr. Dawe," said one of the men as the questioning began, "during the last month a number of highly confidential code words concerning a certain Allied operation have appeared in the *Telegraph* crossword puzzles. Can you tell us what prompted you to use them—or where you got them?"

Before the surprised Dawe could answer, the M.I.5 man pulled a list out of his pocket and said, "We are particularly interested in finding out how you came to choose this word." He pointed to the list. The prize competition crossword in the *Telegraph* for May 27 included the clue (11 across), "But some big-wig like this has stolen some of it at times." This mystifying clue through some strange alchemy made sense to Dawe's devoted followers. The answer, published just two days before on June 2, was the code name for the entire Allied invasion plan—"Overlord."

Dawe did not know what Allied operation they were talking about, so he was not unduly startled or even indignant at these questions. He could not explain, he told them, just how or why he had chosen that particular word. It was quite a common word in history books, he pointed out. "But how," he protested, "can I tell what is being used as a code word and what isn't?"

The two M.1.5 men were extremely courteous: they agreed that it was difficult. But wasn't it strange that all these code words should appear in the same month?

One by one they went over the list with the now slightly harassed bespectacled schoolmaster. In the puzzle for May 2, the clue "One of the U.S." (17 across) had produced the solution "Utah." The answer to three down, "Red Indian on the Missouri," on May 22, turned out to be "Omaha."

In the May 30 crossword (11 across), "This bush is a center of nursery revolutions" required the word "Mulberry"—the code name for the two artificial harbors that were to be placed in position off the beaches. And the solution to 15 down on June 1, "Britannia and he hold to the same thing," had been "Neptune"— the code word for the naval operations in the invasion.

Dawe had no explanation for the use of these words. For all he knew, he said, the crosswords mentioned on the list could have been completed six months before. Was there any explanation? Dawe could suggest only one: fantastic coincidence.

There had been other hair-raising scares. Three months before in Chicago's central post office a bulky, improperly wrapped envelope had burst open on the sorting table, revealing a number of suspicious-looking documents. At least a dozen sorters saw the contents: something about an operation called Overlord.

Intelligence officers were soon swarming all over the scene. The sorters were questioned and told to forget anything they might have seen. Next the completely innocent addressee was interrogated: a girl. She could not explain why these papers were en route to her, but she did recognize the handwriting on the envelope. Through her the papers were traced back to their point of origin, an equally innocent sergeant at American headquarters in London. He had wrongly addressed the envelope. By mistake he had sent it to his sister in Chicago.

Minor as this incident was it might have assumed even greater proportions had Supreme Headquarters known that the German intelligence service, the *Abwehr,* had already discovered the meaning of the code word "Overlord." One of their agents, an Albanian named Diello but better known to the *Abwehr* as "Cicero," had sent Berlin the information in January. At first Cicero had identified the plan as "Overlock," but later he had corrected it. And Berlin believed Cicero—he worked as a valet in the British Embassy in Turkey.

But Cicero was unable to discover the big Overlord secret: the time and place of D Day itself. So scrupulously guarded was this information that up to the end of April only a few hundred Allied officers knew it. But that month, despite constant warnings by counterintelligence that agents were active throughout the British Isles, two senior officers, an American general and a British colonel, carelessly violated security. At a cocktail party in Claridge's Hotel, London, the General mentioned to some brother officers that the invasion would take place before June 15. Elsewhere in England, the colonel, a battalion commander, was even more indiscreet. He told some civilian friends that his men were training to capture a specific target and he hinted that its location was in Normandy. Both officers were immediately demoted and removed from their commands.*

And now, on this tense Sunday, June 4, Supreme Headquarters was stunned by the news that there had been yet another leak, far worse than any that had occurred before. During the night

* Although the American General had been a West Point classmate of General Eisenhower's there was nothing that the Supreme Commander could do but send him home. After D Day the General's case received wide publicity and later, as a colonel, he retired. There is no record that Eisenhower's HQ even heard about the Britisher's indiscretion. It was quietly handled by his own superiors. The Britisher went on to become a Member of Parliament.

an AP teletype operator had been practicing on an idle machine in an effort to improve her speed. By error the perforated tape carrying her practice "flash" somehow preceded the usual nightly Russian communiqué. It was corrected after only thirty seconds, but the word was out. The "bulletin" that reached the U.S. read: "URGENT PRESS ASSOCIATED NYK FLASH EISENHOWER'S HQ ANNOUNCED ALLIED LANDINGS IN FRANCE."

Grave as the consequences of the message might prove to be, it was much too late to do anything about it now. The gigantic machinery of the invasion had moved into high gear. Now, as the hours slipped by and the weather steadily worsened, the greatest airborne and amphibious force ever assembled waited for General Eisenhower's decision. Would Ike confirm June 6 as D Day? Or would he be compelled because of Channel weather—the worst in twenty years—to postpone the invasion once again?

★ 10 ★

In a rain-lashed wood two miles from the naval headquarters at Southwick House, the American who had to make that great decision wrestled with the problem and tried to relax in his sparsely furnished three-and-a-half-ton trailer. Although he could have moved into more comfortable quarters at the big, sprawling Southwick House, Eisenhower had decided against it. He wanted to be as close as possible to the ports where his troops

were loading. Several days before he had ordered a small com-
pact battle headquarters set up—a few tents for his immediate
staff and several trailers, among them his own which he had long
ago named "my circus wagon."

Eisenhower's trailer, a long, low caravan somewhat resembling
a moving van, had three small compartments serving as bedroom,
living room and study. Besides these, neatly fitted into the
trailer's length was a tiny galley, a miniature switchboard, a
chemical toilet and, at one end, a glass-enclosed observation
deck. But the Supreme Commander was rarely around long
enough to make full use of the trailer. He hardly ever used the
living room or the study; when staff conferences were called he
generally held them in a tent next to the trailer. Only his bedroom had a "lived-in" look. It was definitely his: there was a
large pile of Western paperbacks on the table near his bunk, and
here too were the only pictures—photographs of his wife, Mamie,
and his twenty-one-year-old son, John, in West Point cadet's
uniform.

From this trailer Eisenhower commanded almost three million
Allied troops. More than half of his immense command were
American: roughly 1,700,000 soldiers, sailors, airmen and coastguardmen. British and Canadian forces together totaled around
one million and in addition there were Fighting French, Polish,
Czech, Belgian, Norwegian and Dutch contingents. Never before
had an American commanded so many men from so many nations
or shouldered such an awesome burden of responsibility.

Yet despite the magnitude of his assignment and his vast
powers there was little about this tall, sunburned Midwesterner
with the infectious grin to indicate that he was the Supreme
Commander. Unlike many other famous Allied commanders,
who were instantly recognizable by some visible trade-mark such
as eccentric headgear or garish uniforms layered shoulder-high
with decorations, everything about Eisenhower was restrained.
Apart from the four stars of his rank, a single ribbon of deco-

rations above his breast pocket and the flaming-sword shoulder patch of SHAEF (Supreme Headquarters Allied Expeditionary Force) Eisenhower shunned all distinguishing marks. Even in the trailer there was little evidence of his authority: no flags, maps, framed directives, or signed photographs of the great or near-great who often visited him. But in his bedroom, close to his bunk, were three all-important telephones, each a different color; the red was for "scrambled" calls to Washington, the green was a direct line to Winston Churchill's residence at No. 10 Downing Street, London, and the black connected him to his brilliant chief of staff, Major General Walter Bedell Smith, the immediate headquarters, and other senior members of the Allied High Command.

It was on the black phone, to add to all his other worries, that Eisenhower heard of the erroneous "flash" concerning the "landings." He said nothing when he was told the news. His naval aide, Captain Harry C. Butcher, recalls that the Supreme Commander merely grunted an acknowledgment. What was there to say or do now?

Four months before, in the directive appointing him Supreme Commander, the Combined Chiefs of Staff in Washington had spelled out his assignment in one precise paragraph. It read: "You will enter the continent of Europe and, in conjunction with the other United Nations, undertake operations aimed at the heart of Germany and the destruction of her armed forces . . ."

There in one sentence was the aim and purpose of the assault. But to the entire Allied world this was to be more than a military operation. Eisenhower called it "a great crusade"—a crusade to end once and for all a monstrous tyranny that had plunged the world into its bloodiest war, shattered a continent and placed upwards of 300 million people in bondage. (Actually, nobody at this time could even imagine the full extent of the Nazi barbarism that had washed across Europe—the millions who had disappeared into the gas chambers and furnaces of Heinrich Himmler's aseptic crematoria, the millions who had been herded out of their countries to work as slave laborers, a tremendous percentage of whom would never return, the millions more who had been tortured to death, executed as hostages or exterminated by the simple expedient of starvation.) The great crusade's unalterable purpose was not only to win the war, but to destroy Nazism and bring to an end an era of savagery which had never been surpassed in the world's history.

But first the invasion had to succeed. If it failed, the final defeat of Germany might take years.

To prepare for the all-out invasion on which so much depended, intensive military planning had been going on for more than a year. Long before anyone knew that Eisenhower would be named Supreme Commander a small group of Anglo-American officers under Britain's Lieutenant General Sir Frederick Morgan had been laying the groundwork for the assault. Their problems were incredibly involved—there were few guideposts, few military precedents, but a plethora of question marks. Where should the attack be launched and when? How many divisions should be used? If X divisions were needed would they be available, trained and ready to go by Y date? How many transports would be required to carry them? What about naval bombardment, support ships and escorts? Where were all the landing craft going to come from—could some be diverted from the Pacific and Mediterranean theaters of war? How many airfields would be needed to accommodate the thousands of planes necessary for the air attack? How long would it take to stockpile all the supplies, the equipment, guns, ammunition, transport, food, and how much was needed not only for the attack but to follow it up?

These were just a few of the staggering questions that Allied planners had to answer. There were thousands of others. Ultimately their studies, enlarged and modified into the final Overlord plan after Eisenhower took over, called for more men, more ships, more planes, more equipment and matériel than had ever been assembled before for a single military operation.

The build-up was enormous. Even before the plan reached its final form an unprecedented flow of men and supplies began pouring into England. Soon there were so many Americans in the small towns and villages that the British who lived in them were often hopelessly outnumbered. Their movie theaters, hotels, restaurants, dance halls and favorite pubs were suddenly swamped by a flood of troops from every state in the Union.

Airfields blossomed everywhere. For the great air offensive 163 bases were constructed in addition to the scores already in existence, until at last there were so many that a standard gag among 8th and 9th Air Force crewmen was that they could taxi the length and breadth of the island without scratching a wing. Ports were jammed. A great supporting naval fleet of almost nine hundred ships, from battleships to PT boats, began to assemble. Convoys arrived in such great numbers that by spring they had delivered almost two million tons of goods and supplies—so much that 170 miles of new railroad lines had to be laid down to move it.

By May southern England looked like a huge arsenal. Hidden in the forests were mountainous piles of ammunition. Stretching across the moors, bumper to bumper, were tanks, half-tracks, armored cars, trucks, jeeps and ambulances—more than fifty thousand of them. In the fields were long lines of howitzers and antiaircraft guns, great quantities of prefabricated materials from Nissen huts to airstrips, and huge stocks of earth-moving equipment from bulldozers to excavators. At central depots there were immense quantities of food, clothing and medical supplies, from pills for combating seasickness to 124,000 hospital beds. But the most staggering sight of all were the valleys filled with long lines of railroad rolling stock: almost one thousand brand-new locomotives, and nearly twenty thousand tanker cars and freight cars which would be used to replace the shattered French equipment after the beachhead had been established.

There were also strange new devices of war. There were tanks that could swim, others that carried great rolls of lath to be used in antitank ditches or as steppingstones over walls, and yet others equipped with great chain flails that beat the ground in front of them to explode mines. There were flat, block-long ships, each carrying a forest of pipes for the launching of warfare's newest weapon, rockets. Perhaps strangest of all were two man-made harbors that were to be towed across to the Normandy beaches. They were engineering miracles and one of the big Overlord secrets; they assured the constant flow of men and supplies into the beachhead during the first critical weeks until a port could be captured. The harbors, called "Mulberries," consisted first of an outer breakwater made up of great steel floats. Next came 145 huge concrete caissons in various sizes which were to be sunk butt to butt to make an inner breakwater. The largest of these caissons had crew quarters and antiaircraft guns and, when it was being towed, looked like a five-story apartment building lying on its side. Within these man-made harbors freighters as large as Liberty ships could unload into barges ferrying back and forth to the beaches. Smaller ships, like coasters or landing craft, could dump their cargoes at massive steel pierheads where waiting trucks would run them to shore over floating pontoon-supported piers. Beyond the Mulberries a line of sixty concrete blockships was to be sunk as an additional breakwater. In position off the invasion beaches of Normandy, each harbor would be the size of the port of Dover.

All through May men and supplies began to move down to the ports and the loading areas. Congestion was a major problem, but somehow the quartermasters, military police and British railroad authorities kept everything moving and on time.

Trains loaded with troops and supplies backed and filled on every line as they waited to converge on the coast. Convoys jammed every road. Every little village and hamlet was covered with a fine dust, and throughout the quiet spring nights the whole of southern England resounded with the low whining sound of the trucks, the whirring and clacking of tanks and the unmistakable voices of Americans, all of whom seemed to be asking the same question: "How far away is this goddam place?"

Almost overnight, cities of Nissen huts and tents sprang up in the coastal regions as troops began to pour into the embarkation areas. Men slept in bunks stacked three and four deep. Showers and latrines were usually several fields away and the men had to queue up to use them. Chow lines were sometimes a quarter of a mile long. There were so many troops that it took some 54,000 men, 4,500 of them newly trained cooks, just to service American installations. The last week in May troops and supplies began loading onto the transports and the landing ships. The time had finally come.

The statistics staggered the imagination; the force seemed overwhelming. Now this great weapon—the youth of the free world, the resources of the free world—waited on the decision of one man: Eisenhower.

Throughout most of June 4 Eisenhower remained alone in his trailer. He and his commanders had done everything to insure that the invasion would have every possible chance of success at the lowest cost in lives. But now, after all the months of political and military planning, Operation Overlord lay at the mercy of the elements. Eisenhower was helpless; all he could do was to wait and hope that the weather would improve. But no matter what happened he would be forced to make a momentous decision by the end of the day—to go or to postpone the assault once again. Either way the success or failure of Operation Overlord might depend on that decision. And nobody could make that decision for him. The responsibility would be his and his alone.

Eisenhower was faced with a dreadful dilemma. On May 17 he had decided that D Day would have to be one of three days in June—the fifth, sixth or seventh. Meteorological studies had shown that two of the vital weather requirements for the invasion could be expected for Normandy on those days: a late-rising moon and, shortly after dawn, a low tide.

The paratroopers and glider-borne infantry who would launch the assault, some eighteen thousand men of the U.S. 101st and 82nd divisions and the British 6th Division, needed the moonlight. But their surprise attack depended on darkness up to the time they arrived over the dropping zones. Thus their critical demand was for a late-rising moon.

The seaborne landings had to take place when the tide was low enough to expose Rommel's beach obstacles. On this tide the timing of the whole invasion would depend. And to complicate the meteorological calculations further, follow-up troops landing much later in the day would also need a low tide—and it had to come before darkness set in.

These two critical factors of moonlight and tide shackled Eisenhower. Tide alone reduced the number of days in any one month for the attack to six, and three of those were moonless.

But that was not all. There were many other considerations he had to take into account. First, all the services wanted long hours of daylight and good visibility—to identify the beaches; for the naval and air forces to spot their targets; and to reduce the hazard of collision when five thousand ships began maneuvering almost side by side in the Bay of the Seine. Second, a calm sea was required. Apart from the havoc a rough sea might cause to the fleet, seasickness could leave the troops helpless long before they even set foot on the beaches. Third, low winds, blowing inshore, were needed to clear the beaches of smoke so that targets would not be obscured. And finally the Allies required three more quiet days after D Day to facilitate the quick build-up of men and supplies.

Nobody at Supreme Headquarters expected perfect conditions on D Day, least of all Eisenhower. He had schooled himself, in countless dry runs with his meteorological staff, to recognize and weigh all the factors which would give him the bare minimum conditions acceptable for the attack. But according to his meteorologist the chances were about ten to one against Normandy having weather on any one day in June which would meet even the minimal requirements. On this stormy Sunday, as Eisenhower, alone in his trailer, considered every possibility, those odds appeared to have become astronomical.

Of the three possible days for the invasion he had chosen the fifth so that if there was a postponement he could launch the assault on the sixth. But if he ordered the landings for the sixth and then had to cancel them again, the problem of refueling the returning convoys might prevent him from attacking on the seventh. There would then be two alternatives. He could postpone D Day until the next period when the tides were right, June 19. But if he did that the airborne armies would be forced to attack in darkness—June 19 was moonless. The other alternative was to wait until July, and that long a postponement, as he was later to recall, "was too bitter to contemplate."

So terrifying was the thought of postponement that many of Eisenhower's most cautious commanders were even prepared to risk attack instead on the eighth or ninth. They did not see how more than 200,000 men, most of them already briefed, could be kept isolated and bottled up for weeks on ships, in embarkation areas and on airfields without the secret of the invasion leaking out. Even if security remained intact during the period, surely Luftwaffe reconnaissance aircraft would spot the massed fleet (if they hadn't done so already) or German agents would somehow learn of the plan. For everybody the prospect of a postponement was grim. But it was Eisenhower who would have to make the decision.

In the fading light of the afternoon the Supreme Commander occasionally came to the door of his trailer and gazed up through the wind-swept treetops at the blanket of clouds that covered the sky. At other times he would pace up and down outside the trailer, chain-smoking, kicking at the cinders on the little pathway —a tall figure, shoulders slightly hunched, hands rammed deep into his pockets.

On these solitary strolls Eisenhower scarcely seemed to notice anybody, but during the afternoon he spotted one of the four pool correspondents accredited to his advance headquarters— Merrill "Red" Mueller of NBC. "Let's take a walk, Red," said Ike abruptly, and without waiting for Mueller he strode off, hands in his pockets, at his usual brisk pace. The correspondent hurriedly caught up with him as he disappeared into the woods.

It was a strange, silent walk. Eisenhower uttered hardly a word. "Ike seemed completely preoccupied with his own thoughts, completely immersed in all his problems," Mueller remembers. "It was almost as though he had forgotten I was with him." There were many questions that Mueller wanted to put to the Supreme Commander, but he didn't ask them; he felt that he couldn't intrude.

When they returned to the encampment and Eisenhower had said goodbye, the correspondent watched him climb the little aluminum stairs leading to the trailer door. At that moment he appeared to Mueller to be "bowed down with worry . . . as though each of the four stars on either shoulder weighed a ton."

Shortly before nine-thirty that night, Eisenhower's senior commanders and their chiefs of staff gathered in the library of Southwick House. It was a large, comfortable room with a table covered by a green baize cloth, several easy chairs and two sofas. Dark oak bookcases lined three of the walls, but there were few books on the shelves and the room had a bare look. Heavy double blackout curtains hung at the windows and on this night they muffled the drumming of the rain and the flat buckling sound of the wind.

Standing about the room in little groups, the staff officers talked quietly. Near the fireplace Eisenhower's chief of staff,

Major General Walter Bedell Smith, conversed with the pipe-smoking Deputy Supreme Commander, Air Chief Marshal Tedder. Seated to one side was the fiery Allied naval commander. Admiral Ramsay, and close by the Allied air commander, Air Chief Marshal Leigh-Mallory. Only one officer was dressed informally, General Smith recalls. The peppery Montgomery, who would be in charge of the D-Day assault, wore his usual corduroy slacks and roll-necked sweater. These were the men who would translate the order for the attack when Eisenhower gave the word to go. Now they and their staff officers—altogether there were twelve senior officers in the room—waited for the arrival of the Supreme Commander and the decisive conference that would begin at nine-thirty. At that time they would hear the latest forecasts of the meteorologists.

At exactly nine-thirty the door opened and Eisenhower, neat in his dark-green battle dress, strode in. There was just the faintest flicker of the old Eisenhower grin as he greeted his old friends, but the mask of worry quickly returned to his face as he opened the conference. There was no need for a preamble; everybody knew the seriousness of the decision that had to be made. So almost immediately the three senior Overlord meteorologists, led by their chief, Group Captain J. N. Stagg of the Royal Air Force, came into the room.

There was a hushed silence as Stagg opened the briefing. Quickly he sketched the weather picture of the previous twenty-four hours and then he quietly said, "Gentlemen . . . there have been some rapid and unexpected developments in the situation . . ." All eyes were on Stagg now, as he presented the anxious-faced Eisenhower and his commanders with a slender ray of hope.

A new weather front had been spotted which, he said, would move up the Channel within the next few hours and cause a gradual clearing over the assault areas. These improving conditions would last throughout the next day and continue up to the

morning of June 6. After that the weather would begin to deterio-
rate again. During this promised period of fair weather, the winds
would drop appreciably and the skies would clear—enough at
least for bombers to operate on the night of the fifth and throughout the morning of the sixth. By noon the cloud layer would
thicken and the skies would become overcast again. In short,
what Eisenhower was being told was that a barely tolerable
period of fair conditions, far below the minimal requirements,
would prevail *for just a little more than twenty-four hours.*

The moment Stagg had finished, he and the other two meteorologists were subjected to a barrage of questions. Were all of
them confident about the accuracy of their predictions? Could
their forecasts be wrong—had they checked their reports with
every available source? Was there any chance of the weather
continuing to improve in the few days immediately after the
sixth?

Some of the questions were impossible for the weathermen to
answer. Their report had been checked and double-checked and
they were as optimistic as they could be about the forecast, but
there was always the chance that the vagaries of the weather
might prove them wrong. They answered as best they could, then
they withdrew.

For the next fifteen minutes Eisenhower and his commanders
deliberated. The urgency of making a decision was stressed by
Admiral Ramsay. The American task force for Omaha and Utah
beaches under the command of Rear Admiral A. G. Kirk would
have to get the order within a half hour if Overlord was to take
place on Tuesday. Ramsay's concern was prompted by the refueling problem; if those forces sailed later and were then recalled it would be impossible to get them ready again for a possible attack on Wednesday, the seventh.

Eisenhower now polled his commanders one by one. General
Smith thought that the attack should go in on the sixth—it was
a gamble, but one that should be taken. Tedder and Leigh-

Mallory were both fearful that even the predicted cloud cover would prove too much for the air forces to operate effectively. It might mean that the assault would take place without adequate air support. They thought it was going to be "chancy." Montgomery stuck to the decision that he had made the night before when the June 5 D Day had been postponed. "I would say Go," he said.

It was now up to Ike. The moment had come when only he could make the decision. There was a long silence as Eisenhower weighed all the possibilities. General Smith, watching, was struck by the "isolation and loneliness" of the Supreme Commander as he sat, hands clasped before him, looking down at the table. The minutes ticked by; some say two minutes passed, others as many as five. Then Eisenhower, his face strained, looked up and announced his decision. Slowly he said, "I am quite positive we must give the order . . . I don't like it, but there it is. . . . I don't see how we can do anything else."

Eisenhower stood up. He looked tired, but some of the tension had left his face. Six hours later at a brief meeting to review the weather he would hold to his decision and reconfirm it—Tuesday, June 6, would be D Day.

Eisenhower and his commanders left the room, hurrying now to set the great assault in motion. Behind them in the silent library a haze of blue smoke hung over the conference table, the fire reflected itself in the polished floor, and on the mantelpiece the hands of a clock pointed to 9:45.

★ 11 ★

I<small>T WAS</small> about 10 P.M. when Private Arthur B. "Dutch" Schultz of the 82nd Airborne Division decided to get out of the crap game; he might never have this much money again. The game had been going on ever since the announcement that the airborne assault was off for at least twenty-four hours. It had begun behind a tent, next it had moved under the wing of a plane, and now the session was going full blast in the hangar, which had been converted into a huge dormitory. Even here it had done some traveling, moving up and down the corridors created by the rows of double-tiered bunks. And Dutch was one of the big winners.

How much he had won he didn't know. But he guessed that the bundle of crumpled greenbacks, English banknotes and fresh blue-green French invasion currency he held in his fist came to more than $2,500. That was more money than he had seen at any one time in all his twenty-one years.

Physically and spiritually he had done everything to prepare himself for the jump. Services for all denominations had been held on the airfield in the morning and Dutch, a Catholic, had gone to confession and Communion. Now he knew exactly what he was going to do with his winnings. He mentally figured out the distribution. He would leave $1,000 with the adjutant's office; he could use that on pass when he got back to England. Another $1,000 he planned to send to his mother in San Francisco to keep

63

for him, but he wanted her to have $500 of it as a gift—she sure could use it. He had a special purpose for the remainder: that would go on a helluva blowout when his outfit, the 505th, reached Paris.

The young paratrooper felt good; he had taken care of everything—but had he? Why did the incident of the morning keep coming back, filling him with so much uneasiness?

At mail call that morning he had received a letter from his mother. As he tore open the envelope a rosary slid out and fell at his feet. Quickly, so that the wisecracking crowd around him wouldn't notice, he had snatched up the beads and stuffed them into a barracks bag that he was leaving behind.

Now the thought of the rosary beads suddenly gave rise to a question that hadn't struck him before: What was he doing gambling at a time like this? He looked at the folded and crumpled bills sticking out between his fingers—more money than he could have earned in a year. At that moment Private Dutch Schultz *knew* that if he pocketed all this money, he would surely be killed. Dutch decided to take no chances. "Move over," he said, "and let me get at the play." He glanced at his watch and wondered how long it would take to lose $2,500.

Schultz wasn't the only one who acted strangely this night. Nobody, from enlisted men to generals, seemed eager to challenge the fates. Over near Newbury at the headquarters of the 101st Airborne Division, the commander, Major General Maxwell D. Taylor, was holding a long, informal session with his senior officers. There were perhaps half a dozen men in the room and one of them, Brigadier General Don Pratt, the assistant division commander, sat on a bed. While they were talking another officer arrived. Taking off his cap, he tossed it onto the bed. General Pratt leaped up, swept the cap onto the floor and said, "My God, that's damn bad luck!" Everybody laughed, but Pratt didn't sit on the bed again. He had chosen to lead the 101st's glider forces into Normandy.

The Wait

As the night closed in, the invasion forces all over England continued to wait. Keyed up by months of training, they were ready to go, and the postponement had made them jittery. It was now about eighteen hours since the stand-down, and each hour had taken its toll of the patience and readiness of the troops. They did not know that D Day now was barely twenty-six hours away; it was still much too early for the news to filter down. And so, on this stormy Sunday night, men waited, in loneliness, anxiety and secret fear, for something, anything, to happen.

They did precisely what the world expects men to do under such circumstances: They thought of their families, their wives, their children, their sweethearts. And everybody talked about the fighting that lay ahead. What would the beaches really be like? Would the landings be as tough as everybody seemed to think? Nobody could visualize D Day, but each man prepared for it in his own way.

On the dark, wave-tossed Irish Sea, aboard the destroyer U.S.S. *Herndon,* Lieutenant (j.g.) Bartow Farr, Jr., tried to concentrate on a bridge game. It was difficult; there were too many sober reminders all around him that this was not just another social evening. Taped to the walls of the wardroom were large aerial reconnaissance photographs of German gun positions overlooking the Normandy beaches. These guns were the *Herndon's* D-Day targets. It occurred to Farr that the *Herndon* would also be theirs.

Farr was reasonably certain he would survive D Day. There had been a lot of kidding about who would come through and who wouldn't. Back in Belfast Harbor the crew of the *Corry,* their sister ship, had been giving odds of ten to one against the *Herndon's* return. The *Herndon's* crew retaliated by spreading the rumor that when the invasion fleet set out the *Corry* would remain in port, because of low morale aboard ship.

Lieutenant Farr had every confidence that the *Herndon* would return safe, and he with her. Still, he was glad he had written a

long letter to his unborn son. It never occurred to Farr that his
wife, Anne, back in New York, might give birth to a girl instead.
(She didn't. That November the Farrs had a boy.)

In a staging area near Newhaven, Corporal Reginald Dale of
the British 3rd Division sat up in his bunk and worried about his
wife, Hilda. They had been married in 1940, and ever since both
had longed for a child. On his last leave, just a few days before,
Hilda had announced that she was pregnant. Dale was furious;
all along he had sensed that the invasion was close and that he'd
be in on it. "This is a hell of a time, I must say," he had snapped.
In his mind he saw again the quick hurt that had come into her
eyes, and he berated himself once again for the hasty words.

But it was too late now. He could not even telephone her. He
lay back down on his bunk and, like thousands of others in
British staging areas, tried to will himself to sleep.

A few men, nerveless and cool, slept soundly. At a British 50th
Division embarkation area one such man was Company Sergeant
Major Stanley Hollis. Long ago he had learned to sleep whenever
he could. The coming attack didn't worry Hollis too much; he had
a good idea what to expect. He had been evacuated from Dunkirk, had fought with the Eighth Army in North Africa and had
landed on the beaches of Sicily. Among the millions of troops in
Britain that night Hollis was a rarity. He was looking forward to
the invasion; he wanted to get back to France to kill some more
Germans.

It was a personal matter with Hollis. He had been a dispatch
rider at the time of Dunkirk, and in the town of Lille during the
retreat he had seen a sight which he had never forgotten. Cut off
from his unit, Hollis had taken a wrong turn in a part of the town
that the Germans had apparently just passed through. He found
himself in a cul-de-sac filled with the still warm bodies of over a
hundred French men, women and children. They had been machine-gunned. Embedded in the wall behind the bodies and littering the ground were hundreds of spent bullets. From that mo-

ment Stan Hollis had become a superb hunter of the enemy. His score was now over ninety. At D Day's end, he would notch his Sten gun with his one hundred and second victory.

There were others who were also anxious to set foot in France. The waiting seemed interminable to Commander Philippe Kieffer and his 171 tough French commandos. With the exception of the few friends they had made in England, there had been no one for them to say goodbye to—their families were still in France.

In their encampment near the mouth of the Hamble River, they spent the time checking weapons and studying the molded-foam-rubber terrain model of Sword Beach and their targets in the town of Ouistreham. One of the commandos, Count Guy de Montlaur, who was extremely proud to be a sergeant, was delighted to hear this night that there had been a slight change of plan: His squad would be leading the attack on the resort's gambling casino, now believed to be a strongly defended German command post. "It will be a pleasure," he told Commander Kieffer. "I have lost several fortunes in that place."

One hundred fifty miles away, in the U.S. 4th Infantry Division's staging area, near Plymouth, Sergeant Harry Brown came off duty and found a letter waiting for him. Many times he had seen the same sort of thing in war movies, but he never thought it would happen to him: the letter contained an advertisement for Adler Elevator Shoes. The ad particularly galled the sergeant. Everyone was so short in his section that they were called "Brown's midgets." The sergeant was the tallest—five feet five and a half inches.

While he was wondering who had given his name to the Adler Company, one of his squad showed up. Corporal John Gwiadosky had decided to repay a loan. Sergeant Brown couldn't get over it as Gwiadosky solemnly handed him the money. "Don't get any wrong ideas," explained Gwiadosky. "I just don't want you chasing me all over hell trying to collect."

Across the bay, on the transport *New Amsterdam* anchored near Weymouth, Second Lieutenant George Kerchner of the 2nd Ranger Battalion was occupied with a routine chore. He was censoring his platoon's mail. It was particularly heavy tonight; everybody seemed to have written long letters home. The 2nd and 5th Rangers had been given one of the toughest D-Day assignments. They were to scale the almost sheer 100-foot cliffs at a place called Pointe du Hoc and silence a battery of six long-range guns—guns so powerful that they could zero in on Omaha Beach or the transport area of Utah Beach. The Rangers would have just thirty minutes to do the job.

Casualties were expected to be heavy—some thought as high as sixty per cent—unless the air and naval bombardment could knock out the guns before the Rangers got there. Either way, nobody expected the attack to be a breeze. Nobody, that is, except Staff Sergeant Larry Johnson, one of Kerchner's section leaders.

The lieutenant was dumfounded when he read Johnson's letter. Although none of the mail would be sent out until after D Day—whenever that would be—this letter couldn't even be delivered through ordinary channels. Kerchner sent for Johnson and, when the sergeant arrived, gave him back the letter. "Larry," said Kerchner drily, "you better post this yourself—after you get to France." Johnson had written a girl asking for a date early in June. She lived in Paris.

It struck the lieutenant as the sergeant left the cabin that as long as there were optimists like Johnson nothing was impossible.

Almost every man in the invasion forces wrote a letter to someone during the long hours of waiting. They had been penned up for a long time, and the letters seemed to give them emotional release. Many of them recorded their thoughts in a way that men seldom do.

Captain John F. Dulligan of the 1st Infantry Division, slated to land on Omaha Beach, wrote his wife: "I love these men. They sleep all over the ship, on the decks, in, on top, and underneath the vehicles. They smoke, play cards, wrestle around and indulge in general horseplay. They gather around in groups and talk mostly about girls, home and experiences (with and without girls) . . . They are good soldiers, the best in the world . . . Before the invasion of North Africa, I was nervous and a little scared. During the Sicilian invasion I was so busy that the fear passed while I was working. . . . This time we will hit a beach in France and from there on only God knows the answer. I want you to know that I love you with all my heart. . . . I pray that God will see fit to spare me to you and Ann and Pat."

The men on heavy naval vessels or large transports, on airfields or in embarkation areas, were the lucky ones. They were restricted and overcrowded, but they were dry, warm and well. It was a different story for the troops on the flat-bottomed landing ships heaving at anchor outside nearly every harbor. Some men had been on these vessels for more than a week. The ships were overcrowded and foul, the men unbelievably miserable. For them the battle began long before they ever left England. It was a battle against continuous nausea and seasickness. Most of the men still remember that the ships smelled of just three things: diesel oil, backed-up toilets and vomit.

Conditions varied from ship to ship. On LCT 777 Signalman Third Class George Hackett, Jr., was amazed to see waves so high that they smashed over one end of the wallowing craft and rolled out the other. LCT 6, a British landing craft, was so overloaded that Lieutenant Colonel Clarence Hupfer of the U.S. 4th Division thought it would sink. Water lapped at the gunwales and at times washed over into the craft. The galley was flooded and the troops were forced to eat cold food—those who could eat at all.

LST 97, Sergeant Keith Bryan of the 5th Engineer Special Brigade remembers, was so overcrowded that men were stepping over one another, and it rolled so much that those lucky enough to have bunks had difficulty staying in them. And to Sergeant

Morris Magee of the Canadian 3rd Division the heaving of his craft "was worse than being in a rowboat in the center of Lake Champlain." He was so sick he could no longer throw up.

But the troops who suffered most during the waiting period were the men in the recalled convoys. All day they had ridden out the storm in the Channel. Now, waterlogged and weary, they glumly lined the rails as the last of the straggling convoys dropped their anchors. By 11 P.M. all the ships were back.

Outside Plymouth Harbor, Lieutenant Commander Hoffman of the *Corry* stood on his bridge looking at the long lines of dark shadows, blacked-out landing ships of every size and description. It was cold. The wind was still high and he could hear the shallow-draft vessels slopping and slapping the water as they rolled in the trough of every wave.

Hoffman was weary. They had returned to port only a short while before to learn for the first time the reason for the postponement. Now they had been warned to stand to once again.

Below decks the news spread quickly. Bennie Glisson, the radio operator, heard it as he prepared to go on watch. He made his way to the mess hall and when he got there he found more than a dozen men having dinner—tonight it was turkey with all the trimmings. Everybody seemed depressed. "You guys," he said, "act like you're eating your last meal." Bennie was nearly right. At least half of those present would go down with the *Corry* a little after H Hour on D Day.

Nearby, on LCI 408, morale was also very low. The Coast Guard crew were convinced that the false start had been just another dry run. Private William Joseph Phillips of the 29th Infantry Division tried to cheer them up. "This outfit," he solemnly predicted, "will never see combat. We've been in England so long that our job won't start until the war is over. They're going to have us wipe the bluebird shit off the White Cliffs of Dover."

At midnight Coast Guard cutters and naval destroyers began

70

the huge job of reassembling the convoys again. This time there would be no turning back.

Off the coast of France the midget submarine X23 slowly came to the surface. It was 1 A.M., June 5. Lieutenant George Honour quickly undid the hatch. Climbing up into the little conning tower, Honour and another crewman erected the antennae. Below, Lieutenant James Hodges flicked the dial on the radio to 1850 kilocycles and cupped his earphones with his hands. He hadn't long to wait. Very faintly he picked up their call sign: "PADFOOT . . . PADFOOT . . . PADFOOT." As he heard the one-word message that followed, he looked up in disbelief. Pressing his hands more firmly over the earphones, he listened again. But there was no mistake. He told the others. Nobody said anything. Glumly they looked at one another; ahead lay another full day under water.

★ 12 ★

IN THE early-morning light the beaches of Normandy were shrouded in mist. The intermittent rain of the previous day had become a steady drizzle, soaking everything. Beyond the beaches lay the ancient, irregularly shaped fields over which countless battles had been fought and countless more battles would be fought.

For four years the people of Normandy had lived with the Germans. This bondage had meant different things for different Normans. In the three major cities—Le Havre and Cherbourg, the ports which bracketed the area on east and west, and between them (both geographically and in size) Caen, lying ten miles inland—the occupation was a harsh and constant fact of life. Here were the headquarters of the Gestapo and the S.S. Here were the reminders of war—the nightly roundups of hostages, the never ending reprisals against the underground, the welcome but fearful Allied bombing attacks.

Beyond the cities, particularly between Caen and Cherbourg, lay the hedgerow country: the little fields bordered by great mounds of earth, each topped with thick bushes and saplings, that had been used as natural fortifications by invaders and defenders alike since the days of the Romans. Dotting the countryside were the timbered farm buildings with their thatched or red-tiled roofs, and here and there stood the towns and villages like miniature citadels, nearly all with square-cut Norman churches surrounded by centuries-old gray stone houses. To most of the world their names were unknown—Vierville, Colleville, La Madeleine, Ste.-Mère-Église, Chef-du-Pont, Ste.-Marie-du-Mont, Arromanches, Luc. Here, in the sparsely populated countryside, the occupation had a different meaning than in the big cities. Caught up in a kind of pastoral backwash of the war, the Norman peasant had done what he could to adjust to the situation. Thousands of men and women had been shipped out of the towns and villages as slave laborers, and those who remained were forced to work part of their time in labor battalions for the coastal garrisons. But the fiercely independent peasants did no more than was absolutely necessary. They lived from day to day, hating the Germans with Norman tenaciousness, and stoically watching and waiting for the day of liberation.

In his mother's house on a hill overlooking the sleepy village of Vierville, a thirty-one-year-old lawyer, Michel Hardelay, stood at the living-room windows, his binoculars focused on a German soldier riding a large farm horse down the road to the sea front. On either side of his saddle hung several tin cans. It was a preposterous sight: the massive rump of the horse, the bounding cans, and the soldier's bucketlike helmet topping it all.

As Hardelay watched, the German rode through the village, past the church with its tall, slender spire and on down to the concrete wall that sealed the main road off from the beach. Then he dismounted and took down all but one can. Suddenly three or four soldiers appeared mysteriously from around the cliffs and bluffs. They took the cans and disappeared again. Carrying the remaining can, the German climbed the wall and crossed to a large russet-colored summer villa surrounded by trees which stood astride the promenade at the end of the beach. There he got down on his knees and passed the can to a pair of waiting hands that appeared at ground level from under the building.

Every morning it was the same. The German was never late; he always brought the morning coffee down to the Vierville exit at this time. The day had begun for the gun crews in the cliff-side pillboxes and camouflaged bunkers at this end of the beach—a peaceful-looking, gently curving strip of sand that would be known to the world by the next day as Omaha Beach.

Michel Hardelay knew it was exactly 6:15 A.M.

He had watched the ritual many times before. It always struck Hardelay as a little comic, partly because of the soldier's appearance, partly because he found it amusing that the much vaunted technical know-how of the Germans fell apart when it came to a simple job like supplying men in the field with morning coffee. But Hardelay's was a bitter amusement. Like all Normans he had hated the Germans for a long time and he hated them particularly now.

For some months Hardelay had watched German troops and conscripted labor battalions digging, burrowing and tunneling all along the bluffs which backed up the beach and in the cliffs at either end where the sands stopped. He had seen them trellis the sands with obstacles and plant thousands of lethal, ugly mines. And they had not stopped there. With methodical thoroughness, they had demolished the line of pretty pink, white and red summer cottages and villas below the bluffs along the sea front. Now only seven out of ninety buildings remained. They had been destroyed not only to give the gunners clear arcs of fire, but because the Germans wanted the wood to panel their bunkers. Of the seven houses still standing, the largest—an all-year-round house built of stone—belonged to Hardelay. A few days before he had been officially told by the local commandant that his house would be destroyed. The Germans had decided they needed the bricks and the stone.

Hardelay wondered if maybe somebody, somewhere wouldn't countermand the decision. In some matters, the Germans were often unpredictable. He'd know for certain within twenty-four hours; he had been told the house would come down tomorrow —Tuesday, June 6.

At six-thirty, Hardelay switched on his radio to catch the BBC news. It was forbidden, but like hundreds of thousands of Frenchmen he flouted the order. It was just one more way to resist. Still he kept the sound down to a whisper. As usual, at the end of the news "Colonel Britain"—Douglas Ritchie, who was always identified as the voice of Supreme Headquarters Allied Expeditionary Force—read an important message.

"Today, Monday, June fifth," he said, "the Supreme Commander directs me to say this: There now exists in these broadcasts a direct channel of communications between the Supreme Commander and yourselves in the occupied countries. . . . In due course instructions of great importance will be given, but it will not be possible always to give them at a previously announced time; therefore, you must get into the habit, either personally or by arrangement with your friends, of listening at all hours. This is not as difficult as it sounds . . ." Hardelay guessed that the "instructions" would have something to do with the invasion. Everyone knew it was coming. He thought the Allies would attack at the narrowest part of the English Channel—around Dunkirk or Calais, where there were ports. But certainly not here.

The Dubois and Davot families living in Vierville didn't hear the broadcast; they slept late this morning. They had held a big celebration the previous night that had gone on until the early hours. Similar family gatherings had taken place all over Normandy, for Sunday, June 4, had been set aside by the ecclesiastical authorities as First Communion Day. It was always a great occasion, an annual reason for families and relatives to get together.

Togged out in their best clothes, the Dubois and Davot children had made their first Communion in the little Vierville church before their proud parents and relatives. Some of these relatives, each armed with a special pass from the German authorities which had taken months to get, had come all the way from Paris. The trip had been exasperating and dangerous—exasperating because the overcrowded trains no longer ran on time, dangerous because all locomotives were targets for Allied fighter-bombers.

But it had been worth it; a trip to Normandy always was. The region was still rich in all those things that Parisians rarely saw now—fresh butter, cheese, eggs, meat and, of course, Calvados, the heady cider-and-apple-pulp cognac of the Normans. Besides, in these difficult times Normandy was a good place to be. It was quiet and peaceful, too far away from England to be invaded.

The reunion of the two families had been a great success. And it wasn't over yet. This evening everyone would sit down to another great meal with the best wines and cognacs that their hosts had been able to save. That would wind up the celebrations; the relatives would catch the train for Paris at dawn on Tuesday.

Their three-day Normandy vacation was due to last much longer; they would remain trapped in Vierville for the next four months.

Farther down the beach, near the Colleville exit, forty-year-old Fernand Broeckx was doing what he did every morning at six-thirty: he sat in his dripping barn, spectacles askew, head tucked down by the udders of a cow, directing a thin stream of milk into a pail. His farm, lying alongside a narrow dirt road, topped a slight rise barely a half mile from the sea. He hadn't been down that road or onto the beach in a long time—not since the Germans had closed it off.

He had been farming in Normandy for five years. In World War I, Broeckx, a Belgian, had seen his home destroyed. He had never forgotten it. In 1939 when World War II began he promptly gave up his job in an office and moved his wife and daughter to Normandy, where they would be safe.

Ten miles away in the cathedral town of Bayeux his pretty nineteen-year-old daughter Anne Marie prepared to set out for the school where she taught kindergarten. She was looking forward to the end of the day, for then summer vacations began. She would spend her holidays on the farm. She would cycle home tomorrow.

Tomorrow also, a tall, lean American from Rhode Island whom she had never met would land on the beach almost in line with her father's farm. She would marry him.

All along the Normandy coast people went about their usual daily chores. The farmers worked in the fields, tended their apple orchards, herded their white-and-liver-colored cows. In the little villages and towns the shops opened. For everyone it was just another routine day of occupation.

The Wait

In the little hamlet of La Madeleine, back of the dunes and the wide expanse of sand that would soon be known as Utah Beach, Paul Gazengel opened up his tiny store and café as usual, although there was almost no business.

There had been a time when Gazengel had made a fair living—not much, but sufficient for the needs of himself, his wife Marthe and their twelve-year-old daughter Jeannine. But now the entire coastal area was sealed off. The families living just behind the seashore—roughly from the mouth of the Vire (which emptied into the sea nearby) and all along this side of the Cherbourg peninsula—had been moved out. Only those who owned farms had been permitted to remain. The café keeper's livelihood now depended on seven families that remained in La Madeleine and a few German troops in the vicinity whom he was forced to serve.

Gazengel would have liked to move away. As he sat in his café waiting for the first customer, he did not know that within twenty-four hours he would be making a trip. He and all the other men in the village would be rounded up and sent to England for questioning.

One of Gazengel's friends, the baker Pierre Caldron, had more serious problems on his mind this morning. In Dr. Jeanne's clinic at Carentan ten miles from the coast, he sat by the bedside of his five-year-old son Pierre, who had just had his tonsils removed. At midday Dr. Jeanne re-examined his son. "You've nothing to worry about," he told the anxious father. "He's all right. You'll be able to take him home tomorrow." But Caldron had been thinking. "No," he said. "I think his mother will be happier if I take little Pierre home today." Half an hour later, with the little boy in his arms, Caldron set out for his home in the village of Ste.-Marie-du-Mont, back of Utah Beach—where the paratroopers would link up with the men of the 4th Division on D Day.

The day was quiet and uneventful for the Germans too. Nothing was happening and nothing was expected to happen; the weather was much too bad. It was so bad, in fact, that in Paris, at the Luftwaffe's headquarters in the Luxembourg Palace, Colonel Professor Walter Stöbe, the chief meteorologist, told staff officers at the routine daily conference that they could relax. He doubted that Allied planes would even be operational this day. Antiaircraft crews were promptly ordered to stand down.

Next, Stöbe telephoned 20 Boulevard Victor Hugo in St.-Germain-en-Laye, a suburb of Paris just twelve miles away. His call went to an immense, three-floored blockhouse, one hundred yards long, sixty feet deep and embedded in the side of a slope beneath a girl's high school—OB West, Von Rundstedt's headquarters. Stöbe spoke to his liaison officer, weatherman Major Hermann Mueller, who dutifully recorded the forecast and then sent it along to the chief of staff, Major General Blumentritt. Weather reports were taken very seriously at OB West and Blumentritt was particularly anxious to see this one. He was putting the finishing touches to the itinerary of an inspection trip the Commander in Chief West planned to make. The report confirmed his belief that the trip could take place as scheduled. Von Rundstedt, accompanied by his son, a young lieutenant, planned to inspect the coastal defenses in Normandy on Tuesday.

Not many in St.-Germain-en-Laye were aware of the blockhouse's existence and even fewer knew that the most powerful field marshal in the German west lived in a small unpretentious villa back of the high school at 28 Rue Alexandre Dumas. It was surrounded by a high wall, the iron gates permanently closed. Entrance to the villa was by way of a specially constructed corridor that had been cut through the walls of the school, or by

78

way of an unobtrusive door in the wall bordering the Rue Alexandre Dumas.

Von Rundstedt slept late as usual (the aged Field Marshal rarely got up now before ten-thirty) and it was almost noon before he sat down at his desk in the villa's first-floor study. It was there that he conferred with his chief of staff and approved OB West's "Estimate of Allied Intentions" so that it could be forwarded to Hitler's headquarters, OKW, later in the day. The estimate was another typical wrong guess. It read:

The systematic and distinct increase of air attacks indicates that the enemy has reached a high degree of readiness. The probable invasion front still remains the sector from the Scheldt [in Holland] to Normandy . . . and it is not impossible that the north front of Brittany might be included . . . [but] it is still not clear where the enemy will invade within this total area. Concentrated air attacks on the coast defenses between Dunkirk and Dieppe may mean that the main Allied invasion effort will be made there . . . [but] imminence of invasion is not recognizable . . .

With this vague estimate out of the way—an estimate that placed the possible invasion area someplace along almost eight hundred miles of coast—Von Rundstedt and his son set out for the Field Marshal's favorite restaurant, the Coq Hardi at Bougival nearby. It was a little after one; D Day was twelve hours away.

All along the chain of German command the continuing bad weather acted like a tranquilizer. The various headquarters were quite confident that there would be no attack in the immediate future. Their reasoning was based on carefully assessed weather evaluations that had been made of the Allied landings in North Africa, Italy and Sicily. In each case conditions had varied, but meteorologists like Stöbe and his chief in Berlin, Dr. Karl Sonntag, had noted that the Allies had never attempted a landing unless the prospects of favorable weather were almost certain, particularly for covering air operations. To the methodical German mind there was no deviation from this rule; the weather had to be just right or the Allies wouldn't attack. And the weather wasn't just right.

At Army Group B headquarters in La Roche-Guyon the work went on as though Rommel were still there, but the chief of staff, Major General Speidel, thought it was quiet enough to plan a little dinner party. He had invited several guests: Dr. Horst, his brother-in-law; Ernst Junger, the philosopher and author; and an old friend, Major Wilhelm von Schramm, one of the official "war reporters." The intellectual Speidel was looking forward to the dinner. He hoped they'd discuss his favorite subject, French literature. There was something else to be discussed: a twenty-page manuscript that Junger had drafted and secretly passed on to Rommel and Speidel. Both of them fervently believed in the document; it outlined a plan for bringing about peace—after Hitler had either been tried by a German court or been assassinated. "We can really have a night discussing things," Speidel had told Schramm.

In St.-Lô, at the headquarters of the 84th Corps, Major Friedrich Hayn, the intelligence officer, was making arrangements for another kind of party. He had ordered several bottles of excellent Chablis, for at midnight the staff planned to surprise the corps commander, General Erich Marcks. His birthday was June 6.

They were holding the surprise birthday party at midnight because Marcks had to leave for the city of Rennes in Brittany at daybreak. He and all the other senior commanders in Normandy were to take part in a big map exercise that was to begin early on Tuesday morning. Marcks was slightly amused at the role he was supposed to play: he would represent the "Allies." The war games had been arranged by General Eugen Meindl, and perhaps because he was a paratrooper the big feature of the exercise was to be an "invasion" beginning with a paratroop "assault" followed by "landings" from the sea. Everyone thought the *Kriegsspiel* would be interesting—the theoretical invasion was supposed to take place in Normandy.

The *Kriegsspiel* worried the Seventh Army's chief of staff, Major General Max Pemsel. All afternoon at the headquarters in Le Mans he'd been thinking about it. It was bad enough that his senior commanders in Normandy and the Cherbourg peninsula would be away from their commands all at the same time. But it might be extremely dangerous if they were away overnight. Rennes was a long way off for most of them and Pemsel was afraid that some might be planning to leave the front before dawn. It was the dawn that always worried Pemsel; if an invasion ever came in Normandy, he believed, the attack would be launched at first light. He decided to warn all those due to participate in the games. The order he sent out by teletype read: "Commanding generals and others scheduled to attend the *Kriegsspiel* are reminded not to leave for Rennes before dawn on June 6." But it was too late. Some had already gone.

And so it was that, one by one, senior officers from Rommel down had left the front on the very eve of the battle. All of them had reasons, but it was almost as though a capricious fate had manipulated their departure. Rommel was in Germany. So was Army Group B's operations officer, Von Tempelhof. Admiral Theodor Krancke, the naval commander in the west, after informing Rundstedt that patrol boats were unable to leave harbor because of rough seas, set out for Bordeaux. Lieutenant General Heinz Hellmich, commanding the 243rd Division, which was holding one side of the Cherbourg peninsula, departed for Rennes. So did Lieutenant General Karl von Schlieben of the 709th Division. Major General Wilhelm Falley of the tough 91st Air Landing Division, which had just moved into Normandy, prepared to go. Colonel Wilhelm Meyer-Detring, Rundstedt's intelligence officer, was on leave and the chief of staff of one division couldn't be reached at all—he was off hunting with his French mistress.*

At this point, with the officers in charge of beachhead defenses dispersed all over Europe, the German High Command decided to transfer the Luftwaffe's last remaining fighter squadrons in France far out of range of the Normandy beaches. The fliers were aghast.

The principal reason for the withdrawal was that the squadrons were needed for the defense of the Reich, which for months had been coming under increasingly heavy round-the-clock Allied bombing attack. Under the circumstances it just did not seem reasonable to the High Command to leave these vital planes on exposed airfields in France where they were being destroyed by Allied fighters and bombers. Hitler had promised his generals that a thousand Luftwaffe planes would hit the beaches on the day of invasion. Now that was patently impossible. On June 4 there were only 183 day fighter planes in the whole of France,† of which about 160 were considered service-

---

* After D Day the coincidences of these multiple departures from the invasion front struck Hitler so forcibly that there was actually talk of an investigation to see whether British secret service could possibly have had anything to do with it.

The fact is that Hitler himself was no better prepared for the great day than his generals. The Führer was at his Berchtesgaden retreat in Bavaria. His naval aide, Admiral Karl Jesko von Puttkamer, remembers that Hitler got up late, held his usual military conference at noon and then had lunch at 4 P.M. Besides his mistress, Eva Braun, there were a number of Nazi dignitaries and their wives. The vegetarian Hitler apologized to the ladies for the meatless meal with his usual mealtime comment, "The elephant is the strongest animal; he also cannot stand meat." After lunch the group adjourned to the garden, where the Führer sipped lime blossom tea. He napped between six and seven, held another military conference at 11 P.M., then, a little before midnight, the ladies were called back. To the best of Puttkamer's recollection, the group then had to listen to four hours of Wagner, Lehar and Strauss.

† In researching this book I found no less than five different figures for the number of fighter planes in France. The figure of 183 given here I believe to be accurate. My source is a recent Luftwaffe history written by Colonel Josef Priller (see next page), whose work is now considered one of the most authoritative yet written on the Luftwaffe's activities.

able. Of the 160 one wing of 124, the 26th Fighter Wing, was being moved back from the coast this very afternoon.

At the headquarters of the 26th at Lille in the zone of the Fifteenth Army, Colonel Josef "Pips" Priller, one of the Luftwaffe's top aces (he had shot down ninety-six planes), stood on the airfield and fumed. Overhead was one of his three squadrons, heading for Metz in northeast France. His second squadron was about to take off. It had been ordered to Rheims, roughly halfway between Paris and the German border. The third squadron had already left for the south of France.

There was nothing the wing commander could do but protest. Priller was a flamboyant, temperamental pilot renowned in the Luftwaffe for his short temper. He had a reputation for telling off generals, and now he telephoned his group commander. "This is crazy!" Priller shouted. "If we're expecting an invasion the squadrons should be moved up, not back! And what happens if the attack comes during the transfer? My supplies can't reach the new bases until tomorrow or maybe the day after. You're all crazy!"

"Listen, Priller," said the group commander. "The invasion is out of the question. The weather is much too bad."

Priller slammed down the receiver. He walked back out onto the airfield. There were only two planes left, his and the one belonging to Sergeant Heinz Wodarczyk, his wing man. "What can we do?" he said to Wodarczyk. "If the invasion comes they'll probably expect us to hold it off all by ourselves. So we might as well start getting drunk now."

Of all the millions who watched and waited throughout France only a few men and women actually knew that the invasion was imminent. There were less than a dozen of them. They went about their affairs calmly and casually as usual. Being calm and casual was part of their business; they were the leaders of the French underground.

Most of them were in Paris. From there they commanded a vast and complicated organization. It was in fact an army with a full chain of command and countless departments and bureaus handling everything from the rescue of downed Allied pilots to sabotage, from espionage to assassination. There were regional chiefs, area commanders, section leaders and thousands of men and women in the rank and file. On paper the organization had so many overlapping nets of activity that it appeared to be unnecessarily complex. This apparent confusion was deliberate. In it lay the underground's strength. Overlapping commands gave greater protection; multiple nets of activity guaranteed the success of each operation; and so secret was the entire structure that leaders rarely knew one another except by code names and never did one group know what another was doing. It had to be this way if the underground was to survive at all. Even with all those precautions German retaliatory measures had become so crushing that by May of 1944 the life expectancy of an active underground fighter was considered to be less than six months.

This great secret resistance army of men and women had been fighting a silent war for more than four years—a war that was often unspectacular, but always hazardous. Thousands had been executed, thousands more had died in concentration camps. But now, although the rank and file didn't know it yet, the day for which they had been fighting was close at hand.

In the previous days the underground's high command had picked up hundreds of coded messages from the BBC. A few of these had been alerts warning that the invasion might come at any moment. One of these messages had been the first line of the Verlaine poem, "Chanson d'Automne"—the same alert that Lieutenant Colonel Meyer's men at the German Fifteenth Army headquarters had intercepted on June 1. (Canaris had been right.)

Now, even more excited than Meyer, the underground leaders waited for the second line of this poem and for other messages which would confirm the previously received information. None of these alerts was expected to be broadcast until the very last moment in the hours preceding the actual day of invasion. Even then the underground leaders knew that they would not learn from these messages the exact area where the landings were due to take place. For the underground at large the real tip-off would come when the Allies ordered the prearranged sabotage plans to go into effect. Two messages would trigger off the attacks. One, "It is hot in Suez," would put into effect the "Green Plan"—the sabotaging of railroad tracks and equipment. The other, "The dice are on the table," would call for the "Red Plan"—the cutting of telephone lines and cables. All regional, area and sector leaders had been warned to listen for these two messages.

On this Monday evening, the eve of D Day, the first message was broadcast by the BBC at 6:30 P.M. "It is hot in Suez. . . . It is hot in Suez," said the voice of the announcer solemnly.

Guillaume Mercader, the intelligence chief for the Normandy coastal sector between Vierville and Port-en-Bessin (roughly the Omaha Beach area) was crouching by a hidden radio set in the cellar of his bicycle shop in Bayeux when he heard it. He was almost stunned by the impact of the words. It was a moment he would never forget. He didn't know where the invasion would take place or when, but it was coming at long last, after all these years.

There was a pause. Then came the second message that Mercader had been waiting for. "The dice are on the table," said the announcer. "The dice are on the table." This was immediately followed by a long string of messages, each one repeated: "Napoleon's hat is in the ring. . . . John loves Mary. . . . The Arrow will not pass. . . ." Mercader switched off the radio. He had heard the only two messages that concerned him. The others were specific alerts for groups elsewhere in France.

Hurrying upstairs, he said to his wife, Madeleine, "I have to go out. I'll be back late tonight." Then he wheeled out a low racing bike from his bicycle shop and pedaled off to tell his section leaders. Mercader was the former Normandy cycling champion and he had represented the province several times in the famed Tour de France race. He knew the Germans wouldn't stop him. They had given him a special permit so that he could practice.

Everywhere now resistance groups were quietly told the news by their immediate leaders. Each unit had its own plan and knew exactly what had to be done. Albert Augé, the stationmaster at Caen, and his men were to destroy water pumps in the yards, smash the steam injectors on locomotives. André Farine, a café owner from Lieu Fontaine, near Isigny, had the job of strangling Normandy's communications: his forty-man team would cut the massive telephone cable feeding out of Cherbourg. Yves Gresselin, a Cherbourg grocer, had one of the toughest jobs of all: his men were to dynamite a network of railway lines between Cherbourg, St.-Lô and Paris. And these were just a few of the teams. It was a large order for the underground. Time was short and the attacks couldn't begin before dark. But everywhere along the invasion coast from Brittany to the Belgian border men prepared, all hoping that the attack would come in their areas.

For some men the messages posed quite different problems. In the seaside resort town of Grandcamp near the mouth of the Vire and almost centered between Omaha and Utah beaches, sector chief Jean Marion had vital information to pass on to London. He wondered how he'd get it there—and if he still had time. Early in the afternoon his men had reported the arrival of a new antiaircraft battery group barely a mile away. Just to be sure, Marion had casually cycled over to see the guns. Even if he was stopped he knew he'd get through; among the many fake identification cards he had for such occasions was one stating that he was a construction worker on the Atlantic Wall.

Marion was shaken by the size of the unit and the area it covered. It was a motorized flak assault group with heavy, light and mixed antiaircraft guns. There were five batteries, twenty-five guns in all, and they were being moved into positions covering the area from the mouth of the Vire all the way to the outskirts of Grandcamp. Their crews, Marion noted, were toiling feverishly to emplace the guns, almost as though they were working against time. The frantic activity worried Marion. It could mean that the invasion would be here and that somehow the Germans had learned of it.

Although Marion did not know it, the guns covered the precise route the planes and gliders of the 82nd and 101st paratroopers would take within a few hours. Yet, if anybody in the German High Command had any knowledge of the impending attack they hadn't told Colonel Werner von Kistowski, commander of Flak Assault Regiment 1. He was still wondering why his 2,500-man flak unit had been rushed up here. But Kistowski was used to sudden moves. His outfit had once been sent into the Caucasus all by itself. Nothing surprised him any more.

Jean Marion, calmly cycling by the soldiers at work on the guns, began to wrestle with a big problem: how to get this vital information to the secret headquarters of Léonard Gille, Normandy's deputy military intelligence chief, in Caen, fifty miles away. Marion couldn't leave his sector now—there was too much to do. So he decided to take a chance on sending the message by a chain of couriers to Mercader in Bayeux. He knew it might take hours, but if there was still time Marion was sure that Mercader would somehow get it to Caen.

There was one more thing Marion wanted London to know about. It wasn't as important as the antiaircraft gun positions—

simply a confirmation of the many messages he had sent in the previous days about the massive gun emplacements on the top of the nine-story-high cliffs at Pointe du Hoc. Marion wanted to pass on once again the news that the guns had not yet been installed. They were still en route, two miles away from the positions. (Despite Marion's frantic efforts to warn London, on D Day U.S. Rangers would lose 135 men out of 225 in their heroic attack to silence guns that had never been there.)

For some members of the underground, unaware of the imminence of the invasion, Tuesday, June 6, had a special significance of its own. For Léonard Gille it meant a meeting in Paris with his superiors. Even now, Gille was calmly sitting in a train bound for Paris, although he expected Green Plan sabotage teams to derail it at any moment. Gille was quite sure the invasion was not scheduled for Tuesday, at least not in his area. Surely his superiors would have canceled the meeting if the attack was due in Normandy.

But the date did bother him. That afternoon in Caen, one of Gille's section chiefs, the leader of an affiliated Communist group, had told him quite emphatically that the invasion was due at dawn on the sixth. The man's information had proved invariably right in the past. This raised an old question again in Gille's mind. Did the man get his information direct from Moscow? Gille decided not; it seemed inconceivable to him that the Russians would deliberately jeopardize Allied plans by breaking security.

For Janine Boitard, Gille's fiancée, back in Caen, Tuesday couldn't come soon enough. In three years of underground work, she had hidden more than sixty Allied pilots in her little ground-floor apartment at 15 Rue Laplace. It was dangerous, unrewarding, nerve-racking work; a slip could mean the firing squad. After Tuesday Janine could breathe a little easier—until the next time she hid a flier who was down—for on Tuesday she was due to pass along the escape route two R.A.F. pilots who had been shot down over northern France. They had spent the last fifteen days in her apartment. She hoped her luck would continue to hold.

For others, luck had already run out. For Amélie Lechevalier, June 6 could mean nothing, or everything. She and her husband, Louis, had been arrested by the Gestapo on June 2. They had helped more than a hundred Allied fliers to escape; they had been turned in by one of their own farm boys. Now, in her cell in the Caen prison, Amélie Lechevalier sat on the bunk and wondered how soon she and her husband would be executed.

★ 13 ★

OFF THE French coast a little before 9 P.M. a dozen small ships appeared. They moved quietly along the horizon, so close that their crews could clearly see the houses of Normandy. The ships went unnoticed. They finished their job and then moved back. They were British mine sweepers—the vanguard of the mightiest fleet ever assembled.

For now back in the Channel, plowing through the choppy gray waters, a phalanx of ships bore down on Hitler's Europe— the might and fury of the free world unleashed at last. They came, rank after relentless rank, ten lanes wide, twenty miles across, five thousand ships of every description. There were fast new attack transports, slow rust-scarred freighters, small ocean liners, Channel steamers, hospital ships, weather-beaten tank·

ers, coasters and swarms of fussing tugs. There were endless columns of shallow-draft landing ships—great wallowing vessels, some of them almost 350 feet long. Many of these and the other heavier transports carried smaller landing craft for the actual beach assault—more than 1,500 of them. Ahead of the convoys were processions of mine sweepers, Coast Guard cutters, buoy-layers and motor launches. Barrage balloons flew above the ships. Squadrons of fighter planes weaved below the clouds. And surrounding this fantastic cavalcade of ships packed with men, guns, tanks, motor vehicles and supplies, and excluding small naval vessels, was a formidable array of 702 warships.*

There was the heavy cruiser U.S.S. *Augusta*, Rear Admiral Kirk's flagship, leading the American task force—twenty-one convoys bound for Omaha and Utah beaches. Just four months before Pearl Harbor the queenly *Augusta* had carried President Roosevelt to a quiet Newfoundland bay for the first of his many historic meetings with Winston Churchill. Nearby, steaming majestically with all their battle flags flying, were the battleships: H.M.S. *Nelson, Ramillies* and *Warspite,* and U.S.S. *Texas, Arkansas* and the proud *Nevada* which the Japanese had sunk and written off at Pearl Harbor.

Leading the thirty-eight British and Canadian convoys bound for Sword, Juno and Gold beaches was the cruiser H.M.S. *Scylla,* the flagship of Rear Admiral Sir Philip Vian, the man who tracked down the German battleship *Bismarck.* And close by was one of Britain's most famous light cruisers—H.M.S. *Ajax,* one of a trio which had hounded the pride of Hitler's fleet, the

---

* There is considerable controversy as to the exact number of ships in the invasion fleet, but the most accurate military works on D Day—Gordon Harrison's *Cross-Channel Attack* (the official U.S. Army military history) and Admiral Samuel Eliot Morison's naval history *Invasion of France & Germany*—both agree on a figure of about five thousand. This includes the landing craft which were carried on board. *Operation Neptune* by the Royal Navy's Commander Kenneth Edwards gives a lower figure of around 4,500.

Graf Spee, to her doom in Montevideo harbor after the battle of the River Plate in December 1939. There were other famous cruisers—the U.S.S. *Tuscaloosa* and *Quincy,* H.M.S. *Enterprise* and *Black Prince,* France's *Georges Leygues*—twenty-two in all.

Along the edges of the convoys sailed a variety of ships: graceful sloops, chunky corvettes, slim gunboats like the Dutch *Soemba,* antisubmarine patrol craft, fast PT boats, and everywhere sleek destroyers. Besides the scores of American and British destroyers, there were Canada's *Qu'Appelle, Saskatchewan* and *Ristigouche,* Norway's *Svenner,* and even a contribution from the Polish forces, the *Poiron.*

Slowly, ponderously this great armada moved across the Channel. It followed a minute-by-minute traffic pattern of a kind never attempted before. Ships poured out of British ports and, moving down the coasts in two-convoy lanes, converged on the assembly area south of the Isle of Wight. There they sorted themselves out and each took a carefully predetermined position with the force heading for the particular beach to which it had been assigned. Out of the assembly area, which was promptly nicknamed "Piccadilly Circus," the convoys headed for France along five buoy-marked lanes. And as they approached Normandy these five paths split up into ten channels, two for each beach—one for fast traffic, the other for slow. Up front, just behind the spearhead of mine sweepers, battleships and cruisers, were the command ships, five attack transports bristling with radar and radio antennae. These floating command posts would be the nerve centers of the invasion.

Everywhere there were ships. To the men aboard, this historic armada is still remembered as "the most impressive, unforgettable" sight they had ever seen.

For the troops it was good to be on the way at last, despite the discomforts and the dangers ahead. Men were still tense, but some of the strain had lifted. Now everybody simply wanted to get the job over and done with. On the landing ships and transports men wrote last-minute letters, played cards, joined in long bull sessions. "Chaplains," Major Thomas Spencer Dallas of the 29th Division recalls, "did a land-office business."

One minister on a jam-packed landing craft, Captain Lewis Fulmer Koon, chaplain for the 4th Division's 12th Infantry Regiment, found himself serving as pastor for all denominations. A Jewish officer, Captain Irving Gray, asked Chaplain Koon if he would lead his company in prayer "to the God in whom we all believe, whether Protestant, Roman Catholic or Jew, that our mission may be accomplished and that, if possible, we may be brought safely home again." Koon gladly obliged. And in the gathering dusk, Gunner's Mate Third Class William Sweeney of a Coast Guard cutter remembers, the attack transport *Samuel Chase* blinked out a signal, "Mass is going on."

For most of the men the first few hours of the journey were spent quietly. Many grew introspective and talked of things men usually keep to themselves. Hundreds later recalled that they found themselves admitting their fears and talking of other personal matters with unusual candor. They drew closer to one another on this strange night and confided in men they had never even met before. "We talked a lot about home and what we had experienced in the past and what we would experience at the landing and what it would all be like," P.F.C. Earlston Hern of the 146th Engineer Battalion recalls. On the slippery wet deck of his landing craft, Hern and a medic whose name he never learned had such a conversation. "The medic was having trouble at home. His wife, a model, wanted a divorce. He was a pretty worried guy. He said she'd have to wait until he got home. I remember, too, that the whole time we were talking there was a young kid nearby singing softly to himself. This kid made the remark that he could sing better than he ever had in the past and it really seemed to please him."

Aboard H.M.S. *Empire Anvil*, Corporal Michael Kurtz of the U.S. 1st Division, a veteran of the invasions of North Africa,

Sicily and Italy, was approached by a new replacement, Private Joseph Steinber of Wisconsin.

"Corporal," said Steinber, "do you honestly think we've got a chance?"

"Hell, yes, boy," said Kurtz. "Don't ever worry about getting killed. In this outfit we worry about battles when we get to them."

Sergeant Bill "L-Rod" Petty of the 2nd Ranger Battalion was doing his worrying now. With his friend, P.F.C. Bill McHugh, Petty sat on the deck of the old Channel steamer *Isle of Man* watching the darkness close in. Petty took cold comfort from the long lines of ships all about them; his mind was on the cliffs at Pointe du Hoc. Turning to McHugh, he said, "We haven't got a hope in hell of coming out of this alive."

"You're just a goddam pessimist," said McHugh.

"Maybe," replied Petty, "but only one of us will make it, Mac."

McHugh was unimpressed. "When you gotta go, you gotta go," he said.

Some men tried to read. Corporal Alan Bodet of the 1st Division began *Kings Row* by Henry Bellamann, but he found it difficult to concentrate because he was worrying about his jeep. Would the waterproofing hold out when he drove it into three or four feet of water? Gunner Arthur Henry Boon of the Canadian 3rd Division, on board a landing craft loaded with tanks, tried to get through a pocket book intriguingly titled *A Maid and a Million Men*. Chaplain Lawrence E. Deery of the 1st Division on the transport H.M.S. *Empire Anvil* was amazed to see a British naval officer reading Horace's odes in Latin. But Deery himself, who would land on Omaha Beach in the first wave with the 16th Infantry Regiment, spent the evening reading Symond's *Life of Michelangelo*. In another convoy, on a landing craft which was rolling so much that nearly everybody was seasick, Captain James Douglas Gillan, another Canadian, brought out the one volume which made sense this night. To quiet his own nerves and those of a brother officer, he opened to the Twenty-third Psalm and read aloud, "The Lord is my Shepherd; I shall not want. . . ."

It wasn't all solemn. There was lightheartedness too. Aboard the transport H.M.S. *Ben Machree,* some Rangers strung three-quarter-inch ropes from the masts to the decks and began climbing all over the ship, much to the astonishment of the British crew. On another ship, members of the Canadian 3rd Division held an amateur night with assorted recitations, jigs and reels and choral offerings. Sergeant James Percival "Paddy" de Lacy of the King's Regiment became so emotional listening to the "Rose of Tralee" played on the bagpipes that he forgot where he was and stood up and offered a toast to Ireland's Eamon de Valera for "keepin' us out of the war."

Many men who had spent hours worrying about their chances of survival now couldn't wait to reach the beaches. The boat trip was proving more terrible than their worst fear of the Germans. Seasickness had struck through the fifty-nine convoys like a plague, especially in the rolling landing craft. Each man had been supplied with antiseasickness pills, plus an article of equipment which was listed in the loading sheets with typical Army thoroughness as "Bag, vomit, one."

This was military efficiency at its best, but it still wasn't enough. "The puke bags were full, tin hats were full, the fire buckets were emptied of sand and filled," Technical Sergeant William James Wiedefeld of the 29th Division recalls. "The steel decks you couldn't stand on, and everywhere you heard men say, 'If they are going to kill us, get us out of these damn tubs.' " On some landing ships men were so ill that they threatened— possibly more for effect than in earnest—to throw themselves overboard. Private Gordon Laing of the Canadian 3rd Division found himself hanging on to a friend who "begged me to let go his belt." A Royal Marine commando, Sergeant Russell John

Wither, remembers that on his landing ship "the spew bags were soon used up and in the end only one was left." It was passed from hand to hand.

Because of the seasickness thousands of the men lost the best meals they would see for many months to come. Special arrangements had been made to give all ships the finest food possible. The special menus, which the troops dubbed the "last meal," varied from ship to ship, and appetites varied from man to man. On board the attack transport *Charles Carroll*, Captain Carroll B. Smith of the 29th Division had a steak with eggs on top, sunny side up, and then topped it off with ice cream and loganberries. Two hours later he was fighting for a position at the rail. Second Lieutenant Joseph Rosenblatt, Jr., of the 112th Engineer Battalion ate seven helpings of chicken à la king and felt fine. So did Sergeant Keith Bryan of the 5th Engineer Special Brigade. He put away sandwiches and coffee and was still hungry. One of his buddies "lifted" a gallon of fruit cocktail from the galley and four of them finished that.

Aboard the H.M.S. *Prince Charles*, Sergeant Avery J. Thornhill of the 5th Rangers avoided all discomforts. He took an overdose of seasick pills and slept through it all.

Despite the common miseries and fears of the men who were there some memories are etched with surprising clarity. Second Lieutenant Donald Anderson of the 29th Division remembers how the sun broke through about an hour before dark, silhouetting the entire fleet. In honor of Sergeant Tom Ryan of the 2nd Rangers, the men of F Company gathered around him and sang "Happy Birthday." He was twenty-two. And for homesick nineteen-year-old Private Robert Marion Allen of the 1st Division it was "a night ready-made for a boat ride on the Mississippi."

All over, throughout the ships of the fleet, the men who would make history at dawn settled down to get what rest they could.

As Commander Philippe Kieffer of the lone French commando unit rolled himself into his blankets aboard his landing ship, there came to his mind the prayer of Sir Jacob Astley at the battle of Edgehill in England in 1642. "O Lord," prayed Kieffer, "Thou knowest how busy I must be this day. If I forget Thee, do not Thou forget me . . ." He drew up the blankets and was almost immediately asleep.

It was a little after 10:15 P.M. when Lieutenant Colonel Meyer, counterintelligence chief of the German Fifteenth Army, rushed out of his office. In his hand was probably the most important message the Germans had intercepted throughout the whole of World War II. Meyer now knew that the invasion would take place within forty-eight hours. With this information the Allies could be thrown back into the sea. The message picked up from a BBC broadcast to the French underground was the second line of the Verlaine poem: *"Blessent mon coeur d'une langueur monotone* [Wound my heart with a monotonous languor]."

Meyer burst into the dining room where General Hans von Salmuth, the Fifteenth Army's commanding officer, was playing bridge with his chief of staff and two others. "General!" Meyer said breathlessly. "The message, the second part—it's here!"

Von Salmuth thought a moment, then gave the order to put the Fifteenth Army on full alert. As Meyer hurried out of the room, Von Salmuth was again looking at his bridge hand. "I'm too old a bunny," Von Salmuth recalls saying, "to get too excited about this."

Back in his office, Meyer and his staff immediately notified OB West, Von Rundstedt's headquarters, by telephone. They in turn alerted OKW, Hitler's headquarters. Simultaneously all other commands were informed by teletype.

Once again, for reasons that have never been explained satisfactorily, the Seventh Army was not notified.* It would take the Allied fleet a little more than four hours now to reach the transport areas off the five Normandy beaches; within three hours eighteen thousand paratroopers would drop over the darkening fields and hedgerows—into the zone of the one German army never alerted to D Day.

Private Arthur B. "Dutch" Schultz of the 82nd Airborne Division was ready. Like everybody else on the airfield, he was in his jump suit, a parachute hanging over his right arm. His face was blackened with charcoal; his head, in the crazy style affected by paratroopers everywhere this night, was shaven Iroquois fashion, with a narrow tuft of hair running back the center of his scalp. All around him was his gear; he was ready in every respect. Of the $2,500 he had won a few hours before he now had just $20 left.

Now the men waited for the trucks to carry them to the planes. Private Gerald Columbi, one of Dutch's friends, broke away from

* All times in this book are given in British Double Summer Time, which was one hour later than German Central Time. So to Meyer the time his men intercepted the message was 9:15 P.M. Just for the record the Fifteenth Army War Diary carries the exact teletype message that was sent out to the various commands. It reads: "Teletype No. 2117/26 urgent to 67th, 81st, 82nd, 89th Corps; Military Governor Belgium and Northern France; Army Group B; 16th Flak Division; Admiral Channel Coast; Luftwaffe Belgium and Northern France. Message of BBC, 2115, June 5 has been processed. According to our available records it means 'Expect invasion within 48 hours, starting 0000, June 6.'"

It will be noted that neither the Seventh Army nor its 84th Corps is included in the above list. It was not Meyer's job to notify these. The responsibility lay with Rommel's headquarters, as these units came under Army Group B. However, the biggest mystery of all is why OB West, Rundstedt's headquarters, failed to alert the whole invasion front from Holland to the Spanish border. The mystery is further compounded by the fact that at war's end the Germans claimed that at least fifteen messages pertaining to D Day were intercepted and correctly interpreted. The Verlaine messages are the only ones I found entered in the German war diaries.

a small crap game that was still going and came running up. "Lend me twenty bucks quick!" he said.

"What for?" asked Schultz. "You might get killed."

"I'll let you have this," said Columbi, undoing his wrist watch.

"Okay," said Dutch, handing over his last $20.

Columbi ran back to the game. Dutch looked at the watch; it was a gold Bulova graduation model with Columbi's name and an inscription from his parents on the back. Just then someone yelled, "Okay, here we go."

Dutch picked up his gear and with the other paratroopers left the hangar. As he climbed aboard a truck he passed Columbi. "Here," he said, as he gave him back the watch, "I don't need two of them." Now all Dutch had left were the rosary beads his mother had sent him. He had decided to take them after all. The trucks moved across the airfield toward the waiting planes.

All over England the Allied airborne armies boarded their planes and gliders. The planes carrying the pathfinders, the men who would light the dropping zones for the airborne troops, had already left. At the 101st Airborne Division's headquarters at Newbury, the Supreme Commander, General Dwight D. Eisenhower, with a small group of officers and four correspondents, watched the first planes get into position for take-off. He had spent more than an hour talking to the men. He was more worried about the airborne operation than about any other phase of the assault. Some of his commanders were convinced that the airborne assault might produce more than eighty per cent casualties.

Eisenhower had said goodbye to the 101st's commanding officer, Major General Maxwell D. Taylor, who was leading his men into battle. Taylor had walked away carrying himself very straight and stiff. He didn't want the Supreme Commander to know that he had torn a ligament in his right knee that afternoon playing squash. Eisenhower might have refused him permission to go.

The Wait

Now Eisenhower stood watching as the planes trundled down the runways and lifted slowly into the air. One by one they followed each other into the darkness. Above the field they circled as they assembled into formation. Eisenhower, his hands deep in his pockets, gazed up into the night sky. As the huge formation of planes roared one last time over the field and headed toward France, NBC's Red Mueller looked at the Supreme Commander. Eisenhower's eyes were filled with tears.

Minutes later, in the Channel, the men of the invasion fleet heard the roar of the planes. It grew louder by the second, and then wave after wave passed overhead. The formations took a long time to pass. Then the thunder of their engines began to fade. On the bridge of the U.S.S. *Herndon*, Lieutenant Bartow Farr, the watch officers and NEA's war correspondent, Tom Wolf, gazed up into the darkness. Nobody could say a word. And then as the last formation flew over, an amber light blinked down through the clouds on the fleet below. Slowly it flashed out in Morse code three dots and a dash: V for Victory.

PART TWO

The Night

★ 1 ★

Moonlight flooded the bedroom. Madame Angèle Levrault, sixty-year-old schoolmistress in Ste.-Mère-Église, slowly opened her eyes. On the wall opposite her bed bunches of red and white lights were flickering silently. Madame Levrault sat bolt upright and stared. The winking lights seemed to be slowly dripping down the wall.

As full consciousness came to her, the old lady realized she was looking at reflections in the large mirror on her dressing table. At that moment, too, she heard off in the distance the low throbbing of planes, the muffled booming of explosions and the sharp staccato of quick-firing flak batteries. Quickly she went to the window.

Far up the coast, hanging eerily in the sky, were brilliant clusters of flares. A red glow tinged the clouds. In the distance there were bright-pink explosions and streams of orange, green, yellow and white tracer bullets. To Madame Levrault it looked as if Cherbourg, twenty-seven miles away, was being bombed again. She was glad she lived in quiet little Ste.-Mère-Église this night.

The schoolmistress put on her shoes and a dressing gown and headed through the kitchen and out the back door, bound for the outhouse. In the garden everything was peaceful. The flares and the moonlight made it seem bright as day. The neighboring fields with their hedgerows were still and quiet, filled with long shadows.

She had taken only a few steps when she heard the sound of airplanes growing louder, heading for the town. Suddenly every flak battery in the district began firing. Madame Levrault, frightened, rushed wildly for the protection of a tree. The planes came in fast and low, accompanied by a thunderous barrage of anti-aircraft fire, and she was momentarily deafened by the din. Almost immediately the roar of the engines faded, the firing ceased and, as though nothing had happened, there was silence again.

It was then that she heard a strange fluttering sound from somewhere above her. She looked up. Floating down, heading straight for the garden, was a parachute with something bulky swinging beneath it. For a second the light of the moon was cut off, and at that moment Private Robert M. Murphy* of the 82nd Airborne's 505th Regiment, a pathfinder, fell with a thud twenty yards away and tumbled head over heels into the garden. Madame Levrault stood petrified.

Quickly the eighteen-year-old trooper whipped out a knife, cut himself loose from his chute, grabbed a large bag and stood up. Then he saw Madame Levrault. They stood looking at each other for a long moment. To the old Frenchwoman, the paratrooper looked weirdly frightening. He was tall and thin, his face was streaked with war paint, accentuating his cheekbones and nose. He seemed weighted down with weapons and equipment. Then, as the old lady watched in terror, unable to move, the strange apparition put a finger to his lips in a gesture of silence

---

* As a war correspondent I interviewed Madame Levrault in June 1944. She had no idea of the man's name or unit, but she showed me three hundred rounds of ammunition, still in their pouches, which the paratrooper had dropped. In 1958 when I began writing and interviewing D-Day participants for this book I was able to locate only a dozen of the original American pathfinders. One of them, Mr. Murphy, now a prominent Boston lawyer, told me that "after hitting the ground . . . I took my trench knife from my boot and cut myself out of the harness. Without knowing it I also cut away pouches carrying three hundred rounds of ammunition." His story tallied in all respects with Madame Levrault's, told to me fourteen years before.

and swiftly disappeared. At that moment, Madame Levrault was galvanized to action. Grabbing up the skirts of her night-wear, she dashed madly for the house. What she had seen was one of the first Americans to land in Normandy. The time was 12:15 A.M., Tuesday, June 6. D Day had begun.

All over the area the pathfinders had jumped, some from only three hundred feet. The task of this advance guard of the inva-sion, a small, courageous group of volunteers, was to mark "drop zones" in a 50-mile-square area of the Cherbourg peninsula back of Utah Beach for the 82nd and 101st paratroopers and gliders. They had been trained in a special school set up by Brigadier General James M. "Jumpin' Jim" Gavin. "When you land in Normandy," he had told them, "you will have only one friend: God." At all costs they were to avoid trouble. Their vital mission depended on speed and stealth.

But the pathfinders ran into difficulties from the very begin-ning. They plunged into chaos. The Dakotas had swept in over the targets so fast that the Germans at first thought they were fighter planes. Surprised by the suddenness of the attack, flak units opened up blindly, filling the sky with weaving patterns of glowing tracer bullets and deadly bursts of shrapnel. As Sergeant Charles Asay of the 101st floated down, he watched with a curi-ous detachment as "long graceful arcs of multicolored bullets waved up from the ground," reminding him of the Fourth of July. He thought "they were very pretty."

Just before Private Delbert Jones jumped, the plane he was in got a direct hit. The shell slammed through without doing much damage, but it missed Jones by only an inch. And as Private Adrian Doss, burdened with upwards of one hundred pounds of equipment, fell through the air, he was horrified to find tracer bullets weaving all about him. They converged above his head and he felt the tugging of his chute as the bullets ripped through the silk. Then a stream of bullets passed through the equipment hanging in front of him. Miraculously he wasn't hit, but a hole

105

was ripped in his musette bag "large enough for everything to fall out."

So intense was the flak fire that many planes were forced off course. Only thirty-eight of the 120 pathfinders landed directly on their targets. The remainder came down miles away. They dropped into fields, gardens, streams and swamps. They crashed into trees and hedgerows and onto rooftops. Most of these men were veteran paratroopers, but even so they were utterly confused when they tried to get their initial bearings. The fields were smaller, the hedgerows higher and the roads narrower than those they had studied for so many months on terrain maps. In those first awful moments of disorientation, some men did foolhardy and even dangerous things. P.F.C. Frederick Wilhelm was so dazed when he landed that he forgot he was behind enemy lines and switched on one of the large marker lights he was carrying. He wanted to see if it still worked. It did. Suddenly the field was flooded with light, scaring Wilhelm more than if the Germans had actually opened fire on him. And Captain Frank Lillyman, leader of the 101st teams, almost gave his position away. Dropping into a pasture, he was suddenly confronted by a huge bulk that bore down on him out of the darkness. He almost shot it before it identified itself with a low moo.

Besides frightening themselves and startling the Normans, the pathfinders surprised and confused the few Germans who saw them. Two troopers actually landed outside the headquarters of Captain Ernst Düring of the German 352nd Division, more than five miles from the nearest drop zone. Düring, who commanded a heavy machine gun company stationed at Brevands, had been awakened by the low-flying formations and the flak barrage. Leaping out of bed, he dressed so quickly that he put his boots on the wrong feet (something he didn't notice until the end of D Day). In the street Düring saw the shadowy figures of the two men some distance away. He challenged them but got no answer. Immediately he sprayed the area with his *Schmeisser* submachine gun. There was no answering fire from the two well-trained pathfinders. They simply vanished. Rushing back to his headquarters, Düring called his battalion commander. Breathlessly he said into the phone, *"Fallschirmjäger* [Paratroopers]! *Fallschirmjäger!"*

Other pathfinders weren't as lucky. As Private Robert Murphy of the 82nd, lugging his bag (which contained a portable radar set), headed out of Madame Levrault's garden and started toward his drop zone north of Ste.-Mère-Église, he heard a short burst of firing off to his right. He was to learn later that his buddy, Private Leonard Devorchak, had been shot at that moment. Devorchak, who had sworn to "win a medal a day just to prove to myself that I can make it," may have been the first American to be killed on D Day.

All over the area pathfinders like Murphy tried to get their bearings. Silently moving from hedgerow to hedgerow, these fierce-looking paratroopers, bulky in their jump smocks and overloaded with guns, mines, lights, radar sets and fluorescent panels, set out for rendezvous points. They had barely one hour to mark the drop zones for the full-scale American airborne assault that would begin at 1:15 A.M.

Fifty miles away, at the eastern end of the Normandy battlefield, six planeloads of British pathfinders and six R.A.F. bombers towing gliders swept in over the coast. Ahead of them the sky stormed with vicious flak fire, and ghostly chandeliers of flares hung everywhere. In the little village of Ranville, a few miles from Caen, eleven-year-old Alain Doix had seen the flares, too. The firing had awakened him and now he stared transfixed, as had Madame Levrault, utterly fascinated by the kaleidoscopic reflections which he could see in the great brass knobs on the posts at the end of the bed. Shaking his grandmother, Madame Mathilde Doix, who was sleeping with him, Alain said excitedly, "Wake up! Wake up, Grandmama, I think something is happening."

Just then Alain's father, René Doix, rushed into the room. "Get dressed quickly," he urged them. "I think it's a heavy raid." From the window, father and son could see the planes coming in over the fields, but as he watched René realized that these planes made no sound. Suddenly it dawned on him what they were. "My God," he exclaimed, "these aren't planes! They're gliders!"

Like huge bats, the six gliders, each carrying approximately thirty men, swooped silently down. Immediately on crossing the coast, at a point some five miles from Ranville, they had been cast off by their tow planes from five to six thousand feet up. Now they headed for two parallel waterways shimmering in the moonlight, the Caen Canal and the Orne River. Two heavily guarded bridges, one leading to the other, crossed the twin channels just above and between Ranville and the village of Bénouville. These bridges were the objectives for this small band of British 6th Airborne glider infantry—volunteers from such proud units as the Oxfordshire and Buckinghamshire Light Infantry and the Royal Engineers. Their hazardous mission was to seize the bridges and overwhelm the garrison. If their task could be achieved a major artery between Caen and the sea would be severed, preventing the east-west movement of German reinforcements, particularly panzer units, from driving into the flank of the British and Canadian invasion area. Because the bridges were needed to expand the invasion bridgehead, they had to be captured intact before the guards could set off demolitions. A swift surprise assault was called for. The British had come up with a bold and dangerous solution. The men who now linked arms and held their breath as their gliders rustled softly down through the moonlit night were about to crash-land on the very approaches to the bridges.

Private Bill Gray, a Bren gunner, in one of three gliders heading for the Caen Canal bridge, closed his eyes and braced himself for the crash. It was eerily silent. There was no firing from the ground. The only sound came from the big machine, sighing gently through the air. Near the door, ready to push it open the moment they touched down, was Major John Howard, in charge of the assault. Gray remembers his platoon leader, Lieutenant H. D. "Danny" Brotheridge, saying, "Here we go, chaps." Then there was a splintering, rending crash. The undercarriage ripped off, splinters showered back from the smashed cockpit canopy, and, swaying from side to side like a truck out of control, the glider screeched across the ground, throwing up a hail of sparks. With a sickening half swing, the wrecked machine smashed to a halt, as Gray recalls, "with the nose buried in barbed wire and almost on the bridge."

Someone yelled, "Come on, lads!" and men came scrambling out, some piling through the door, others tumbling down from the stove-in nose. Almost at the same time and only yards away, the other two gliders skidded to a crashing halt and out of them poured the remainder of the assault force. Now everybody stormed the bridge. There was bedlam. The Germans were shocked and disorganized. Grenades came hurtling into their dugouts and communications trenches. Some Germans who were actually asleep in gun pits woke to the blinding crash of explosions and found themselves gazing into the business ends of Sten guns. Others, still dazed, grabbed rifles and machine guns and began firing haphazardly at the shadowy figures who seemed to have materialized from nowhere.

While teams mopped up resistance on the near side of the bridge, Gray and some forty men led by Lieutenant Brotheridge charged across to seize the all-important far bank. Halfway over, Gray saw a German sentry with a Very pistol in his right hand, ready to fire a warning flare. It was the last act of a courageous man. Gray fired from the hip with his Bren gun and, he thinks, so did everyone else. The sentry fell dead even as the flare burst over the bridge and arched into the night sky.

His warning, presumably intended for the Germans on the Orne bridge a few hundred yards ahead, was fired much too late. The garrison there had already been overrun, even though in that attack only two of the assaulting gliders found the target (the third came down seven miles away on the wrong bridge— a crossing over the Dives River). Both target bridges fell almost simultaneously. Stunned by the swiftness of the assault, the Germans were overwhelmed. Ironically, the Wehrmacht garrisons couldn't have destroyed the crossings even if they had had the time. Swarming over the bridges, the British sappers found that although demolition preparations had been completed, explosive charges had never been placed in position. They were found in a nearby hut.

Now there was that strange silence that seems always to follow a battle, when men partly dazed by the speed of events try to figure out how they lived through it and everybody wonders who else survived. The nineteen-year-old Gray, elated by his part in the assault, eagerly sought out his platoon leader, "Danny" Brotheridge, whom he had last seen leading the attack across the bridge. But there had been casualties, and one of them was the twenty-eight-year-old lieutenant. Gray found Brotheridge's body lying in front of a small café near the canal bridge. "He had been shot in the throat," Gray recalls, "and apparently hit by a phosphorous smoke grenade. His airborne smock was still burning."

Close by, in a captured pillbox, Lance Corporal Edward Tappenden sent out the success signal. Over and over he called into his walkie-talkie-like radio the code message, "Ham and jam . . . Ham and jam . . ." D Day's first battle was over. It had lasted barely fifteen minutes. Now Major Howard and his 150-odd men, deep in enemy territory and cut off for the moment from reinforcements, prepared to hold the vital bridges.

At least they knew where they were. The same couldn't be said for the majority of the sixty British paratroop pathfinders who jumped from six light bombers at 12:20 A.M.—the same time that Howard's gliders touched down.

The Night

These men took on one of the toughest of all D-Day jobs. The vanguard of the British 6th Airborne assault, they had volunteered to jump into the unknown and to mark three drop zones west of the Orne River with flashing lights, radar beacons and other guidance apparatus. These areas, all lying in a rectangle of roughly twenty square miles, were close to three small villages—Varaville, less than three miles from the coast; Ranville, near the bridges which Howard's men now held; and Touffréville, barely five miles from the eastern outskirts of Caen. At twelve-fifty British paratroopers would begin dropping on these zones. The pathfinders had just thirty minutes to set them up.

Even in England in daylight, it would have been tricky to find and mark drop zones in thirty minutes. But at night, in enemy territory and in a country where few of them had ever been, their task was awesome. Like their comrades fifty miles away, the British pathfinders dropped headlong into trouble. They, too, were scattered widely and their drop was even more chaotic.

Their difficulties began with the weather. An unaccountable wind had sprung up (which the American pathfinders did not experience) and some areas were obscured by light patches of fog. The planes carrying the British pathfinder teams ran into curtains of flak fire. Their pilots instinctively took evasive action, with the result that targets were overshot or couldn't be found at all. Some pilots made two and three runs over the designated areas before all the pathfinders were dropped. One plane, flying very low, swept doggedly back and forth through intense anti-aircraft fire for fourteen hair-raising minutes before unloading its pathfinders. The result of all this was that many pathfinders or their equipment plummeted down in the wrong places.

The troopers bound for Varaville landed accurately enough, but they soon discovered that most of their equipment had been smashed in the fall or had been dropped elsewhere. None of the Ranville pathfinders landed even close to their area in the initial drop; they were scattered miles away. But most unfortunate of all were the Touffréville teams. Two 10-man groups were to mark that area with lights, each one flashing up into the night sky the code letter K. One of these teams dropped on the Ranville zone. They assembled easily enough, found what they thought was their right area and a few minutes later flashed out the wrong signal.

The second Touffréville team did not reach the right area either. Of the ten men in this "stick," only four reached the ground safely. One of them, Private James Morrissey, watched with horror as the other six, suddenly caught by a heavy wind, sailed far off to the east. Helplessly Morrissey watched the men being swept away toward the flooded Dives valley, gleaming in the moonlight off in the distance—the area the Germans had inundated as part of their defenses. Morrissey never saw any of the men again.

Morrissey and the remaining three men landed quite close to Touffréville. They assembled and Lance Corporal Patrick O'Sullivan set out to reconnoiter the drop zone. Within minutes he was hit by fire which came from the very edge of the area they were supposed to mark. So Morrissey and the other two men positioned the Touffréville lights in the cornfield where they had landed.

Actually in these first confusing minutes few of the pathfinders encountered the enemy. Here and there men startled sentries and drew fire, and inevitably some became casualties. But it was the ominous silence of their surroundings which created the greatest terror. Men had expected to meet heavy German opposition the moment they landed. Instead, for the majority all was quiet—so quiet that men passed through nightmarish experiences of their own making. In several instances pathfinders stalked one another in fields and hedgerows, each man thinking the other was a German.

Groping through the Normandy night, near darkened farmhouses and on the outskirts of sleeping villages, the pathfinders and 210 men of the battalions' advance parties tried to get their bearings. As always, their immediate task was to find out exactly where they were. Those dropped accurately recognized the landmarks they had been shown on terrain maps back in England. Others, completely lost, tried to locate themselves with maps and compasses. Captain Anthony Windrum of an advance signal unit solved the problem in a more direct way. Like a motorist who has taken the wrong road on a dark night, Windrum shinnied up a signpost, calmly struck a match and discovered that Ranville, his rendezvous point, was only a few miles off.

But some pathfinders were irretrievably lost. Two of them plunged out of the night sky and dropped squarely on the lawn before the headquarters of Major General Josef Reichert, commanding officer of the German 711th Division. Reichert was playing cards when the planes roared over, and he and the other officers rushed out onto the veranda—just in time to see the two Britishers land on the lawn.

It would have been hard to tell who was the more astonished, Reichert or the two pathfinders. The General's intelligence officer captured and disarmed the two men and brought them up to the veranda. The astounded Reichert could only blurt out, "Where have you come from?" to which one of the pathfinders, with all the aplomb of a man who had just crashed a cocktail party, replied, "Awfully sorry, old man, but we simply landed here by accident."

Even as they were led away to be interrogated, 570 American and British paratroopers, the first of the Allied forces of liberation, were setting the stage for the battle of D Day. On the landing zones lights were already beginning to flash up into the night sky.

★ 2 ★

Whats happening?" yelled Major Werner Pluskat into the phone. Dazed and only half awake, he was still in his underwear. The racket of planes and gunfire had awakened him, and every instinct told him that this was more than a raid. Two years of bitter experience on the Russian front had taught the major to rely heavily on his instincts.

Lieutenant Colonel Ocker, his regimental commander, seemed annoyed at Pluskat's phone call. "My dear Pluskat," he said icily, "we don't know yet what's going on. We'll let you know when we find out." There was a sharp click as Ocker hung up.

The reply didn't satisfy Pluskat. For the past twenty minutes planes had been droning through the flare-studded sky, bombing the coast to the east and the west. Pluskat's coastal area in the middle was uncomfortably quiet. From his headquarters at Etreham, four miles from the coast, he commanded four batteries of the German 352nd Division—twenty guns in all. They covered one half of Omaha Beach.

Nervously, Pluskat decided to go over his regimental commander's head; he phoned division headquarters and spoke with the 352nd's intelligence officer, Major Block. "Probably just another bombing raid, Pluskat," Block told him. "It's not clear yet."

Feeling a little foolish, Pluskat hung up. He wondered if he had been too impetuous. After all, there had been no alarm. In

114

fact, Pluskat recalls, after weeks of on-again, off-again alerts this was one of the few nights when his men had been ordered to stand down.

Pluskat was wide-awake now, too uneasy for sleep. He sat on the edge of his cot for some time. At his feet, Harras, his German shepherd, lay quietly. In the château all was still, but off in the distance Pluskat could still hear the droning of planes.

Suddenly the field telephone rang. Pluskat grabbed it. "Paratroopers are reported on the peninsula," said the calm voice of Colonel Ocker. "Alert your men and get down to the coast right away. This could be the invasion."

Minutes later Pluskat, Captain Ludz Wilkening, the commander of his second battery, and Lieutenant Fritz Theen, his gunnery officer, started out for their advance headquarters, an observation bunker built into the cliffs near the village of Ste.-Honorine. Harras went with them. It was crowded in the jeep-like Volkswagen and Pluskat recalls that in the few minutes it took them to reach the coast nobody talked. He had one big worry: his batteries had only enough ammunition for twenty-four hours. A few days before, General Marcks of the 84th Corps had inspected the guns and Pluskat had raised the question. "If an invasion ever does come in your area," Marcks had assured him, "you'll get more ammunition than you can fire."

Passing through the outer perimeter of the coastal defense zone, the Volkswagen reached Ste.-Honorine. There, with Harras on a leash, and followed by his men, Pluskat slowly climbed a narrow track back of the cliffs leading to the hidden headquarters. The path was clearly marked by several strands of barbed wire. It was the only entrance to the post and there were mine fields on either side. Almost at the top of the cliff the major dropped into a slit trench, went down a flight of concrete steps, followed a twisting tunnel and finally entered a large, single-roomed bunker manned by three men.

Quickly Pluskat positioned himself before the high-powered

artillery glasses which stood on a pedestal opposite one of the bunker's two narrow apertures. The observation post couldn't have been better sited: it was more than one hundred feet above Omaha Beach and almost directly in the center of what was soon to be the Normandy beachhead. On a clear day from this vantage point, a spotter could see the whole Bay of the Seine, from the tip of the Cherbourg peninsula off to the left to Le Havre and beyond on the right.

Even now, in the moonlight, Pluskat had a remarkable view. Slowly moving the glasses from left to right, he scanned the bay. There was some mist. Black clouds occasionally blanketed out the dazzling moonlight and threw dark shadows on the sea, but there was nothing unusual to be seen. There were no lights, no sound. Several times he traversed the bay with the glasses, but it was quite empty of ships.

Finally Pluskat stood back. "There's nothing out there," he said to Lieutenant Theen as he called regimental headquarters. But Pluskat was still uneasy. "I'm going to stay here," he told Ocker. "Maybe it's just a false alarm, but something still could happen."

By now vague and contradictory reports were filtering into Seventh Army command posts all over Normandy, and everywhere officers were trying to assess them. They had little to go on—shadowy figures seen here, shots fired there, a parachute hanging from a tree somewhere else. Clues to something—but what? Only 570 Allied airborne troops had landed. This was just enough to create the worst kind of confusion.

Reports were fragmentary, inconclusive and so scattered that even experienced soldiers were skeptical and plagued by doubts. How many men had landed—two or two hundred? Were they bomber crews that had bailed out? Was this a series of French underground attacks? Nobody was sure, not even those like General Reichert of the 711th Division who had seen paratroopers face to face. Reichert thought that it was an airborne raid on his headquarters and that was the report he passed on to his corps commander. Much later the news reached Fifteenth Army headquarters, where it was duly recorded in the war diary with the cryptic note, "No details given."

There had been so many false alarms in the past that everyone was painfully cautious. Company commanders thought twice before passing reports on to battalion. They sent out patrols to check and recheck. Battalion commanders were even more careful before informing regimental officers. As to what actually transpired at the various headquarters in these first minutes of D Day, there are as many accounts as there were participants. But one fact seems clear: On the basis of such spotty reports nobody at this time was willing to raise the alarm—an alarm that later might be proved wrong. And so the minutes ticked by.

On the Cherbourg peninsula two generals had already departed for the map exercise in Rennes. Now a third, Major General Wilhelm Falley of the 91st Air Landing Division, chose this time to set out. Despite the order issued from Seventh Army headquarters forbidding commanding officers to leave before dawn, Falley did not see how he could make the *Kriegsspiel* unless he departed earlier. His decision was to cost him his life.

At Seventh Army headquarters in Le Mans, the commanding officer, Colonel General Friedrich Dollmann, was asleep. Presumably because of the weather, he had actually canceled a practice alert scheduled for this very night. Tired out, he had gone to bed early. His chief of staff, the very able and conscientious Major General Max Pemsel, was preparing for bed.

In St.-Lô, at the headquarters of the 84th Corps, the next level of command below army headquarters, all was set for General Erich Marcks's surprise birthday party. Major Friedrich Hayn, the corps intelligence officer, had the wine ready. The plan was for Hayn, Lieutenant Colonel Friedrich von Criegern, the chief of staff, and several other senior officers to walk into the General's room as the clock in St.-Lô Cathedral struck midnight (1 A.M. British Double Summer Time). Everybody wondered how the stern-faced, one-legged Marcks (he had lost a leg in Russia) would react. He was considered one of the finest generals in Normandy, but he was also an austere man not given to demonstrations of any kind. Still, the plans were set and although everybody felt a little childish about the whole idea the staff officers were determined to go through with the party. They were almost ready to enter the General's room when suddenly they heard a nearby flak battery open up. Rushing outside, they were just in time to see an Allied bomber spiraling down in flames and to hear the jubilant gun crew yelling, "We got it! We got it!" General Marcks remained in his room.

As the cathedral bells began chiming, the little group, with Major Hayn in the lead carrying the Chablis and several glasses, marched into the General's room, perhaps a shade self-consciously, to do honor to their commander. There was a slight pause as Marcks looked up and gazed at them mildly through his glasses. "His artificial leg creaked," recalls Hayn, "as he rose to greet us." With a friendly wave of the hand he immediately put everybody at ease. The wine was opened and, standing in a little group around the fifty-three-year-old general, his staff officers came to attention. Stiffly raising their glasses, they drank his health, blissfully unaware that forty miles away 4,255 British paratroopers were dropping on French soil.

★ *3* ★

Across the moonlit fields of Normandy rolled the hoarse, haunting notes of an English hunting horn. The sound hung in the air, lonely, incongruous. Again and again the horn sounded. Scores of shadowy helmeted figures, in green-brown-and-yellow camouflaged jump smocks festooned with equipment, struggled across fields, along ditches, by the sides of hedgerows, all heading in the direction of the call. Other horns took up the chorus. Suddenly a bugle began trumpeting. For hundreds of men of the British 6th Airborne Division this was the overture to battle.

The strange cacophony came from the Ranville area. The calls were the assembly signals for two battalions of the 5th Parachute Brigade and they had to move fast. One was to rush to the assistance of Major Howard's tiny glider-borne force holding the bridges. The other was to seize and hold Ranville, at the eastern approaches to this vital crossing. Never before had paratroop commanders assembled men in this manner, but speed this night was essential. The 6th Airborne was racing against time. The first waves of American and British troops would land on Normandy's five invasion beaches between 6:30 and 7:30 A.M. The "Red Devils" had five and a half hours to secure the initial foothold and anchor the left flank of the entire invasion area.

The division had a variety of complex tasks, each one demanding almost minute-by-minute synchronization. The plan called for paratroopers to dominate the heights northeast of

Caen, hold the bridges over the Orne and the Caen Canal, demolish five more on the Dives River and thus block enemy forces, particularly panzers, from driving into the side of the invasion bridgehead.

But the lightly armed paratroopers didn't have enough fire power to stop a concentrated armored attack. So the success of the holding action depended on the speedy and safe arrival of antitank guns and special armor-piercing ammunition. Because of the weight and size of the guns there was only one way of getting them safely into Normandy: by glider train. At 3:20 A.M. a fleet of sixty-nine gliders was due to sweep down out of the Normandy skies carrying men, vehicles, heavy equipment and the precious guns.

Their arrival posed a mammoth problem all by itself. The gliders were immense—each one larger than a DC-3. Four of them, the Hamilcars, were so big that they could even carry light tanks. To get the sixty-nine gliders in, the paratroopers had first to secure the chosen landing zones from enemy attack. Next they had to create a huge landing field out of the obstacle-studded meadows. This meant clearing a forest of mined tree trunks and railroad ties, in the dead of night, and in just under two and a half hours. The same field would be used for a second glider train due to land in the evening.

There was one more job to be done. It was perhaps the most important of all the 6th Airborne's missions: the destruction of a massive coastal battery near Merville. Allied intelligence believed that this battery's four powerful guns could harass the assembling invasion fleet and massacre the troops landing on Sword Beach. The 6th had been ordered to destroy the guns by 5 A.M.

To accomplish these tasks 4,255 paratroopers of the 3rd and 5th parachute brigades had jumped into Normandy. They dropped over a huge area, victims of navigational errors, bucketing planes forced off course by flak fire, badly marked drop zones and gusty winds. Some were fortunate, but thousands fell anywhere from five to thirty-five miles from the drop zones.

Of the two brigades the 5th fared best. Most of its soldiers were dropped close to their objectives near Ranville. Even so, it would take company commanders the better part of two hours to assemble even half their men. Scores of troopers, however, were already en route, guided in by the wavering notes of the horns.

Private Raymond Batten of the 13th Battalion heard the horns, but although he was almost at the edge of his drop zone he was momentarily unable to do anything about it. Batten had crashed through the thick, leafy roof of a small woods. He was hanging from a tree, slowly swaying back and forth in his harness, just fifteen feet from the ground. It was very still in the woods, but Batten could hear prolonged bursts of machine gun fire, the droning of planes and the firing of flak batteries off in the distance. As he pulled out his knife, ready to cut himself down, Batten heard the abrupt stutter of a *Schmeisser* machine pistol nearby. A minute later, there was a rustling of underbrush and somebody moved slowly toward him. Batten had lost his Sten gun in the drop and he didn't have a pistol. Helplessly he hung there, not knowing whether it was a German or another paratrooper moving toward him. "Whoever it was came and looked up at me," Batten recalls. "All I could do was to keep perfectly still and he, probably thinking I was dead, as I hoped he would, went away."

Batten got down from the tree as fast as he could and headed toward the rallying horns. But his ordeal was far from over. At the edge of the woods he found the corpse of a young paratrooper whose parachute had failed to open. Next, as he moved along a road a man rushed past him shouting crazily, "They got my mate! They got my mate!" And finally, catching up with a group of paratroopers heading toward the assembly point, Batten found himself beside a man who seemed to be in a state of complete shock. He strode along, looking neither to his left or right, totally oblivious of the fact that the rifle which he gripped tightly in his right hand was bent almost double.

In many places this night men like Batten were shocked almost immediately into the harsh realities of war. As he was struggling to get out of his harness, Lance Corporal Harold Tait of the 8th Battalion saw one of the Dakota transports hit by flak. The plane careened over his head like a searing comet and exploded with a tremendous noise about a mile away. Tait wondered if the stick of troopers it carried had already jumped.

Private Percival Liggins of the Canadian 1st Battalion saw another flaming plane. It was "at full power, with pieces falling off it, blazing from end to end," and seemed to be heading for him. He was so fascinated by the sight that he was unable to move. It swept overhead and crashed in a field behind him. He and others tried to get to the plane in an effort to rescue anybody still in it, but "the ammo started to go and we couldn't get near it."

To twenty-year-old Private Colin Powell of the 12th Battalion, miles from his drop zone, the first sound of war was a moaning in the night. He knelt down beside a badly wounded trooper, an Irishman, who softly pleaded with Powell to "finish me off, lad, please." Powell could not do it. He made the trooper as comfortable as he could and hurried off, promising to send back help.

In these first few minutes their own resourcefulness became the measure of survival for many men. One paratrooper, Lieutenant Richard Hilborn of the Canadian 1st Battalion remembers, crashed through the top of a greenhouse, "shattering glass all over the place and making a hell of a lot of noise, but he was out and running before the glass had stopped falling." Another fell with pinpoint accuracy into a well. Hauling himself up hand over hand on his shroud lines, he set out for his assembly point as though nothing had happened.

Everywhere men extricated themselves from extraordinary

predicaments. Most of their situations would have been bad enough in daylight; at night, in hostile territory, they were compounded by fear and imagination. Such was the case with Private Godfrey Maddison. He sat at the edge of a field imprisoned by a barbed-wire fence, unable to move. Both legs were twisted in the wire and the weight of his equipment—125 pounds, including four 10-pound mortar shells—had driven him so far forward into the wire that he was almost completely enmeshed. Maddison had been heading toward the rallying horns of the 5th when he missed his footing and crashed into the fence. "I started to panic a bit," he remembers, "and it was very dark and I felt sure someone would take a potshot at me." For a few moments he did nothing but wait and listen. Then, satisfied that he had escaped notice, Maddison began a slow and painful struggle to free himself. It seemed hours before he finally worked one arm free enough to get a pair of wire cutters from the back of his belt. In a few minutes he was out and heading in the direction of the horns again.

At about that same time Major Donald Wilkins of the Canadian 1st Battalion was crawling past what appeared to him to be a small factory building. Suddenly he saw a group of figures on the lawn. He instantly threw himself to the ground. The shadowy figures did not move. Wilkins stared hard at them and, after a minute, got up cursing and went over to confirm his suspicions. They were stone garden statues.

A sergeant of the same unit had a somewhat similar experience, except that the figures he saw were only too real. Private Henry Churchill, in a nearby ditch, saw the sergeant, who had landed in knee-deep water, shrug out of his harness and look about in desperation as two men approached. "The sergeant waited," Churchill remembers, "trying to decide whether they were British or Germans." The men came closer and their voices were unmistakably German. The sergeant's Sten gun barked and "he brought them down with a single fast burst."

The most sinister enemy in these opening minutes of D Day was not man but nature. Rommel's antiparatroop precautions had paid off well: the waters and swamps of the flooded Dives valley were deathtraps. Many of the men of the 3rd Brigade came down in this area like so much confetti shaken haphazardly out of a bag. For these paratroopers, mishap followed tragic mishap. Some pilots, caught in heavy cloud, mistook the mouth of the Dives for that of the Orne and let men out over a maze of marshes and swamps. One entire battalion of seven hundred whose drop was to be concentrated in an area roughly a mile square was scattered, instead, over fifty miles of countryside, most of it swampland. And this battalion, the highly trained 9th, had been given the toughest, most urgent job of the night—the assault on the Merville battery. It would take some of these men days to rejoin their unit; many would never return at all.

The number of troopers who died in the wastes of the Dives will never be known. Survivors say that the marshes were intersected by a maze of ditches about seven feet deep, four feet wide and bottomed with sticky slime. A man alone, weighed down with guns, ammunition and heavy equipment, could not negotiate these ditches. Wet kitbags nearly doubled in weight and men had to discard them in order to survive. Many men who somehow struggled through the marshes drowned in the river with dry land only a few yards away.

Private Henry Humberstone of the 224th Parachute Field Ambulance narrowly missed such a death. Humberstone landed waist-deep in the marshes, with no idea of where he was. He had expected to come down in the orchard area west of Varaville; instead he had landed on the east side of the drop zone. Between him and Varaville were not only the marshes but the Dives River itself. A low mist covered the area like a dirty white blanket, and all around Humberstone could hear the croaking of frogs. Then, ahead, came the unmistakable sound of rushing water. Humberstone stumbled on through the flooded fields and came upon the Dives. While he looked for some way to cross the river, he spotted two men on the opposite bank. They were members of the Canadian 1st Battalion. "How do I get across?" yelled Humberstone. "It's quite safe," one of them called back. The Canadian waded into the river, apparently to show him. "I was watching him one minute and the next minute he was gone," Humberstone remembers. "He didn't yell or scream or anything. He just drowned before either me or his buddy on the other bank could do anything."

Captain John Gwinnett, the chaplain of the 9th Battalion, was completely lost. He, too, had landed in the marshes. He was all alone and the silence around him was unnerving. Gwinnett had to get out of the swamps. He was certain the Merville assault would be a bloody one and he wanted to be with his men. "Fear," he had told them at the airfield just before take-off, "knocked at the door. Faith opened it, and there was nothing there." Gwinnett did not know it now, but it would be a full seventeen hours before he found his way out of the swamps.

At this moment the 9th's commander, Lieutenant Colonel Terence Otway, was in a towering rage. He had been dropped miles from the rendezvous point, and he knew that his battalion must have been thoroughly scattered. As Otway marched quickly through the night, small groups of his men appeared everywhere, confirming his worst suspicions. He wondered just how bad the drop had been. Had his special glider train been scattered, too?

Otway badly needed the glider-borne guns and other equipment if his plan of assault was to succeed, for Merville was no ordinary battery. Around it ranged a formidable series of defenses in depth. To get to the heart of the battery—four heavy guns in massive concrete emplacements—the 9th would have to pass through mine fields and over antitank ditches, penetrate a 15-foot-thick hedge of barbed wire, cross more mine fields and then fight through a maze of machine-gun-filled trenches. The Germans considered this deadly fortification with its garrison of two hundred men almost impregnable.

Otway didn't think it was, and his plan to destroy it was elaborate and incredibly detailed. He wanted to leave nothing to chance. One hundred Lancaster bombers were to saturate the battery first with 4,000-pound bombs. The glider trains were to bring in jeeps, antitank guns, flame throwers, "Bangalore" torpedoes (lengths of explosive-filled pipe to destroy the wire), mine detectors, mortars, and even lightweight aluminum scaling ladders. After collecting this special equipment from the gliders, Otway's men were to set out for the battery in eleven teams to begin the assault.

This called for dovetailed timing. Reconnaissance teams would lead off and scout the area. "Taping" parties would remove the mines and mark the approaches through the cleared areas. "Breaching" teams with the Bangalore torpedoes would destroy the barbed wire. Snipers, mortar men and machine gunners were to take up positions to cover the main charge.

Otway's plan had one final surprise: At the same time that his assault troops rushed the battery from the ground, three gliders filled with more troopers were to crash-land *on the top of the battery*, in a combined massive rush on the defenses from ground and air.

Parts of the plan seemed suicidal, but the risks were worth taking, for the Merville guns could kill thousands of British troops as they touched down on Sword Beach. Even if everything went according to schedule in the next few hours, by the time Otway and his men assembled, moved out and reached the battery they would have barely an hour to destroy the guns. He had been told plainly that if the 9th could not complete the task on time, naval gunfire would try to do it. That meant that Otway and his men had to be away from the battery, no matter what the outcome, by 5:30 A.M. At that time, if the signal of success had not come from Otway, the bombardment would begin.

That was the strategy. But, as Otway hurried anxiously toward the assembly point, the first part of the plan had already misfired. The air attack which had taken place at twelve-thirty had been a complete failure; not one bomb had hit the battery. And the errors were multiplying: the gliders with the vital supplies had failed to arrive.

In the center of the Normandy beachhead, in the German observation bunker overlooking Omaha Beach, Major Werner Pluskat still watched. He saw the white tops of the waves, nothing more. His uneasiness had not lessened; if anything, Pluskat felt more certain than ever that something was happening. Soon after he reached the bunker, formation after formation of planes had thundered over the coast far off to the right; Pluskat thought there must have been hundreds. From the first moment he heard them, he had expected a sudden call from regiment confirming his suspicions that the invasion was in fact beginning. But the phone had remained silent. There had been nothing from Ocker since the first call. Now Pluskat heard something else—the slowly swelling roar of a great number of planes off to his left. This time the sound was coming from behind him. The planes seemed to be approaching the Cherbourg peninsula from the west. Pluskat was more bewildered than ever. Instinctively he looked out through his glasses once again. The bay was completely empty. There was nothing to be seen.

★ 4 ★

I<small>N</small> S<small>TE.</small>-M<small>ÈRE</small>-É<small>GLISE</small> the sound of bombing was very close. Alexandre Renaud, the mayor and town pharmacist, could feel the very ground shaking. It seemed to him that planes were attacking the batteries at St.-Marcouf and St.-Martin-de-Varreville, and both places were only a few miles away. He was quite worried about the town and its people. About all the inhabitants could do was take shelter in garden trenches or cellars, for they could not leave their homes because of the curfew. Renaud herded his wife, Simone, and their three children to the passageway leading off the living room. Its heavy timbers afforded good protection. It was about 1:10 A.M. when the family collected in the makeshift air raid shelter. Renaud remembers the time (it was 12:10 A.M. to him), because just then there was a persistent, urgent knocking at the street door.

Renaud left his family in their living quarters and walked through his darkened pharmacist's shop, which fronted on the Place de l'Église. Even before he reached the door, he could see what the trouble was. Through the windows of his shop the square, with its edging of chestnut trees and its great Norman church, appeared brilliantly lit up. M. Hairon's villa across the square was on fire and blazing fiercely.

Renaud got the door open. The town's fire chief, resplendent in his polished, shoulder-length brass helmet, stood before him. "I think it was hit by a stray incendiary from one of the planes," the man said without any preamble, motioning toward the burn-

ing house. "The fire is spreading fast. Can you get the commandant to lift the curfew? We need as much help as we can get for
the bucket brigade."

The mayor ran to the nearby German headquarters. He
quickly explained the situation to the sergeant on duty, who, on
his own authority, gave permission. At the same time the German called out the guard, to watch the volunteers when they
assembled. Then Renaud went to the parish house and told
Father Louis Roulland. The curé sent his sexton to the church to
toll the bell, while he, Renaud and the others banged on doors,
calling for the inhabitants to help. Above them the bell began to
clang, booming out over the town. People started to appear,
some in their nightwear, others half dressed, and soon more than
one hundred men and women in two long lines were passing
buckets of water from hand to hand. Surrounding them were
about thirty German guards armed with rifles and *Schmeissers*.

In the midst of this confusion, Renaud remembers, Father
Roulland took him aside. "I must talk to you—something very
important," the priest said. He led Renaud to the kitchen of the
parish house. There Madame Angèle Levrault, the aged schoolmistress, awaited them. She was in a state of shock. "A man has
landed in my pea patch," she announced in a wavering voice.
Renaud had almost more trouble than he could handle, but he
tried to calm her. "Don't worry," he said. "Please go home and
stay indoors." Then he raced back to the fire.

The noise and confusion had intensified in his absence. The
flames were higher now. Showers of sparks had spread to the
outbuildings and they were already starting to burn. To Renaud
the scene had a nightmarish quality. He stood almost rooted to
the spot, seeing the flushed, excited faces of the fire fighters, the
overdressed, ponderous German guards with their rifles and
machine guns. And above the square the bell still tolled, adding
its persistent clanging to the din. It was then they all heard the
droning of the planes.

129

The sound came from the west—a steadily mounting roar, and with it the approaching racket of antiaircraft fire as battery after battery across the peninsula picked up the formations. In the square of Ste.-Mère-Église everybody looked up, transfixed, the burning house forgotten. Then the guns of the town began firing and the roaring was on top of them. The aircraft swept in, almost wing tip to wing tip, through a crisscrossing barrage of fire that hammered up from the ground. The planes' lights were on. They came in so low that people in the square instinctively ducked and Renaud remembers that the airplanes cast "great shadows on the ground and red lights seemed to be glowing inside them."

In wave after wave the formations flew over, the first planes of the biggest airborne operation ever attempted—882 planes carrying thirteen thousand men. These men of the U.S. 101st and veteran 82nd airborne divisions were heading for six drop zones all within a few miles of Ste.-Mère-Église. The troopers tumbled out of their planes, stick after stick. And as those destined for the zone outside the town drifted down, scores of them heard an incongruous sound over the clatter of battle: a church bell tolling in the night. For many it was the last sound they ever heard. Caught by a heavy wind, a number of soldiers floated down toward the inferno of the Place de l'Église—and the guns of the German guards that a twist of fate had placed there. Lieutenant Charles Santarsiero of the 101st's 506th Regiment was standing in the door of his plane as it passed over Ste.-Mère-Église. "We were about four hundred feet up," he remembers, "and I could see fires burning and Krauts running about. There seemed to be total confusion on the ground. All hell had broken loose. Flak and small-arms fire was coming up and those poor guys were caught right in the middle of it."

Almost as soon as he left his plane, Private John Steele of the 82nd's 505th Regiment saw that instead of landing in a lighted drop zone he was heading for the center of a town that seemed to be on fire. Then he saw German soldiers and French civilians running frantically about. Most of them, it seemed to Steele, were looking up at him. The next moment he was hit by something that felt "like the bite of a sharp knife." A bullet had smashed into his foot. Then Steele saw something that alarmed him even more. Swinging in his harness, unable to veer away from the town, he dangled helplessly as his chute carried him straight toward the church steeple at the edge of the square.

Above Steele, P.F.C. Ernest Blanchard heard the church bell ringing and saw the maelstrom of fire coming up all around him. The next minute he watched horrified as a man floating down almost beside him "exploded and completely disintegrated before my eyes," presumably a victim of the explosives he was carrying.

Blanchard began desperately to swing on his risers, trying to veer away from the mob in the square below. But it was too late. He landed with a crash in one of the trees. Around him men were being machine-gunned to death. There were shouts, yells, screams and moans—sounds that Blanchard will never forget. Frantically, as the machine-gunning came closer, Blanchard sawed at his harness. Then he dropped out of the tree and ran in panic, unaware that he had also sawed off the top of his thumb.

It must have seemed to the Germans that Ste.-Mère-Église was being smothered by paratroop assault, and certainly the townspeople in the square thought that they were at the center of a major battle. Actually very few Americans—perhaps thirty —dropped into the town, and no more than twenty came down in and about the square. But they were enough to cause the German garrison of slightly less than one hundred men to panic. Reinforcements rushed to the square, which seemed to be the focal point of the attack, and there some Germans, coming suddenly upon the bloody, burning scene, seemed to Renaud to lose all control.

About fifteen yards from where the mayor stood in the square a paratrooper plunged into a tree and almost immediately, as he tried frantically to get out of his harness, he was spotted. As Renaud watched, "about half a dozen Germans emptied the magazines of their submachine guns into him and the boy hung there with his eyes open, as though looking down at his own bullet holes."

Caught up in the slaughter all around them, the people in the square were now oblivious to the mighty airborne armada that was still droning ceaselessly overhead. Thousands of men were jumping for the 82nd's drop zones northwest of the town, and the 101st's zones east and slightly west, between Ste.-Mère-Église and the Utah invasion area. But every now and then, because the drop was so widely scattered, stray paratroopers from almost every regiment drifted into the holocaust of the little town. One or two of these men, loaded down with ammunition, grenades and plastic explosives, actually fell into the burning house. There were brief screams and then a fusillade of shots and explosions as the ammunition went up.

In all this horror and confusion one man tenaciously and precariously clung to life. Private Steele, his parachute draped over the steeple of the church, hung just under the eaves. He heard the shouts and the screams. He saw Germans and Americans firing at each other in the square and the streets. And, almost paralyzed by terror, he saw winking red flashes of machine guns as streams of stray bullets shot past and over him. Steele had tried to cut himself down, but his knife had somehow slipped out of his hand and dropped to the square below. Steele then decided that his only hope lay in playing dead. On the roof, only a few yards away from him, German machine gunners fired at everything in sight, but not at Steele. He hung so realistically "dead" in his harness that Lieutenant Willard Young of the 82nd, who passed by during the height of the fighting, still remembers "the dead man hanging from the steeple." In all, Steele dangled there for more than two hours before being cut down and taken

captive by the Germans. Shocked and in pain from his shattered
foot, he has absolutely no recollection of the tolling of the bell,
only a few feet from his head.

The encounter at Ste.-Mère-Église was the prelude to the
main American airborne assault. But in the scheme of things this
initial and bloody skirmish* was quite accidental. Although the
town was one of the principal objectives of the 82nd Airborne,
the real battle for Ste.-Mère-Église was still to come. Much had
to be accomplished before then, for the 101st and 82nd divisions,
like the British, were racing the clock.

To the Americans went the job of holding the right flank of
the invasion area just as their British counterparts were holding
on the left. But much more was riding on the American paratroopers: on them hung the fate of the whole Utah Beach operation.

The main obstacle to the success of the Utah landing was a
body of water known as the Douve River. As part of their anti-
invasion measures Rommel's engineers had taken brilliant advantage of the Douve and its principal tributary, the Merderet.
These water barriers veining the lower part of the thumblike
Cherbourg land mass flow south and southeast through low-
lying land, link up with the Carentan Canal at the base of the
peninsula and, flowing almost parallel with the Vire River,

* I have not been able to determine how many were killed and wounded
in the square, because sporadic fighting continued all over the town until
the actual attack which resulted in its capture. But the best estimates put
casualties at about twelve killed, wounded and missing. Most of these men
were from F Company, 2nd Battalion, 505th Regiment, and there is a
pathetic little note in their official records which reads: "2nd Lt. Cadish and
the following enlisted men dropped in the town and were killed almost
instantly: Shearer, Blankenship, Bryant, Van Holsbeck and Tlapa." Private
John Steele saw two men fall into the burning house, and one of those
he believes was Private White of his own mortar squad, who dropped behind him.

Lieutenant Colonel William E. Ekman, commanding the 505th, also
says that "one of the chaplains of the regiment . . . who dropped in
Ste.-Mère-Église was captured and executed within minutes."

empty into the English Channel. By manipulating the century-old La Barquette locks just a few miles above the town of Carentan, the Germans had inundated so much ground that the peninsula, marshy to begin with, was almost isolated from the remainder of Normandy. Thus, by holding the few roads, bridges and causeways through these wastes the Germans could bottle up an invading force and eventually wipe it out. In the event of landings on the eastern coast German forces attacking from the north and west could close the trap and drive the invaders back into the sea.

That, at least, was the general strategy. But the Germans had no intention of allowing an invasion to get even that far; as a further defense measure they had flooded more than twelve square miles of low-lying land behind the beaches on the eastern coast. Utah Beach lay almost in the center of these man-made lakes. There was only one way that the men of the 4th Infantry Division (plus their tanks, guns, vehicles and supplies) could force their way inland: along five causeways running through the floods. And German guns controlled these.

Holding the peninsula and these natural defense barriers were three German divisions: the 709th in the north and along the east coast, the 243rd defending the west coast, and the recently arrived 91st in the middle and spread about the base. Also, lying south of Carentan and within striking distance was one of the finest and toughest German units in Normandy—Baron von der Heydte's 6th Parachute Regiment. Exclusive of naval units manning coastal batteries, Luftwaffe antiaircraft contingents and a variety of personnel in the Cherbourg vicinity, the Germans could throw about forty thousand men almost immediately at an Allied attack of any sort. In this heavily defended area Major General Maxwell D. Taylor's 101st Airborne Division and Major General Matthew B. Ridgway's 82nd had been given the enormous task of carving out and holding an "airhead"—an island of defense running from the Utah Beach area to a point far to the west across the base of the peninsula. They were to open up the way for the 4th Division and hold until relieved. In and about the peninsula the American paratroopers were outnumbered more than three to one.

On the map the airhead looked like the imprint of a short, broad left foot with the small toes lying along the coast, the big toe at the La Barquette locks above Carentan, and the heel back and beyond the Merderet and Douve marshes. It was roughly twelve miles long, seven miles wide at the toes and four miles in width across the heel. It was a huge area to be held by thirteen thousand men, but it had to be taken in less than five hours.

Taylor's men were to seize a six-gun battery at St.-Martin-de-Varreville, almost directly behind Utah, and race for four of the five causeways between there and the coastal hamlet of Pouppeville. At the same time crossings and bridges along the Douve and the Carentan Canal, particularly the La Barquette locks, had to be seized or destroyed. While the Screaming Eagles of the 101st secured these objectives, Ridgway's men were to hold the heel and the left side of the foot. They were to defend crossings over the Douve and the Merderet, capture Ste.-Mère-Église and hold positions north of the town to prevent counterattacks from driving into the side of the bridgehead.

The men of the airborne divisions had one other vital mission. The enemy had to be cleared off glider landing areas, for big glider trains were coming in to reinforce the Americans, just as they were the British, before dawn and again in the evening. The first flight, more than one hundred gliders, was scheduled to arrive at 4 A.M.

From the beginning the Americans worked against staggering odds. Like the British, the U.S. divisions were critically scattered. Only one regiment, the 505th of the 82nd, fell accurately. Sixty per cent of all equipment was lost, including most of the radios, mortars and ammunition. Worse still, many of the men were lost too. They came down miles from any recognizable landmarks, confused and alone. The route of the planes was from west to east and it took just twelve minutes to cross the peninsula. Jumping too late meant landing in the English Channel; too early meant coming down somewhere between the west coast and the flooded areas. Some sticks were dropped so badly they actually landed closer to the western side of the peninsula than to their zones on the east. Hundreds of men, heavily weighted with equipment, fell into the treacherous swamps of the Merderet and the Douve. Many drowned, some in less than two feet of water. Others, jumping too late, fell into the darkness over what they thought was Normandy and were lost in the Channel.

One entire stick of 101st paratroopers—some fifteen or eighteen soldiers—met such a death. In the next plane Corporal Louis Merlano fell on a sandy beach in front of a sign reading *"Achtung Minen!"* He had been the second man in his stick to jump. Off in the darkness Merlano could hear the quiet slapping sound of waves. He was lying in sand dunes surrounded by Rommel's anti-invasion obstacles, just a few yards above Utah Beach. As he lay there, trying to get his breath, he heard screams far off in the distance. Merlano was not to find out until later that the screams were coming from the Channel, where the last eleven men from his plane were at that moment drowning.

Merlano got off the beach fast, ignoring the possibility that it was mined. He climbed over a barbed-wire fence and ran for a hedgerow. Someone else was already there; Merlano didn't stop. He ran across a road and started to climb a stone wall. Just then he heard an agonized cry behind him. He whirled around. A flame thrower was hosing the hedgerow he had just passed, and outlined in the flame was the figure of a fellow paratrooper. Stunned, Merlano crouched down by the wall. From the other side came the shouts of German voices and the firing of machine guns. Merlano was caught in a heavily fortified area, with Germans on all sides of him. He prepared to fight for his life. There was one thing he had to do first. Merlano, who was attached to a signal unit, pulled from his pocket a two-by-two-inch communications log containing codes and passwords for three days. Carefully he tore up the log and, page by page, ate it all.

On the other side of the airhead men were floundering in the dark swamps. The Merderet and the Douve were dotted with parachutes of all colors and the little lights on equipment bundles gleamed eerily from out of the marshes and the water. Men plummeted down from the sky, barely missing one another as they splashed beneath the surface of the water. Some never appeared again. Others came up gasping, fighting for air and sawing desperately at chutes and equipment that could drag them under again.

Like Chaplain John Gwinnett of the British 6th Airborne fifty miles away, the 101st chaplain, Captain Francis Sampson, landed in the wastes. The water was over his head. The priest was pinned by his equipment and his parachute, caught by a strong wind, remained open above him. Frantically he cut away the equipment hanging from him—including his Mass kit. Then, with his parachute acting like a great sail, he was blown along for about a hundred yards until he finally came to rest in shallow water. Exhausted, he lay there for about twenty minutes. At last, disregarding the machine gun and mortar fire that was beginning to come in, Father Sampson set out for the area where he had first gone under and doggedly began diving for his Mass kit. He got it on the fifth try.

It wasn't until much later that Father Sampson, thinking back about the experience, realized that the Act of Contrition he had so hurriedly said as he struggled in the water was actually the grace before meals.

In countless small fields and pastures between the Channel and the flooded areas, Americans came together in the night, drawn not by hunting horns but by the sound of a toy cricket. Their lives depended on a few cents' worth of tin fashioned in the shape of a child's snapper. One snap of the cricket had to be answered by a double snap and—for the 82nd alone—a password. Two snaps required one in reply. On these signals men came out of hiding, from trees and ditches, around the sides of buildings, to greet one another. Major General Maxwell D. Taylor and a bareheaded, unidentified rifleman met at the corner of a hedgerow and warmly hugged each other. Some paratroopers found their units right away. Others saw strange faces in the night and then the familiar, comforting sight of the tiny American flag stitched above the shoulder patch.

As confused as things were these men adapted quickly. The battle-tested troopers of the 82nd, with airborne assaults in Sicily and Salerno under their belts, knew what to expect. The 101st, on its first combat jump, was fiercely determined not to be outdone by its more illustrious partner. All these men wasted as little time as possible, for they had no time to waste. The lucky ones who knew where they were assembled promptly and set out for their objectives. The lost ones joined with small groups made up of men from different companies, battalions and regiments. 82nd troopers found themselves being led by 101st officers and vice versa. Men from both divisions fought side by side, often for objectives they had never heard of.

Hundreds of men found themselves in small fields, surrounded on all sides by tall hedgerows. The fields were silent little worlds, isolated and scary. In them every shadow, every rustle, every breaking twig was the enemy. Private Dutch Schultz, in one such shadowy world, was unable to find his way out. He decided to try his cricket. On the very first click he got a response he hadn't bargained for: machine gun fire. He threw himself to the ground, aimed his MI rifle in the direction of the machine gun position, and pressed the trigger. Nothing happened. He had forgotten to load it. The machine gun opened up again and Dutch ran for cover in the nearest hedgerow.

He made another careful reconnaissance of the field. Then he heard a twig crackle. Dutch felt a moment's panic, but he calmed down as his company commander, Lieutenant Jack Tallerday, came through the hedgerow. "Is that you, Dutch?" Tallerday called softly. Schultz hurried over to him. Together they left the field and joined a group that Tallerday had already assembled. There were men from the 101st Division and from all three of the 82nd's regiments. For the first time since the jump Dutch felt easy. He was no longer alone.

Tallerday moved down along the side of a hedgerow with his little group fanning out behind him. A short while later they heard and then saw a group of men coming toward them. Tallerday snapped his cricket and thought he heard an answering click. "As our two groups approached each other," Tallerday says, "it was quite evident by the configuration of their steel helmets that they were Germans." And then there occurred one of those curious and rare happenings in war. Each group silently walked past the other in a kind of frozen shock, without firing a shot. As the distance between them grew, the darkness obliterated the figures as though they had never existed.

All over Normandy this night paratroopers and German soldiers met unexpectedly. In these encounters men's lives depended on their keeping their wits and often on the fraction of a second it took to pull a trigger. Three miles from Ste.-Mère-Église, Lieutenant John Walas of the 82nd almost tripped over a German sentry who was in front of a machine gun nest. For a terrible moment, each man stared at the other. Then the German reacted. He fired a shot at Walas at point-blank range. The bullet struck the bolt mechanism of the lieutenant's rifle, which was directly in front of his stomach, nicked his hand and ricocheted off. Both men turned and fled.

One man, Major Lawrence Legere of the 101st, talked his

way out of trouble. In a field between Ste.-Mère-Église and Utah Beach, Legere had collected a little group of men and was leading them toward the rendezvous point. Suddenly Legere was challenged in German. He knew no German but he was fluent in French. As the other men were some distance behind him and had not been seen, Legere, in the darkness of the field, posed as a young farmer and explained rapidly in French that he had been visiting his girl and was on his way home. He apologized for being out after curfew. As he talked, he was busily removing a strip of adhesive tape from a grenade, placed there to prevent the accidental release of the pin. Still talking, he yanked the pin, threw the grenade and hit the ground as it went off. He found he had killed three Germans. "When I backtracked to pick up my brave little band," Legere recalls, "I found they had scattered to the four winds."

There were many ludicrous moments. In a dark orchard one mile from Ste.-Mère-Église, Captain Lyle Putnam, one of the 82nd's battalion surgeons, found himself utterly alone. He gathered up all his medical equipment and began searching for a way out. Near one of the hedgerows he saw a figure approaching cautiously. Putnam froze in his tracks, leaned forward and loudly whispered the 82nd's password, "Flash." There was a moment of electric silence as Putnam waited for the countersign, "Thunder." Instead, to his amazement, Putnam recalls, the other man yelled, "Jesus Christ!" and turned and "fled like a maniac." The doctor was so angry he forgot to be frightened. Half a mile away his friend Captain George Wood, the 82nd's chaplain, was also alone and busily snapping his cricket. No one answered him. Then he jumped with fright as a voice behind him said: "For God's sake, Padre, stop that damn noise." Chastened, Chaplain Wood followed the paratrooper out of the field.

By afternoon these two men would be in Madame Angèle Levrault's schoolhouse in Ste.-Mère-Église fighting their own war—a war where uniforms made no difference. They would be tending the wounded and dying of both sides.

By 2 A.M., although more than an hour would pass before all the paratroopers were on the ground, many small groups of determined men were closing in on their objectives. One group was actually attacking its target, an enemy stronghold of dugouts and machine gun and antitank gun positions in the village of Foucarville just above Utah Beach. The position was of extreme importance, for it controlled all movement on the main road running behind the Utah Beach area—a road which enemy tanks would have to use to reach the beachhead. Storming Foucarville called for a full company, but only eleven men under Captain Cleveland Fitzgerald had as yet arrived. So determined were Fitzgerald and his little group that they assaulted the position without waiting for more men. In this, the first recorded 101st unit battle of the D-Day airborne assault, Fitzgerald and his men got as far as the enemy command post. There was a short, bloody battle. Fitzgerald was shot in the lung by a sentry, but as he fell he killed the German. At last the outnumbered Americans had to pull back to the outskirts to await dawn and reinforcements. Unknown to them nine paratroopers had reached Foucarville some forty minutes earlier. They had dropped into the strongpoint itself. Now, under the eyes of their captors, they were sitting in a dugout, oblivious of the battle, listening to a German practicing on his harmonica.

These were crazy moments for everyone—particularly the generals. They were men without staffs, without communications, and without men to command. Major General Maxwell Taylor found himself with several officers but only two or three enlisted men. "Never," he told them, "have so few been commanded by so many."

Major General Matthew B. Ridgway was alone in a field, pistol in hand, counting himself lucky. As he was later to recall, "at least if no friends were visible neither were any foes." His assistant, Brigadier General James M. "Jumpin' Jim" Gavin, who at this time was in complete charge of the 82nd's parachute assault, was miles away in the swamps of the Merderet.

Gavin and a number of paratroopers were trying to salvage equipment bundles from the marshes. In them were the radios, bazookas, mortars and ammunition Gavin so desperately needed. He knew that by dawn the heel of the airhead which his men were to hold would be under heavy attack. As he stood knee-deep in cold water, alongside the troopers, other worries were crowding in on Gavin. He was not sure where he was, and he wondered what to do about the number of injured men who had found their way to his little group and were now lying along the edge of the swamp.

Nearly an hour earlier, seeing red and green lights on the far edge of the water, Gavin had sent his aide, Lieutenant Hugo Olson, to find out what they meant. He hoped they were the assembly lights of two of the 82nd's battalions. Olson had not returned and Gavin was getting anxious. One of his officers, Lieutenant John Devine, was out in the middle of the river, stark naked, diving for bundles. "Whenever he came up, he stood out like a white statue," Gavin recalls, "and I couldn't help thinking that he'd be a dead turkey if he was spotted by the Germans."

Suddenly a lone figure came struggling out of the swamps. He was covered with mud and slime and was wringing wet. It was Olson coming to report that there was a railroad directly across from Gavin and his men, on a high embankment which snaked through the marshes. It was the first good news of the night. Gavin knew there was only one railroad in the district —the Cherbourg-Carentan track, which passed down the Merderet valley. The general began to feel better. For the first time he knew where he was.

The Night

In an apple orchard outside Ste.-Mère-Église, the man who was to hold the northern approaches to the town—the flank of the Utah invasion bridgehead—was in pain and trying not to show it. Lieutenant Colonel Benjamin Vandervoort of the 82nd had broken his ankle on the jump, but he had made up his mind to stay in the fighting no matter what happened.

Bad luck had dogged Vandervoort. He had always taken his job seriously, sometimes too seriously. Unlike many another Army officer, Vandervoort had never had a popular nickname, nor had he permitted himself the kind of close, easy relationship with his men that other officers enjoyed. Normandy was to change all that—and more. It was to make him, as General Matthew B. Ridgway later recalled, "one of the bravest, toughest battle commanders I ever knew." Vandervoort was to fight on his broken ankle for forty days, side by side with the men whose approval he wanted most.

Vandervoort's battalion surgeon, Captain Putnam, still fuming from his encounter with the strange paratrooper in the hedgerow, came across the colonel and some of his troopers in the orchard. Putnam still vividly remembers his first sight of Vandervoort: "He was seated with a rain cape over him, reading a map by flashlight. He recognized me and, calling me close, quietly asked that I take a look at his ankle with as little demonstration as possible. His ankle was obviously broken. He insisted on replacing his jump boot, and we laced it tightly." Then, as Putnam watched, Vandervoort picked up his rifle and, using it as a crutch, took a step forward. He looked at the men around him. "Well," he said, "let's go." He moved out across the field.

Like the British paratroopers to the east, the Americans—in humor, in sorrow, in terror and in pain—began the work they had come to Normandy to do.

This, then, was the beginning. The first invaders of D Day, almost eighteen thousand Americans, British and Canadians, were on the flanks of the Normandy battlefield. In between lay the five invasion beaches and beyond the horizon, steadily approaching, the mighty 5,000-ship invasion fleet. The first of the vessels, the U.S.S. *Bayfield,* carrying the commander of the Navy's Force U, Rear Admiral D. P. Moon, was now within twelve miles of Utah Beach and preparing to drop anchor.

Slowly the great invasion plan was beginning to unfold—and still the Germans remained blind. There were many reasons. The weather, their lack of reconnaissance (only a few planes had been sent over the embarkation areas in the preceding weeks, and all had been shot down), their stubborn belief that the invasion *must* come at the Pas-de-Calais, the confusion and overlapping of their own commands, and their failure to take the decoded underground messages seriously all played a part. Even their radar stations failed them this night. Those that had not been bombed had been confused by Allied planes flying along the coast dropping bundles of "window"—strips of tinfoil which snowed the screens. Only one station had made a report. It saw only "normal Channel traffic."

More than two hours had elapsed since the first paratroopers had landed. Only now were the German commanders in Normandy beginning to realize that something important might be happening. The first scattered reports were beginning to come in and slowly, like a patient coming out of an anesthetic, the Germans were awakening.

★ 5 ★

GENERAL ERICH MARCKS stood at a long table studying the
war maps spread out before him. He was surrounded by his
staff. They had been with him ever since his birthday party,
briefing the 84th Corps commander for the war games in Rennes.
Every now and then the General called for another map. It
seemed to his intelligence officer, Major Friedrich Hayn, that
Marcks was preparing for the *Kriegsspiel* as though it was a real
battle, instead of merely a theoretical invasion of Normandy.

In the midst of their discussion, the phone rang. The conversation ceased as Marcks picked up the receiver. Hayn recalls that
"as he listened, the General's body seemed to stiffen." Marcks
motioned to his chief of staff to pick up the extension phone.
The man who was calling was Major General Wilhelm Richter,
commander of the 716th Division, holding the coast above Caen.
"Parachutists have landed east of the Orne," Richter told
Marcks. "The area seems to be around Bréville and Ranville
. . . along the northern fringe of the Bavent Forest . . ."

This was the first official report of the Allied attack to reach
a major German headquarters. "It struck us," Hayn says, "like
lightning." The time was 2:11 A.M. (British Double Summer
Time).

Marcks immediately telephoned Major General Max Pemsel,
chief of staff of the Seventh Army. At 2:15 A.M. Pemsel placed
the Seventh on *Alarmstruffe II*, the highest state of readiness

145

It was four hours since the second Verlaine message had been intercepted. Now at last the Seventh Army, in whose area the invasion had already begun, had been alerted.

Pemsel was taking no chances. He wakened the Seventh's commanding officer, Colonel General Friedrich Dollmann. "General," said Pemsel, "I believe this is the invasion. Will you please come over immediately?"

As he put down the phone, Pemsel suddenly remembered something. Among a sheaf of intelligence bulletins that had come in during the afternoon, one had been from an agent in Casablanca. He had specifically stated that the invasion would take place in Normandy on June 6.

As Pemsel waited for Dollmann to arrive, the 84th Corps reported again: ". . . Parachute drops near Montebourg and St.-Marcouf [on the Cherbourg peninsula] . . . Troops partly already engaged in battle."* Pemsel promptly called Rommel's chief of staff, Major General Dr. Hans Speidel at Army Group B. It was 2:35 A.M.

At about the same time, General Hans von Salmuth, from his Fifteenth Army headquarters near the Belgian border, was trying to get some firsthand information. Although the bulk of his army was far removed from the airborne attacks, one division, Major General Josef Reichert's 711th, held positions east of the Orne River on the boundary line between the Seventh and Fifteenth armies. Several messages had come in from the 711th. One reported that paratroopers actually were landing near the

* There has been considerable controversy over the timing of the German reaction to the invasion and over the messages that were passed from one headquarters to another. When I began my research, Colonel General Franz Halder, the former Chief of the German General Staff (now attached to the U.S. Army's historical section in Germany) told me to "believe nothing on our side unless it tallies with the official war diaries of each headquarters." I have followed his advice. All times (corrected to British Double Summer Time), reports and telephone calls as they pertain to German activities come from these sources.

headquarters at Cabourg; a second announced that fighting was going on all around the command post.

Von Salmuth decided to find out for himself. He rang Reichert. "What the devil is going on down there?" Von Salmuth demanded.

"My General," came Reichert's harassed voice on the other end of the wire, "if you'll permit me, I'll let you hear for yourself." There was a pause, and then Von Salmuth could clearly hear the clatter of machine gun fire.

"Thank you," said Von Salmuth, and he hung up. Immediately he too called Army Group B, reporting that at the 711th's headquarters "the din of battle can be heard."

Pemsel's and Von Salmuth's calls, arriving almost simultaneously, gave Rommel's headquarters the first news of the Allied attack. Was it the long-expected invasion? Nobody at Army Group B at this time was prepared to say. In fact, Rommel's naval aide, Vice-Admiral Friedrich Ruge, distinctly remembers that as more reports came in of airborne troops "some said they were only dolls disguised as paratroopers."

Whoever made the observation was partly right. To add to the German confusion, the Allies had dropped hundreds of life-like rubber dummies, dressed as paratroopers, south of the Normandy invasion area. Attached to each were strings of fire-crackers which exploded on landing, giving the impression of a small-arms fight. For more than three hours a few of these dummies were to deceive General Marcks into believing that paratroopers had landed at Lessay some twenty-five miles southwest of his headquarters.

These were strange, confusing minutes for Von Rundstedt's staff at OB West in Paris and for Rommel's officers at La Roche-Guyon. Reports came piling in from everywhere—reports that were often inaccurate, sometimes incomprehensible, and always contradictory.

Luftwaffe headquarters in Paris announced that "fifty to sixty two-engined planes are coming in" over the Cherbourg peninsula and that paratroopers had landed "near Caen." Admiral Theodor Krancke's headquarters—*Marinegruppenkommando West*—confirmed the British paratroop landings, nervously pointed out that the enemy had fallen close to one of their coastal batteries, and then added that "part of the parachute drop consists of straw dummies." Neither report mentioned the Americans on the Cherbourg peninsula—yet at this time one of the naval batteries at St.-Marcouf, just above Utah Beach, had informed Cherbourg headquarters that a dozen Americans had been captured. Within minutes of their first message, the Luftwaffe phoned in another bulletin. Parachutists, they said, were down near Bayeux. Actually none had landed there at all.

At both headquarters men tried desperately to evaluate the rash of red spots sprouting over their maps. Officers at Army Group B rang their opposite numbers at OB West, hashed the situation over and came up with conclusions many of which, in the light of what was actually happening, seem incredible. When OB West's acting intelligence officer, Major Doertenbach, called Army Group B for a report, for example, he was told that "the Chief of Staff views the situation with equanimity" and that "there is a possibility that parachutists who have been reported are merely bailed-out bomber crews."

The Seventh Army didn't think so. By 3 A.M. Pemsel was convinced that the *Schwerpunkt*—the main thrust—was driving into Normandy. His maps showed paratroopers at each end of the Seventh's area—on the Cherbourg peninsula and east of the Orne. Now, too, there were alarming reports from naval stations at Cherbourg. Using sound direction apparatus and some radar equipment, the stations were picking up ships maneuvering in the Bay of the Seine.

There was no doubt now in Pemsel's mind—the invasion was on. He called Speidel. "The air landings," Pemsel said, "con-

148

stitute the first phase of a larger enemy action." Then he added, "Engine noises are audible from out at sea." But Pemsel could not convince Rommel's chief of staff. Speidel's answer, as recorded in the Seventh Army telephone log, was that "the affair is still locally confined." The estimate that he gave Pemsel at this time was summarized in the war diary and reads: "Chief of Staff Army Group B believes that for the time being this is not to be considered as a large operation."

Even as Pemsel and Speidel talked, the last paratroopers of the 18,000-man airborne assault were floating down over the Cherbourg peninsula. Sixty-nine gliders, carrying men, guns and heavy equipment, were just crossing the coast of France, headed for the British landing areas near Ranville. And twelve miles off Normandy's five invasion beaches, the *Ancon*, headquarters ship of Task Force O, under the command of Rear Admiral John L. Hall, dropped anchor. Lining up behind her were the transports carrying the men who would land in the first wave on Omaha Beach.

But at La Roche-Guyon there was still nothing to indicate the immensity of the Allied attack, and in Paris OB West endorsed Speidel's first estimate of the situation. Rundstedt's able operations chief, Lieutenant General Bodo Zimmermann, informed of Speidel's conversation with Pemsel, sent back a message agreeing with Speidel: "Operations OB West holds that this is not a large-scale airborne operation, all the more because Admiral Channel Coast (Krancke's headquarters) has reported that the enemy has dropped straw dummies."

These officers can hardly be blamed for being so utterly confused. They were miles away from the actual fighting, entirely dependent on the reports coming in. These were so spotty and so misleading that even the most experienced officers found it impossible to gauge the magnitude of the airborne assault—or, for that matter, to see an over-all pattern emerging from the Allied attacks. If this was the invasion, was it aimed at Normandy? Only the Seventh Army seemed to think so. Perhaps the paratroop attacks were simply a diversion intended to draw attention from the real invasion—against General Hans von Salmuth's massive Fifteenth Army in the Pas-de-Calais, where nearly everybody thought the Allies would strike. The Fifteenth's chief of staff, Major General Rudolf Hofmann was so sure the main attack would come in the Fifteenth's area that he called Pemsel and bet him a dinner that he was right. "This is one bet you're going to lose," said Pemsel. Yet at this time neither Army Group B nor OB West had sufficient evidence to draw any conclusions. They alerted the invasion coast and ordered measures taken against the paratroop attacks. Then everybody waited for more information. There was little else they could do.

By now, messages were flooding into command posts all over Normandy. One of the first problems for some of the divisions was to find their own commanders—the generals who had already left for the *Kriegsspiel* in Rennes. Although most of them were located quickly, two—Lieutenant General Karl von Schlieben and Major General Wilhelm Falley, both commanding divisions in the Cherbourg peninsula—couldn't be found. Von Schlieben was asleep in his hotel in Rennes and Falley was still en route there by car.

Admiral Krancke, the naval commander in the west, was on an inspection trip to Bordeaux. His chief of staff awakened him in his hotel room. "Paratroop landings are taking place near Caen," Krancke was informed. "OB West insists that this is only a diversionary attack and not the real invasion, but we're picking up ships. We think it's the real thing." Krancke immediately alerted the few naval forces he had and then quickly set out for his headquarters in Paris.

One of the men who got his orders at Le Havre was already a legend in the German Navy. Lieutenant Commander Heinrich Hoffmann had made his name as an E-boat commander.

Almost from the beginning of the war, his speedy, powerful flotillas of torpedo craft had ranged up and down the English Channel, attacking shipping wherever they found it. Hoffmann also had been in action during the Dieppe raid and had boldly escorted the German battleships *Scharnhorst, Gneisenau* and *Prinz Eugen* in their dramatic dash from Brest to Norway in 1942.

When the message from headquarters came in, Hoffmann was in the cabin of T-28, the lead E-boat of his 5th Flotilla, preparing to go out on a mine-laying operation. Immediately he called together the commanders of the other boats. They were all young men and although Hoffmann told them that "this must be the invasion," it did not surprise them. They had expected it. Only three of his six boats were ready, but Hoffmann could not wait for the others to be loaded with torpedoes. A few minutes later the three small boats left Le Havre. On the bridge of T-28, his white sailor's cap pushed back on his head as usual, the thirty-four-year-old Hoffmann peered out into the darkness. Behind him, the two little boats bounced along in Indian file, following the lead boat's every maneuver. They raced through the night at more than twenty-three knots—blindly heading straight toward the mightiest fleet ever assembled.

At least they were in action. Probably the most baffled men in Normandy this night were the 16,242 seasoned troops of the tough 21st Panzer Division, once a part of Rommel's famed *Afrika Korps.* Clogging every small village, hamlet and wood in the area just twenty-five miles southeast of Caen, these men were sitting almost on the edge of the battlefield, the only panzer division within immediate striking distance of the British airborne assault and the only veteran troops in that area.

Ever since the alert, officers and men had been standing alongside their tanks and vehicles, engines running, waiting for the order to move out. Colonel Hermann von Oppeln-Bronikowski, in command of the division's regiment of tanks, couldn't understand the delay. He had been awakened shortly after 2 A.M. by the 21st's commander, Lieutenant General Edgar Feuchtinger. "Oppeln," Feuchtinger had said breathlessly, "imagine! *They* have landed." He had briefed Bronikowski on the situation and told him that as soon as the division got its orders it would "clean out the area between Caen and the coast immediately." But no further word had come. With growing anger and impatience, Bronikowski continued to wait.

Miles away, the most puzzling reports of all were being received by the Luftwaffe's Lieutenant Colonel Priller. He and his wing man, Sergeant Wodarczyk, had stumbled into their beds about 1 A.M. at the 26th Fighter Wing's now deserted airfield near Lille. They had succeeded in drowning their anger at the Luftwaffe High Command with several bottles of excellent cognac. Now, in his drunken sleep, Priller heard the phone ring as though from a long way off. He came to slowly, his left hand groping over the bedside table for the phone.

Second Fighter Corps headquarters was on the wire. "Priller," said the operations officer, "it seems that some sort of an invasion is taking place. I suggest you put your wing on the alert."

Sleepy as he was, Pips Priller's temper promptly boiled over again. The 124 planes of his command had been moved away from the Lille area the previous afternoon and now the very thing he had feared was happening. Priller's language, as he remembers the conversation, is unprintable, but after telling his caller what was wrong with corps headquarters and the entire Luftwaffe High Command, the fighter ace roared, "Who in hell am I supposed to alert? *I'm* alert. Wodarczyk is alert! But you fatheads *know* I have only two damned planes!" With that he slammed down the receiver.

A few minutes later the phone rang again. "Now what?" yelled Priller. It was the same officer. "My dear Priller," he said, "I'm awfully sorry. It was all a mistake. We somehow got a wrong report. Everything is fine—there's no invasion." Priller was so furious he couldn't answer. Worse than that, he couldn't get back to sleep.

Despite the confusion, hesitancy and indecision in the higher levels of command, the German soldiers in actual contact with the enemy were reacting swiftly. Thousands of troops were already on the move and, unlike the generals at Army Group B and OB West, these soldiers had no doubts that the invasion was upon them. Many of them had been fighting it off in isolated, face-to-face skirmishes ever since the first British and Americans had dropped out of the sky. Thousands of other alerted troops waited behind their formidable coastal defenses, ready to repel an invasion no matter where it might come. They were apprehensive, but they were also determined.

At Seventh Army headquarters, the one top commander who was not confused called his staff together. In the brightly lighted map room, General Pemsel stood before his officers. His voice was as calm and quiet as usual. Only his words betrayed the deep concern he felt. "Gentlemen," he told them, "I am convinced the invasion will be upon us by dawn. Our future will depend on how we fight this day. I request of you all the effort and pain that you can give."

In Germany, five hundred miles away, the man who might have agreed with Pemsel—the one officer who had won many a battle by his uncanny ability to see clearly through the most confusing situations—was asleep. At Army Group B the situation was not considered serious enough yet to call Field Marshal Erwin Rommel.

★ 6 ★

ALREADY the first reinforcements had reached the airborne troops. In the British 6th Airborne's area sixty-nine gliders had landed, forty-nine of them on the correct landing strip near Ranville. Other small glider units had landed earlier—notably Major Howard's force on the bridges and a formation carrying heavy equipment for the division—but this was the main glider train. The sappers had done a good job. They had not had time to completely clear the long glider field of all its obstructions, but enough of these had been dynamited for the force to come in. After the arrival of the gliders the landing zone presented a fantastic sight. In the moonlight it looked like a Daliesque graveyard. Wrecked machines, with crumpled wings, squashed cabins and crazily canted tails, lay everywhere. It did not seem possible that anyone could have survived the splintering crashes, yet casualties had been low. More men had been injured from antiaircraft fire than in the landings.

The train had brought in the 6th Airborne's commander, Major General Richard Gale, and his headquarters staff with more troops, heavy equipment and the all-important antitank guns. Men had poured out of the gliders expecting to find the field under harassing enemy fire; instead they found a strange, pastoral silence. Sergeant John Hutley, piloting a Horsa, had expected a hot reception and had warned his copilot, "Get out as quick as you can the moment we hit, and make a dash for

154

cover." But the only sign of battle was off in the distance where Hutley could see the multicolored flash of tracers and hear the sound of machine gun fire coming from nearby Ranville. Around him the landing field was bustling with activity as men salvaged equipment from the wrecks and hitched up the antitank guns to the backs of jeeps. There was even an air of cheerfulness now that the glider ride was over. Hutley and the men he had carried sat down in the wrecked cabin of their glider and had a cup of tea before setting out for Ranville.

On the other side of the Normandy battlefield, on the Cherbourg peninsula, the first American glider trains were just coming in. Sitting in the copilot's seat of the 101st lead glider was the assistant division commander, Brigadier General Don Pratt, the officer who had been so alarmed back in England when a hat was tossed on the bed where he was sitting. Pratt was, reportedly, "as tickled as a schoolboy" to be making his first glider flight. Strung out behind was a procession of fifty-two gliders in formations of four, each towed by a Dakota. The train carried jeeps, antitank guns, an entire airborne medical unit, even a small bulldozer. High on the nose of Pratt's glider a big No. 1 was painted. A huge "Screaming Eagle," insignia of the 101st, and a U.S. flag adorned the canvas on either side of the pilots' compartment. In the same formation, Surgical Technician Emile Natalle looked down on shell bursts and burning vehicles below and saw "a wall of fire coming up to greet us." Still hitched to their planes, the gliders lurched from side to side scudding through "flak thick enough to land on."

Unlike the paratroopers' planes, the gliders came in from the Channel and approached the peninsula from the east. They were only seconds past the coast when they saw the lights of the landing zone at Hiesville, four miles from Ste.-Mère-Église. One by one the 300-yard-long nylon tow ropes parted and the gliders came soughing down. Natalle's glider overshot the zone and crashed into a field studded with "Rommel's asparagus"—lines

155

of heavy posts embedded in the ground as antiglider obstacles. Sitting in a jeep inside the glider, Natalle gazed out through one of the small windows and watched with horrified fascination as the wings sheared off and the posts whizzed past. Then there was a ripping sound and the glider broke in two—directly behind the jeep in which Natalle was sitting. "It made it very easy to get out," he recalls.

A short distance away lay the wreckage of glider No. 1. Skidding down a sloping pasture, its brakes unable to halt its 100-m.p.h. rush, it had smashed headlong into a hedgerow. Natalle found the pilot, who had been hurled from the cockpit, lying in the hedgerow with both legs broken. General Pratt had been killed instantly, crushed by the crumpled framework of the cockpit. He was the first general officer on either side to be killed on D Day.

Pratt was one of the few casualties in the 101st landings. Almost all the division's gliders came down on or close to the field at Hiesville. Although most of them were totally wrecked, their equipment arrived largely intact. It was a remarkable achievement. Few of the pilots had made more than three or four practice landings and these had all been in daylight.*

Although the 101st was lucky, the 82nd was not. The inexperience of the pilots produced near-disaster in the 82nd's 50-glider train. Fewer than half their formations found the right landing zone northwest of Ste.-Mère-Église; the remainder plowed into hedgerows and buildings, dove into rivers or came down in the marshes of the Merderet. Equipment and vehicles

* There was also a shortage of glider pilots. "At one time," General Gavin recalls, "we didn't think we'd have enough. In the invasion each copilot's seat was occupied by an airborne trooper. Incredible as it may seem, these troopers had been given no training in either flying or landing gliders. Some found themselves with a wounded pilot and a fully loaded glider on their hands as they came hurtling in through flak-filled space on June 6. Fortunately the type glider we were using was not too hard to fly or land. But having to do it for the first time in combat was a chastening experience; it really gave a man religion."

so urgently needed were strewn everywhere and casualties were high. Eighteen pilots alone were killed within the first few minutes. One glider loaded with troops sailed directly over the head of Captain Robert Piper, the 505th Regiment's adjutant and, to his horror, "careened off the chimney of a house, dropped into the back yard, cartwheeled across the ground and smashed into a thick stone wall. There was not even a moan from the wreckage."

For the hard-pressed 82nd, the wide dispersion of the glider train was calamitous. It would take hours to salvage and collect the few guns and supplies that had arrived safely. In the meantime, troopers would have to fight on with the weapons they had carried with them. But this, after all, was standard operating procedure for paratroopers: they fought with what they had until relieved.

Now the 82nd men holding the rear of the airhead—the bridges over the Douve and the Merderet—were in position and already encountering the Germans' first probings. These paratroopers had no vehicles, no antitank guns, few bazookas, machine guns or mortars. Worse, they had no communications. They did not know what was happening around them, what positions were being held, what objectives had been taken. It was the same with the men of the 101st, except that the fortunes of war had given them most of their equipment. The soldiers of both divisions were still scattered and isolated, but little groups were fighting toward the principal objectives—and strongholds were beginning to fall.

In Ste.-Mère-Église, as the stunned townspeople watched from behind their shuttered windows, paratroopers of the 82nd's 505th Regiment slipped cautiously through the empty streets. The church bell was silent now. On the steeple Private John Steele's empty parachute hung limp, and every now and then the glowing embers of M. Hairon's villa erupted, briefly outlining the trees in the square. Occasionally a sniper's bullet whined angrily into the night, but that was the only sound; everywhere there was an uneasy silence.

Lieutenant Colonel Edward Krause, leading the attack, had expected to fight hard for Ste.-Mère-Église, but apart from a few snipers it appeared that the German garrison had pulled out. Krause's men swiftly took advantage of the situation: They occupied buildings, set up road blocks and machine gun posts, cut telephone cables and wires. Other squads continued the slow sweep through the town, moving like shadows from hedge to hedge and doorway to doorway, all converging on the town's center, the Place de l'Église.

Passing around the back of the church, P.F.C. William Tucker reached the square and set up his machine gun behind a tree. Then as he looked out on the moonlit square he saw a parachute and, lying next to him, a dead German. On the far side were the crumpled, sprawled shapes of other bodies. As Tucker sat there in the semidarkness trying to figure out what had happened, he began to feel that he was not alone—that somebody was standing behind him. Grabbing the cumbersome machine gun, he whirled around. His eyes came level with a pair of boots slowly swaying back and forth. Tucker hastily stepped back. A dead paratrooper was hanging in the tree looking down at him.

Now other paratroopers came into the square and suddenly they too saw the bodies hanging in the trees. Lieutenant Gus Sanders remembers that "men just stood there staring, filled with a terrible anger." Lieutenant Colonel Krause reached the square. As he stood looking at the dead troopers, he said just three words: "Oh, my God."

Then Krause pulled an American flag from his pocket. It was old and worn—the same flag that the 505th had raised over Naples. Krause had promised his men that "before dawn of D Day this flag will fly over Ste.-Mère-Église." He walked to the town hall and, on the flagpole by the side of the door, ran up the colors. There was no ceremony. In the square of the dead paratroopers the fighting was over. The Stars and Stripes flew over the first town to be liberated by the Americans in France.

At the German Seventh Army headquarters in Le Mans a message was received from General Marcks's 84th Corps. It read: "Communications with Ste.-Mère-Église cut off . . ." The time was 4:30 A.M.

The Îles-St.-Marcouf are two barren piles of rock just three miles off Utah Beach. In the vast and intricate invasion plan the islands had gone unnoticed until three weeks before D Day. Then Supreme Headquarters had decided that they could be the sites of heavy gun batteries. To ignore the islands, then, was a risk that no one was prepared to take. Hurriedly 132 men of the U.S. 4th and 24th cavalry squadrons were trained for a pre-H-Hour assault. These men had landed on the isles at about 4:30 A.M. They found no guns, no troops—only sudden death. For as Lieutenant Colonel Edward C. Dunn's men moved off the beaches they were trapped in a hideous labyrinth of mine fields. S mines—which bound into the air when stepped on and gut the attacker with bulletlike ball bearings—had been sown like grass seed. Within minutes the night was ripped by the flash of explosions, the screams of mangled men. Three lieutenants were injured almost immediately, two enlisted men were killed, and Lieutenant Alfred Rubin, who was also a casualty, would never forget "the sight of one man lying on the ground spitting up ball bearings." By the end of the day their losses would be nineteen killed and wounded. Surrounded by the dead and the dying, Lieutenant Colonel Dunn sent out the success signal, "Mission accomplished." These were the first Allied troops to invade Hitler's Europe from the sea. But in the scheme of things, their action was merely a D-Day footnote, a bitter and useless victory.

In the British zone, almost on the coast and just three miles east of Sword Beach, Lieutenant Colonel Terence Otway and his men lay under heavy machine gun fire at the edge of the barbed wire and the mine fields protecting the massive Merville battery. Otway's situation was desperate. In all the months of training he had never expected every phase of his elaborate land-and-air assault of the coastal battery to work out exactly as planned. But neither had he been prepared for its total disintegration. Yet, somehow, it had happened.

The bombing attack had failed. The special glider train had been lost and with it artillery, flame throwers, mortars, mine detectors and scaling ladders. Of his 700-man battalion, Otway had found only 150 soldiers and, to take the battery with its garrison of 200, these soldiers had only their rifles, Sten guns, grenades, a few Bangalore torpedoes and one heavy machine gun. Despite these handicaps, Otway's men had grappled with each problem, improvising brilliantly.

With wire cutters they had already cut gaps through the outer barricade of wire and placed their few Bangalore torpedoes in position ready to blow the rest. One group of men had cleared a path through the mine fields. It had been a hair-raising job. They had crawled on hands and knees across the moonlit approaches to the battery, feeling for trip wires and prodding the ground ahead of them with bayonets. Now Otway's 150 men crouched in ditches and bomb craters and along the sides of hedges, waiting for the order to attack. The 6th Airborne's commander, General Gale, had instructed Otway, "Your attitude of mind must be that you cannot contemplate failure in the direct assault . . ." As he looked around at his men, Otway knew that his casualties would be high. But the guns of the battery had to be silenced—they could slaughter the troops crossing Sword Beach. The situation was, he thought, desper-

Hitler's "Atlantic Wall" was formidable. Never before had an attacking force encountered such defenses—yet the Wall was only partially completed. These photos (enlargements from a 16 mm. German propaganda film) give some idea of the heavily gunned steel and concrete fortifications which girdled the invasion coast. Communication trenches, machine-gun nests, mortar pits and mine fields supplemented the heavy gun blockhouses, and the sands were strewn with a maze of mined anti-invasion obstacles.   WIDE WORLD

Rommel inspects defenses along French coast in February 1944. On his right (almost out of picture) is Maj. Gen. Alfred Gause, his Chief of Staff up to March 1944. Facing camera, directly behind unidentified officer who is pointing, is Rommel's aide, Capt. Hellmuth Lang.

One of Rommel's simple but deadly anti-invasion beach obstacles—a stake topped by Teller mine. Rommel designed most of these devices and proudly called them "my inventions."

162

"Usually Rommel would explain his ideas by whipping out a pad and making a sketch," recalls his aide. Shortly after his first inspection trip of the invasion coast in the fall of 1943, Rommel sketched the diagram above. It outlined his beach-obstacle plan more clearly than if his engineers had written a pamphlet. It was distributed by the thousands, and Rommel drove his troops so hard to get his program finished that some generals complained. Gen. Marcks of the 84th Corps once told Rommel that his troops were getting "neither training nor rest." Replied Rommel: "My dear Marcks, which would they rather be—tired or dead?" Rommel's drive paid off. Below, the way the beaches looked by April 1944. AUTHOR'S COLLECTION

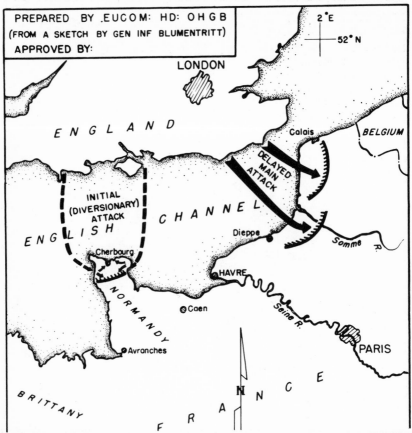

PREPARED BY EUCOM: HD: OHGB
(FROM A SKETCH BY GEN INF BLUMENTRITT)
APPROVED BY:

2°E
52°N

LONDON

E N G L A N D

Calais   BELGIUM

INITIAL
(DIVERSIONARY)
ATTACK

DELAYED
MAIN
ATTACK

C H A N N E L

E N G L I S H

Cherbourg

Dieppe

Somme R.

N O R M A N D Y

HAVRE

Caen

Seine R.

Avranches

PARIS

B R I T T A N Y

F R A N C E

Field Marshall von Rundstedt [BELOW, LEFT] *expected a two-pronged Allied invasion. The first, a diversionary attack against the Cherbourg peninsula and, later, the main assault against the Pas-de-Calais area, where Gen. Hans von Salmuth's massive 15th Army lay waiting. Even after D Day Hitler believed that the Pas-de-Calais attack would still come, and held the 15th Army in its positions until late July. Map prepared from sketches by Rundstedt's Chief of Staff, Maj. Gen. Gunther Blumentritt* [BELOW, RIGHT].

Field Marshal Gerd von Rundstedt, German Supreme Commander in the West.

Maj. Gen. Gunther Blumentritt, Rundstedt's Chief of Staff.

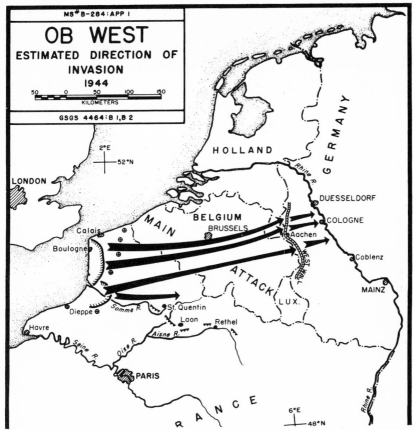

MS#B-284:APP I

OB WEST
ESTIMATED DIRECTION OF
INVASION
1944

50   0   50   100   150
KILOMETERS

GSGS 4464:B1,B2

2°E
52°N
HOLLAND
GERMANY
Rhine R.
LONDON
DUESSELDORF
MAIN
BELGIUM
COLOGNE
BRUSSELS
Calais
Aachen
Boulogne
WEST WALL
Coblenz
ATTACK
MAINZ
LUX.
Dieppe
Somme R.
St. Quentin
Laon
Rethel
Havre
Seine R.
Oise R.
Aisne R.
PARIS
FRANCE
6°E
48°N
Rhine R.

Blumentritt map, above, shows one reason why invasion was expected at
Pas-de-Calais: it was the nearest point to the German border. Germans rea-
soned that Allies would pick the shortest route for their drive toward the
Reich. Even after the Normandy invasion began, Rommel's Chief of Staff,
Maj. Gen. Hans Speidel [BELOW, LEFT], thought it was a diversionary attack.
The 7th Army's Chief of Staff, Maj. Gen. Max Pemsel [BELOW, RIGHT], was
first German general to warn that Normandy assault was the real invasion.

Maj. Gen. Dr. Hans
Speidel, Rommel's
Chief of Staff.

Maj. Gen. Max Pem-
sel, 7th Army's Chief
of Staff.

165

General Dwight D. Eisenhower, the Supreme Commander, and Allied chiefs. Left to right: Lt. Gen. Omar N. Bradley, U.S. 1st Army Commander; Admiral Bertram Ramsey, Allied Naval Commander; Air Chief Marshal Tedder, Deputy Supreme Commander; Eisenhower; Field Marshal Bernard Montgomery, D Day's Assault Commander; Air Chief Marshal Leigh-Mallory, Allied Air Commander; Maj. Gen. Walter Bedell Smith, Eisenhower's Chief of Staff.

In last weeks of May, ports were jammed as men and equipment loaded for D Day attack. Picture at right shows troops and vehicles going aboard three LSTs at Brixham. Notice concrete "hards," which were specially laid down to facilitate loading of shallow-draft landing craft.

No. 5,775

ACROSS

1 A cause of post-scripts (13)
10 Very attentive commonly (two words—3, 4)
11 A fool's weapon (7)
12 But this isn't to be bought at this shop (6)
15 Foils start thus (two words—3, 3) (4)
16 Definite (7)
17 One of the U.S. (4)
18 Achievement that the guardians of the Tower always have at heart (4)
19 Proper behaviour (7)
20 But cook has a practical use for this old weapon (4)
22 Part of one's last will and testament (6)
27 The ceremonious part (6)
30 Fifty fifty (7)
31 White wine (7)

(grid — UTAH filled in)

No. 5,801

ACROSS

1 "Lid on slang" (anag.) (but is all 15 across so pure in speech?) (two words—4, 6)
8 Doing nothing because there's nothing doing, possibly (4)
10 The kind of constitution that laughs at doctors of the Goebbels type! (10)
11 Our supposed portion in 1940, but we never tumbled to it (4)
12 —though coming to the this of it (4)
15 Where the work of the architect stands very high (two words—3, 4)
18 The girl who went into her own reflections very amusingly (5)
19 You must be plumb right! (5)
20 Just a note (5)
21 Got in wrongly to the bar (5)
22 Would this problem be a sitter to an artist? (5)
23 A joint affair (5)
24 Not a forbidding hue (5)
25 She is in an ancient city (official) (5)
26 Of Eastern origin, but serious (7)
30 Cast a skin (4)
33 Points in favour of some players? (4)
34 A submarine should be, of course (10)
35 He gets his wings on false pretences (4)
36 Where to look for Maud's friend? (two words—6, 4)

DOWN

1 Sign of appeal to men (4)
2 Cause of the hidden hand? (5)
4 Like a bear with a sore head (5)
5 He may be the curate's egg, good in parts (4)
6 Outcast agent of fickle chance (4)
7 Flower one might well salute (4)
9 End of a term for losing cohesion (two words—8, 2)
10 Those working in it are sunk in the work (10)
13 It may be seen at the front feeding time (4)
14 See printer for an adventure (4)
15 Britannia and same thing (7)
16 Sphere of down (5)
17 An exclusive notice (two words—4, 3)
20 The root of smokers' pleasures (5)
27 It comes from the rates—blooming scandal! (5)
28 Choice of directions of tongue (5)
29 Was an arm, might support one (5)
31 No good man will live up to (5)

(grid — NEPTUNE filled in)

No. 5,799

ACROSS

1 "Wandering near her secret bower molest her ancient reign" (Gray) (8)
5 Danger courted by billiard players (6)
9 His weapon is the pen (8)
10 Tenant of a kind (6)
11 This bush is a centre of nursery revolutions (8)
12 It is no use asking a jazz band to play for this dance (6)
14 An early example of the N.A.A.F.I. girl? (10)
18 The stronger his team the less this member of it has to do (10)
22 The dim distance (6)
23 "Eager set" (anag.) (8)
24 The words that stick in the mouth of the suffragette who has found a husband? (two words—2, 4)
25 Courteous though exercising compulsion (8)
26 Epithet for that story of the ivy that strangled a sleeper (6)
27 An old week (8)

DOWN

1 A suitable opening word (6)
2 Not so long ago (6)
3 This great English painter does down in times of drought (5)
17 Drink upset in 10 across (3)
18 To get this fabulous lady just ponder (4)
19 Ecclesiastical assembly (5)
22 Its sole work is to produce some effect (5)
23 Not obsolete (two words—2, 3)
24 Battle of the last Great War (5)
26 One probably this these represented at a 19 across (4)

(grid — MULBERRY filled in)

No. 5,792

ACROSS

1 A shot that falls short is not thus satisfactory (four words—2, 2, 3, 4)
9 Town of Germany (5)
10 "Call In a home" (anag.) (11)
11 The Derby winner to start a branch of mathematics (5)
12 Tree used in the building of the Temple (5)
15 Town to go down in times of drought (5)
17 Drink upset in 10 across (3)
18 To get this fabulous lady just ponder (4)
19 Ecclesiastical assembly (5)
22 Its sole work is to produce some effect (5)
23 Not obsolete (two words—2, 3)
24 Battle of the last Great War (5)
26 One probably this these represented at a 19 across (4)
27 The start of 35 across (it's given you) (3)
28 This worker is as good as five in the R.N. (5)
30 The way in which a tasty lemon might come in useful (5)
33 An overworked word nowadays for 'rate' (5)
35 This gives vagueness to place or number (11)
36 Lightweight of the animal world (5)
37 The credit for a joint thus perfectly cooked should go to the turnspit (four words—4, 2, 1, 4)

DOWN

2 This meal would be bit by bit (5)
3 Red Indian on the Missouri (5)
4 None (4)
5 No small deer (5)
6 He wrote "A thing of beauty is a joy for ever" (5)
7 By sticking to one's work (11)
8 A mere jumble of words (11)
12 At any rate a writer of music should have this to offer importunate creditors (11)
13 Kind of absent-mindedness (11)
14 Gathering in which all take part (5)
15 This continental river might easily become a drain (5)
16 Sign of the Zodiac (3)
20 Displeasing (5)
21 One of the worldly wealthy (5)
25 Stands for the control of the lower Thames (3)
28 Well-known refusal given to the lad (5)
29 Edge (5)
31 Fish that resists your getting him his tail (5)
32 Afterwards (5)
34 This term for a European of sorts seems to be 500 years old (4)

(grid — OMAHA filled in)

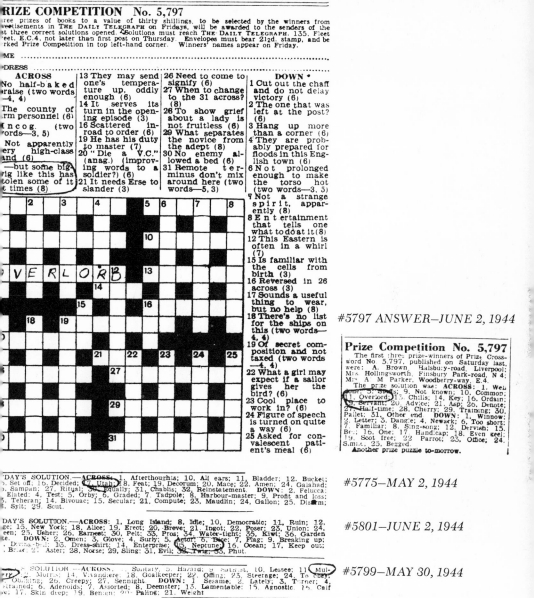

ree prizes of books to a value of thirty shillings, to be selected by the winners from
veetisements in THE DAILY TELEGRAPH on Fridays, will be awarded to the senders of the
st three correct solutions opened. Solutions must reach THE DAILY TELEGRAPH. 135. Fleet
eet. E.C.4, not later than first post on Thursday. Envelopes must bear 2½d. stamp, and be
rked Prize Competition in top left-hand corner. Winners' names appear on Friday.

ME ....

DRESS ....

ACROSS

No half-baked
raise (two words
—4, 4)

The county of
rm personnel (6)

ncog. (two
ords—3, 5)

Not apparently
ery high-class
and (6)

—but some big
ig like this has
tolen some of it
t times (8)

13 They may send
one's tempera-
ture up. oddly
enough (6)

14 It serves its
turn in the open-
ing episode (3)

16 Scattered in-
road to order (6)

19 He has his duty
to master (7)

20 "Die a V.C."
(anag.) (improv-
ing words to a
soldier?) (6)

21 It needs Erse to
slander (3)

26 Need to come to
signify (6)

27 When to change
to the 31 across?
(8)

28 To show grief
about a lady is
not fruitless (6)

29 What separates
the novice from
the adept (8)

30 No enemy al-
lowed a bed (6)

31 Remote ter-
minus don't mix
around here (two
words—5, 3)

DOWN

1 Cut out the chaff
and do not delay
victory (6)

2 The one that was
left at the post?
(6)

3 Hang up more
than a corner (6)

4 They are prob-
ably prepared for
floods in this Eng-
lish town (6)

6 Not prolonged
enough to make
the torso end
(two words—3, 5)

7 Not a strange
spirit, appar-
ently (8)

8 Entertainment
that tells one
what to do at it (8)

12 This Eastern is
often in a whirl
(7)

15 Is familiar with
the cells from
birth (3)

16 Reversed in 26
across (3)

17 Sounds a useful
thing to wear,
but no help (8)

18 There's no list
for the ships on
this (two words—
4, 4)

19 Of secret com-
position and not
taxed (two words
—4, 4)

22 What a girl may
expect if a sailor
gives her the
bird? (6)

23 Cool place to
work in? (6)

24 Figure of speech
is turned on quite
a way (6)

25 Asked for con-
valescent pati-
ent's meal (6)

#5797 ANSWER–JUNE 2, 1944

DAY'S SOLUTION.—ACROSS: 1. Afterthoughts; 10. All ears; 11. Bladder; 12. Bucket;
5. Set off; 16. Decided; 17. Utah; 18. Feat; 19. Decorum; 20. Mace; 22. Amen; 24. Galahad;
5. Sampan; 27. Ritual; 30. Equally; 31. Chablis; 32. Reinstatement. DOWN: 2. Felucca:
Elated; 4. Test; 5. Orby; 6. Graded; 7. Tadpole; 8. Harbour-master; 9. Profit and loss;
3. Teheran; 14. Bivouac; 15. Secular; 21. Compute; 23. Maudlin; 24. Gallon; 25. Disarm;
3. Sylt; 29. Scut.

#5775–MAY 2, 1944

DAY'S SOLUTION.—ACROSS: 1. Long Island; 8. Idle; 10. Democratic; 11. Ruin; 12.
ge; 15. New York; 18. Alice; 19. Erect; 20. Breve; 21. Ingot; 22. Poser; 23. Union; 24.
een; 25. Usher; 26. Earnest; 30. Pelt; 33. Pros; 34. Water-tight; 35. Kiwi; 36. Garden
te. DOWN: 2. Omen; 3. Glove; 4. Surly; 5. Actor; 6. Dice; 7. Flag; 9. Breaking up;
. Diving-bell; 13. Dress-shirt; 14. Enterprise; 15. Neptune; 16. Ocean; 17. Keep out;
Briac; 27. Aster; 28. Norse; 29. Sling; 31. Evil; 32. Twig; 33. Phut.

#5801–JUNE 2, 1944

SOLUTION —ACROSS. 1. Sanitary; 5. Hazard; 9. Sawdust; 10. Lessee; 11. Mul-
try; 12. Morris; 16. Vivandiere; 18. Goalkeeper; 22. Offing; 23. Steerage; 24. To copy;
Obtaining; 26. Creepy; 27. Sennight. DOWN: 1. Sesame, 2. Lately; 3. Turner; 4.
strained; 6. Adenoids; 7. Assorted; 8. Deemster; 15. Lamentable; 15. Agnostic. 16. Calf
ve; 17. Skin deep; 19. Benign; 20. Paling; 21. Weight

#5799–MAY 30, 1944

DAY'S SOLUTION.—ACROSS: 1. Up to the mark; 9. Essen; 10. Melancholia; 11. Trace;
. Cedar; 15. Wells; 17. Aile; 18. Muse; 19. Synod; 22. Pedal; 23. Ava; 24. Ypres; 25. Sees;
. The; 28. Navy; 30. Style; 33. Tempo; 35. Thereabouts; 36. Ounce; 37. Done to a turn.
WN: 2. Piece; 3. Omaha; 4. Hock; 5. Moose; 6. Keats; 7. Assiduously; 8. Incoherence; 12.
mposition; 13. Daydreaming; 14. Rally; 15. Weser; 16. Leo; 20. Nasty; 21. Dives; 25. P.L.A.;
. Noted; 29. Verge; 31. Trout; 32. Later; 34. Dago.

#5792–MAY 22, 1944

*Here are the five Daily Telegraph crossword puzzles containing key D-Day
code words, which scared Allied HQ. Although prepared months before, by
some strange quirk of fate they all appeared in tense days prior to invasion.
Note that "Overlord" and "Neptune," the principal code words, showed up
on same day, June 2, four days before attack.*

Reproductions courtesy Michael Berry, Editor, London Daily Telegraph

This photo showing Eisenhower talking to 101st Division paratroops just before they boarded their planes on the evening of June 5 is probably the best known of all the pre-invasion pictures, but I have always wondered about the identities of the men. The 101st Airborne Association traced them for me. Among those surrounding the Supreme Commander are: Pfc. William Boyle, Cpl. Hans Sannes, Pfc. Ralph Pombano, Pfc. S. W. Jackson, Sgt. Delbert Williams, Cpl. William E. Hayes, Pfc. Carl Wickers, 1st Lt. William Strebel, Pfc. Henry Fuller, Pfc. Michael Babich and Pfc. William Noll.

Lt. Col. Hellmuth Meyer, 15th Army Intelligence chief, who picked up the Verlaine messages going to the French underground [SEE OPPOSITE PAGE], correctly interpreted them, and warned that the Allied invasion would take place in 48 hours. AUTHOR'S COLLECTION

Tag Uhrzeit Ort und Art der Unterkunft	Darstellung der Ereignisse (Dabei wichtig: Beurteilung der Lage [Feind- und eigene], Eingangs- und Abgangs-zeiten von Meldungen und Befehlen)
5.6.44	Am 1., 2. und 3.6.44 ist durch die Nast innerhalb der "Messages personelles" der französischen Sendungen des britischen Rundfunks folgende Meldung abgehört worden : "Les sanglots longs des violons de l'automme ". Nach vorhandenen Unterlagen soll dieser Spruch am 1. oder 15. eines Monats durchgegeben werden, nur die erste Hälfte eines ganzen Spruches darstellen und ankündigen, dass binnen 48 Stunden nach Durchgabe der zweiten Hälfte des Spruches, gerechnet von 00.00 Uhr des auf die Durchsage folgenden Tages ab, die anglo-amerikanische Invasion beginnt.
21.15 Uhr	Zweite Hälfte des Spruches "Blessent mon coeur d'une longeur monotone" wird durch Nast abgehört.
21.20 Uhr	Spruch an Ic-AO durchgegeben. Danach mit Invasionsbeginn ab 6.6. 00.00 Uhr innerhalb 48 Stunden zu rechnen. Überprüfung der Meldung durch Rückfrage beim Militärbefehlshaber Belgien/Nordfrankreich in Brüssel (Major von Wangenheim).
22.00 Uhr	Meldung an O.B. und Chef des Generalstabes.
22.15 Uhr	Weitergabe gemäss Fernschreiben (Anlage 1) an Generalkommandos. Mündliche. Weitergabe an 16.Flak-Division.

Photo of actual 15th Army War Diary page showing entries of two-part Verlaine message which indicated to Col. Meyer that invasion was imminent (see text). Note vital second line of the verse "Blessent mon coeur d'une longeur [sic] monotone" was picked up from BBC broadcast to French Underground at 9:15 (10:15 British time) and its meaning—that the invasion would begin within 48 hours starting 00:00, 6 June—was recorded five minutes later. Although other D-Day messages were decoded, this is the only one recorded in German War Diaries. Ample evidence supports Col. Meyer's claim that Germans considered the Verlaine verse the all-important message. On June 8 Hitler's HQ demanded explanation from Rundstedt as to why full alert had not been ordered, and specifically referred to Verlaine passages. AUTHOR'S COLLECTION

Destination Normandy. Above, a "stick" of 101st Division paratroopers make final check before boarding DC 3. Below, the convoys, protected by barrage balloons and fighter escorts, set sail for the beaches. Wide World

DC 3s of the 316th Troup Carrier Group towing Waco gliders over France.

First U.S. generals to land in Normandy. [LEFT TO RIGHT] *Maj. Gen. Matthew B. Ridgway, 82nd Airborne's commanding officer; Brig. Gen. James M. Gavin, 82nd's Assistant Division Commander; Maj. Gen. Maxwell D. Taylor, 101st Airborne Commander. First senior British officer was 6th Airborne's Commander, Maj. Gen. Richard Gale.*

Alexandre Renaud, Mayor of Ste.-Mère-Eglise, who witnessed slaughter in town square, and Father Louis Roulland, who ordered church bell rung.

This rare photo, the only one known to exist, shows a group of 82nd Airborne Pathfinders just before they took off for Normandy. These were among the first Americans to land in France. How many of the men pictured above survived the war and how many are still living? I was able to find only two 82nd Pathfinders. One of them, Pvt. Robert M. Murphy, who landed in Madame Levrault's back garden, is standing, third from right, wearing woolen cap.

Courtesy Robert M. Murphy

PATHFINDER GROUP 1944 50.5%

JUNE 5 '44 NORMANDY JUMP

SGT. HANNICK: RACLO: LES. ANKO: JONES: JORDAN: CURRAN OM: "MUD" NYE: DESSCHEN
PURCELL: WYNGARE: LESLIE D. FREE XIA: BOWMAN: STOUT: R. MURPHY: COOPING
YOUNG: IN PLANE DOOR: CHARLES TODISCO JR: "LT" MIKE CHESTER.
FRONT ROW: AIR CORP OFFICERS: REUTER: CAPT. SCOTTLE.

Wrecked 30-man Horsa glider in field near Ste.-Mère-Eglise. Eight paratroopers died in crash.

Flooded areas at both ends of Normandy battlefield claimed greatest number of British and American paratroopers. In darkness, weighed down by equipment and often unable to extricate themselves from chutes, many men became casualties and drowned, often like the trooper below, in less than three feet of water.   *Courtesy Lt. Gen. James M. Gavin*

Father Edward Waters conducts dockside service for 1st Division assault troops. The next stop would be Omaha Beach.

ately unfair, but there was no alternative. He had to attack. He
knew this even as he knew that the last part of his carefully detailed plan was also doomed to failure. The three gliders due to
crash-land on the battery as the ground attack went in would
not come down unless they received a special signal—a star
shell fired from a mortar. Otway had neither the shell nor the
mortar. He did have flares for a Very pistol, but they were to be
used only to signal the success of the assault. His last chance for
help was gone.

The gliders were on time. The tow planes signaled with
their landing lights and then cast off the machines. There were
only two gliders, each carrying about twenty men. The third,
parting from its tow rope over the Channel, had glided safely
back to England. Now the paratroopers heard the soft rustle of
the machines as they came over the battery. Helplessly Otway
watched as the gliders, silhouetted against the moon, gradually
lost height and wheeled back and forth, their pilots searching
desperately for the signal he could not send. As the gliders
circled lower the Germans opened up. The machine guns which
had pinned down the troopers now turned on the gliders.
Streams of 20-millimeter tracers ripped into the unprotected
canvas sides. Still the gliders circled, following the plan, doggedly looking for the signal. And Otway, agonized, almost in
tears, could do nothing.

Then the gliders gave it up. One veered off, to land four miles
away. The other passed so low over the waiting, anxious men
that Privates Alan Mower and Pat Hawkins thought it was going
to smash into the battery. At the last moment it lifted and
crashed instead into a wood some distance away. Instinctively
a few men pushed themselves up from hiding to go help the
survivors. But they were stopped immediately. "Don't move!
Don't leave your positions!" whispered their harassed officers.
There was now nothing more to wait for. Otway ordered the at-

tack. Private Mower heard him yell, "Everybody in! We're going to take this bloody battery!"

And in they went.

With a blinding roar the Bangalore torpedoes blasted great gaps in the wire. Lieutenant Mike Dowling yelled, "Move up! Move up!" Once again a hunting horn sounded in the night. Yelling and firing, Otway's paratroopers plunged into the smoke of the explosions and through the wire. Ahead of them, across the no man's land of mine fields, manned trenches and gun pits, loomed the battery. Suddenly red flares burst over the heads of the advancing paratroopers and immediately machine gun, *Schmeisser* and rifle fire poured out to meet them. Through the deadly barrage, the paratroopers crouched and crawled, ran, dropped to the ground, got up and ran some more. They dived into shell craters, pulled themselves out and went forward again. Mines exploded. Private Mower heard a scream and then someone yelled, "Stop! Stop! There's mines everywhere!" Over on his right, Mower saw a badly wounded corporal sitting on the ground waving men away, and shouting, "Don't come near me! Don't come near me!"

Above the firing, the bursting of mines and the yells of the men, Lieutenant Alan Jefferson, out ahead, continued to blow his hunting horn. Suddenly Private Sid Capon heard a mine explode and saw Jefferson go down. He ran toward the lieutenant, but Jefferson shouted at him, "Get in! Get in!" Then, lying on the ground, Jefferson raised the horn to his lips and began blowing it again. Now there were yells and screams and the flash of grenades as paratroopers piled into the trenches and fought hand to hand with the enemy. Private Capon, reaching one of the trenches, suddenly found himself facing two Germans. One of them hastily raised a Red Cross box high above his head in a token of surrender and said, "*Russki, Russki.*" They were Russian "volunteers." For a moment, Capon didn't know what to do. Then he saw other Germans surrendering and paratroopers leading them down the trench. He handed over his two captives and continued on toward the battery.

There Otway, Lieutenant Dowling and about forty men were already fighting fiercely. Troopers who had cleaned out trenches and gun pits were running around the sides of the earth-banked concrete fortifications, emptying their Sten guns and tossing grenades into the apertures. The battle was gory and wild. Privates Mower, Hawkins and a Bren gunner, racing through a torrent of mortar and machine gun fire, reached one side of the battery, found a door open and plunged inside. A dead German gunner was lying in the passageway; there seemed to be nobody else around. Mower left the other two men by the door and went along the passage. He came to a large room and saw a heavy field piece on a platform. Next to it great stacks of shells were piled. Mower rushed back to his friends and excitedly outlined his plan to "blow the whole business up by detonating grenades among the shells." But they didn't get the chance. As the three men stood talking there was the blast of an explosion. The Bren gunner died instantly. Hawkins was hit in the stomach. Mower thought his back had been "ripped open by a thousand red-hot needles." He couldn't control his legs. They twitched involuntarily—the way he had seen dead bodies twitch. He was sure he was going to die and he didn't want to end this way and he began to call out for help. He called for his mother.

Elsewhere in the battery Germans were surrendering. Private Capon caught up with Dowling's men just in time to see "Germans pushing each other out of a doorway and almost begging to surrender." Dowling's party split the barrels of two guns by firing two shells simultaneously through each barrel, and temporarily knocked out the other two. Then Dowling found Otway. He stood before the colonel, his right hand holding the left side of his chest. He said, "Battery taken as ordered, sir. Guns destroyed." The battle was over; it had taken just fifteen minutes. Otway fired a yellow flare—the success signal—from the Very pistol. It was seen by a R.A.F. spotting plane and radioed to H.M.S. *Arethusa* offshore exactly a quarter of an hour before the cruiser was to start bombarding the battery. At the same time Otway's signal officer sent a confirming message out by pigeon. He had carried the bird all through the battle. On its leg in a plastic capsule was a strip of paper with the code word "Hammer." Moments later Otway found the lifeless body of Lieutenant Dowling. He had been dying at the time he made his report.

Otway led his battered battalion out of the bloody Merville battery. He had not been told to hold the battery once the guns were knocked out. His men had other D-Day missions. They took only twenty-two prisoners. Of the two hundred Germans, no fewer than 178 were dead or dying, and Otway had lost almost half of his own men—seventy killed or wounded. Ironically, the four guns were only half the reported size. And within forty-eight hours the Germans would be back in the battery and two of the guns would be firing on the beaches. But for the critical few hours ahead the Merville battery would be silent and deserted.

Most of the badly injured had to be left behind, for Otway's men had neither sufficient medical supplies nor transport to carry them. Mower was carried out on a board. Hawkins was too terribly wounded to be moved. Both men would survive—even Mower, with fifty-seven pieces of shrapnel in his body. The last thing Mower remembers as they moved away from the battery was Hawkins yelling, "Mates, for God's sake, don't leave me!" Then the voice grew fainter and fainter and Mower mercifully drifted into unconsciousness.

It was nearly dawn—the dawn that eighteen thousand paratroopers had been fighting toward. In less than five hours they had more than fulfilled the expectations of General Eisenhower and his commanders. The airborne armies had confused the enemy and disrupted his communications, and now, holding the flanks at either end of the Normandy invasion area, they had to a great extent blocked the movement of enemy reinforcements.

In the British zone Major Howard's glider-borne troops were firmly astride the vital Caen and Orne bridges. By dawn the five crossings over the Dives would be demolished. Lieutenant Colonel Otway and his emaciated battalion had knocked out the Merville battery, and paratroopers were now in position on the heights overlooking Caen. Thus the principal British assignments had been completed, and as long as the various arteries could be held German counterattacks would be slowed down or stopped altogether.

At the other end of Normandy's five invasion beaches the Americans, despite more difficult terrain and a greater variety of missions, had done equally well. Lieutenant Colonel Krause's men held the key communications center of Ste.-Mère-Église. North of the town Lieutenant Colonel Vandervoort's battalion had cut the main Cherbourg highway running down the peninsula and stood ready to repel attacks driving in from there. Brigadier General Gavin and his troops were dug in around the strategic Merderet and Douve crossings and were holding the rear of the Utah invasion beachhead. General Maxwell Taylor's 101st was still widely scattered; by dawn the division's assembled strength would be only 1,100 out of a total of 6,600 men. Despite this handicap troopers had reached the St.-Martin-de-Varreville gun battery, only to discover that the guns had been removed. Others were in sight of the vital La Barquette locks, the key to the flooding across the neck of the peninsula. And although none of the causeways leading off Utah had been reached, groups of soldiers were driving for them and already held the western edge of the inundated areas back of the beach itself.

The men of the Allied airborne armies had invaded the Continent from the air and secured the initial foothold for the invasion from the sea. Now they awaited the arrival of the seaborne forces with whom they would drive into Hitler's Europe. The American task forces were already lying twelve miles off Utah and Omaha beaches. For U.S. troops H Hour—6:30 A.M. —was exactly one hour and forty-five minutes away.

<h1 style="text-align:center">★ 7 ★</h1>

A̲T 4:45 A.M., Lieutenant George Honour's midget submarine X23 broke the surface of a heaving sea one mile off the Normandy coast. Twenty miles away its sister sub the X20 also surfaced. These two 57-foot craft were now in position, each marking one end of the British-Canadian invasion area—the three beaches, Sword, Juno and Gold. Now each crew had to erect a mast with a flashing light, set up all the other visual and radio signaling apparatus and wait for the first British ships to home in on their signals.

On the X23 Honour pushed up the hatch and climbed stiffly out onto the narrow catwalk. Waves rolled over the little deck and he had to hang on to avoid being washed overboard. Behind him came his weary crew. They clung to the guide rails, water washing about their legs, and hungrily gulped in the cool night air. They had been off Sword Beach since before dawn on June 4 and they had been submerged for more than twenty-one hours out of each day. In all, since leaving Portsmouth on June 2 they had been under water some sixty-four hours.

Even now their ordeal was far from over. On the British beaches H Hour varied from 7 to 7:30 A.M. So for two more hours, until the first wave of assault craft came in, the midget subs would have to hold their positions. Until then the X23 and X20 would be exposed on the surface—small, fixed targets for the German beach batteries. And soon it would be daylight.

★ 8 ★

Everywhere men waited for this dawn, but none so anxiously as the Germans. For by now a new and ominous note had begun to creep into the welter of messages pouring into Rommel's and Rundstedt's headquarters. All along the invasion coast Admiral Krancke's naval stations were picking up the sound of ships— not just one or two as before, but ships by the score. For more than an hour the reports had been mounting. At last a little before 5 A.M. the persistent Major General Pemsel of the Seventh Army telephoned Rommel's chief of staff, Major General Speidel, and told him bluntly, "Ships are concentrating between the mouths of the Vire and the Orne. They lead to the conclusion that an enemy landing and large-scale attack against Normandy is imminent."

Field Marshal Gerd von Rundstedt at his headquarters, OB West, outside Paris had already reached a similar conclusion. To him the impending Normandy assault still looked like a "diversionary attack" and not the real invasion. Even so Rundstedt had moved fast. He had already ordered two massive panzer divisions—the 12th S.S. and the *Panzer Lehr,* both lying in reserve near Paris—to assemble and rush to the coast. Technically both these divisions came under Hitler's headquarters, OKW, and they were not to be committed without the Führer's specific approval. But Rundstedt had taken the chance; he could not believe that Hitler would object or countermand the order. Now, convinced that all the evidence pointed to Normandy as the area for the Allied "diversionary attack," Rundstedt sent an official request to OKW for the reserves. "OB West," explained his teletype message, "is fully aware that if this is actually a large-scale enemy operation it can only be met successfully if immediate action is taken. This involves the commitment on this day of the available strategic reserves . . . these are the 12th S.S. and *Panzer Lehr* divisions. If they assemble quickly and get an early start they can enter the battle on the coast during the day. Under the circumstances OB West therefore requests OKW to release the reserves . . ." It was a perfunctory message, simply for the record.

At Hitler's headquarters in Berchtesgaden in the balmy unrealistic climate of southern Bavaria, the message was delivered to the office of Colonel General Alfred Jodl, Chief of Operations. Jodl was asleep and his staff believed that the situation had not developed sufficiently enough yet for his sleep to be disturbed. The message could wait until later.

Not more than three miles away at Hitler's mountain retreat, the Führer and his mistress Eva Braun were also asleep. Hitler had retired as usual at 4 A.M. and his personal physician, Dr. Morell, had given him a sleeping draught (he was unable to sleep now without it). At about 5 A.M. Hitler's naval aide, Admiral Karl Jesko von Puttkamer, was awakened by a call from Jodl's headquarters. Puttkamer's caller—he cannot recall now who it was—said that there had been "some sort of landings in France." Nothing precise was known yet—in fact, Puttkamer was told, "the first messages are extremely vague." Did Puttkamer think that the Führer should be informed? Both men hashed it over and then decided not to wake Hitler. Puttkamer remembers that "there wasn't much to tell him anyway and we both feared that if I woke him at this time he might start one of his endless nervous scenes which often led to the wildest decisions." Puttkamer decided that the morning would be time enough to give Hitler the news. He switched off the light and went back to sleep.

In France the generals at OB West and Army Group B sat down to wait. They had alerted their forces and called up the panzer reserves; now the next move was up to the Allies. Nobody could estimate the magnitude of the impending assault. Nobody knew—or could even guess—the size of the Allied fleet. And although everything pointed toward Normandy, nobody was really sure where the main attack would come. The German generals had done all they could. The rest depended on the ordinary Wehrmacht soldiers holding the coast. They had suddenly become important. From the coastal fortifications the soldiers of the Reich looked out toward the sea, wondering if this was a practice alert or the real thing at last.

Major Werner Pluskat in his bunker overlooking Omaha Beach had heard nothing from his superiors since 1 A.M. He was cold, tired and exasperated. He felt isolated. He couldn't understand why there had been no reports from either regimental or division headquarters. To be sure, the very fact that his phone had remained silent all night was a good sign; it must mean that nothing serious was happening. But what about the paratroopers, the massed formations of planes? Pluskat could not rid himself of his gnawing uneasiness. Once more he swung the artillery glasses over to the left, picked up the dark mass of the Cherbourg peninsula and began another slow sweep of the horizon. The same low banks of mist came into view, the same patches of shimmering moonlight, the same restless, white-flecked sea. Nothing was changed. Everything seemed peaceful.

Behind him in the bunker his dog, Harras, was stretched out asleep. Nearby, Captain Ludz Wilkening and Lieutenant Fritz Theen were talking quietly. Pluskat joined them. "Still nothing out there," he told them. "I'm about to give it up." But he walked back to the aperture and stood looking out as the first streaks of light began to lighten the sky. He decided to make another routine sweep.

Wearily, he swung the glasses over to the left again. Slowly he tracked across the horizon. He reached the dead center of the bay. The glasses stopped moving. Pluskat tensed, stared hard.

Through the scattering, thinning mist the horizon was magically filling with ships—ships of every size and description, ships that casually maneuvered back and forth as though they had been there for hours. There appeared to be thousands of them. It was a ghostly armada that somehow had appeared from nowhere. Pluskat stared in frozen disbelief, speechless, moved as he had never been before in his life. At that moment the world of the good soldier Pluskat began falling apart. He says that in those first few moments he knew, calmly and surely, that "this was the end for Germany."

He turned to Wilkening and Theen and, with a strange detachment, said simply, "It's the invasion. See for yourselves." Then he picked up the phone and called Major Block at the 352nd Division's headquarters.

"Block," said Pluskat, "it's the invasion. There must be ten thousand ships out here." Even as he said it, he knew his words must sound incredible.

"Get hold of yourself, Pluskat!" snapped Block. "The Americans and the British together don't have that many ships. Nobody has that many ships!"

Block's disbelief brought Pluskat out of his daze. "If you don't believe me," he suddenly yelled, "come up here and see for yourself. It's fantastic! It's unbelievable!"

There was a slight pause and then Block said, "What way are these ships heading?"

Pluskat, phone in hand, looked out the aperture of the bunker and replied, "Right for me."

PART THREE

The Day

★ 1 ★

NEVER had there been a dawn like this. In the murky, gray light, in majestic, fearful grandeur, the great Allied fleet lay off Normandy's five invasion beaches. The sea teemed with ships. Battle ensigns snapped in the wind all the way across the horizon from the edge of the Utah area on the Cherbourg peninsula to Sword Beach near the mouth of the Orne. Outlined against the sky were the big battlewagons, the menacing cruisers, the whippetlike destroyers. Behind them were the squat command ships, sprouting their forests of antennae. And behind them came the convoys of troop-filled transports and landing ships, lying low and sluggish in the water. Circling the lead transports, waiting for the signal to head for the beaches, were swarms of bobbing landing craft, jam-packed with the men who would land in the first waves.

The great spreading mass of ships seethed with noise and activity. Engines throbbed and whined as patrol boats dashed back and forth through the milling assault craft. Windlasses whirred as booms swung out amphibious vehicles. Chains rattled in the davits as assault boats were lowered away. Landing craft loaded with pallid-faced men shuddered and banged against the high steel sides of transports. Loud-hailers blared out, "Keep in line! Keep in line!" as coastguardmen shepherded the bobbing assault boats into formations. On the transports men jammed the rails, waiting their turn to climb down slippery ladders or scramble-nets into the heaving, spray-washed beaching craft.

And through it all, over the ships' public-address systems came a steady flow of messages and exhortations: "Fight to get your troops ashore, fight to save your ships, and if you've got any strength left, fight to save yourselves." . . . "Get in there, Fourth Division, and give 'em hell!" . . . "Don't forget, the Big Red One is leading the way." . . . "U.S. Rangers, man your stations." . . . "Remember Dunkirk! Remember Coventry! God bless you all." . . . *"Nous mourrons sur le sable de notre France chérie, mais nous ne retournerons pas* [We shall die on the sands of our dear France but we shall not turn back]." . . . "This is it, men, pick it up and put it on, you've only got a one-way ticket and this is the end of the line. Twenty-nine, let's go!" And then the two messages that most men still remember: "Away all boats," and "Our Father, which art in Heaven, hallowed be Thy Name . . ."

Along the crowded rails many men left their positions to say goodbye to buddies going in on other boats. Soldiers and seamen, who had become firm friends after the long hours spent aboard ships, wished one another good luck. And hundreds of men took time to exchange home addresses "just in case." Technical Sergeant Roy Stevens of the 29th Division fought his way across a crowded deck in search of his twin brother. "I finally found him," he says. "He smiled and extended his hand. I said, 'No, we will shake hands at the crossroads in France like we planned.' We said goodbye, and I never saw him again." On H.M.S. *Prince Leopold*, Lieutenant Joseph Lacy, the chaplain of the 5th and 2nd Ranger battalions, walked among the waiting men and P.F.C. Max Coleman heard him say, "I'll do your praying for you from here on in. What you're going to do today will be a prayer in itself."

All over the ships, officers wound up their pep talks with the kind of colorful or memorable phrases that they felt best suited the occasion—sometimes with unexpected results. Lieutenant Colonel John O'Neill, whose special combat engineers were to land on Omaha and Utah beaches in the first wave and destroy the mined obstacles, thought he had the ideal conclusion to his debarking talk when he thundered, "Come hell or high water, get those damned obstacles out!" From somewhere nearby, a voice remarked, "I believe that s.o.b. is scared, too." Captain Sherman Burroughs of the 29th Division told Captain Charles Cawthon that he planned to recite "The Shooting of Dan Mc-Grew" on the way in to the beach. Lieutenant Colonel Elzie Moore, heading up an engineer brigade bound for Utah, was without a speech. He had wanted to recite a most appropriate excerpt from the story of another invasion of France, a battle scene from Shakespeare's *Henry V*, but all he could remember was the opening line, "Once more unto the breach, dear friends . . ." He decided to give up the idea. Major C. K. "Banger" King of the British 3rd Division, going in on the first wave to Sword Beach, planned to read from the same play. He had gone to the trouble of writing down the lines he wanted. They closed with the passage, "He that outlives this day, and comes safe home/Will stand a tip-toe when this day is named . . ."

The tempo was increasing. Off the American beaches more and more troop-filled boats were joining the churning assault craft endlessly circling the mother ships. Sodden, seasick and miserable, the men in these boats would lead the way into Normandy, across Omaha and Utah beaches. In the transport areas, debarking was now in full swing. It was a complex and hazardous operation. Soldiers carried so much equipment that they were barely able to move. Each had a rubber-tube life preserver and, besides weapons, musette bags, entrenching tools, gas masks, first-aid kits, canteens, knives and rations, everybody had extra quantities of grenades, explosives and ammunition—often as much as 250 rounds. In addition, many men were burdened with the special equipment that their particular jobs demanded. Some men estimate that they weighed at least three hundred pounds as they waddled across decks and prepared to get into the boats. All this paraphernalia was necessary, but it seemed to Major Gerden Johnson of the 4th Infantry Division that his men were "slowed down to the pace of a turtle." Lieutenant Bill Williams of the 29th thought his men were so overburdened that "they wouldn't be able to do much fighting," and Private Rudolph Mozgo, looking down the side of his transport at the assault craft that smashed against the hull and rose sickeningly up and down on the swells, figured that if he and his equipment could just get into a boat "half the battle would be won."

Many men, trying to balance themselves and their equipment as they climbed down the weblike scramble-nets, became casualties long before they were even fired on. Corporal Harold Janzen of a mortar unit, loaded down with two reels of cable and several field phones, tried to time the rise and fall of the assault craft beneath him. He jumped at what he thought was the right moment, misjudged, fell twelve feet to the bottom of the boat and knocked himself out with his carbine. There were more serious injuries. Sergeant Romeo Pompei heard someone scream below him, looked down and saw a man hanging in agony on the net as the assault boat ground his foot against the side of the transport. Pompei himself fell headlong from the net into the boat and smashed his front teeth.

Troops that boarded craft on the decks and were lowered down from davits were no better off. Major Thomas Dallas, one of the 29th's battalion commanders, and his headquarters staff were suspended about halfway between the rail and the water when the davits lowering their boat jammed. They hung there for about twenty minutes—just four feet beneath the sewage outlet from the "heads." "The heads were in constant use," he recalls, "and during these twenty minutes we received the entire discharge."

The waves were so high that many assault craft bounced like monstrous Yo-yos up and down on the davit chains. One boat-

load of Rangers got halfway down the side of H.M.S. *Prince
Charles* when a huge swell surged up and almost pitched them
back on the deck. The swell receded and the boat dropped sickeningly down again on its cables, bouncing its seasick occupants
about like so many dolls.

As they went into the small boats veteran soldiers told the new
men with them what to expect. On H.M.S. *Empire Anvil*, Corporal Michael Kurtz of the 1st Division gathered his squad
about him. "I want all of you Joes to keep your heads down below the gunwale," he warned them. "As soon as we're spotted
we'll catch enemy fire. If you make it, O.K. If you don't, it's a
helluva good place to die. Now let's go." As Kurtz and his men
loaded into their boat in the davits they heard yells below them.
Another boat had upended, spilling its men into the sea. Kurtz's
boat was lowered away without trouble. Then they all saw the
men swimming near the side of the transport. As Kurtz's boat
moved off, one of the soldiers floating in the water yelled, "So
long, suckers!" Kurtz looked at the men in his boat. On each face
he saw the same waxy, expressionless look.

It was 5:30 A.M. Already the first-wave troops were well on the
way to the beaches. For this great seaborne assault which the
free world had toiled so hard to mount, only about three thousand men were leading the attack. They were the combat teams
of the 1st, 29th and 4th divisions and attached units—Army and
Navy underwater demolition teams, tank battalion groups, and
Rangers. Each combat team was given a specific landing zone.
For example, the 16th Regiment of Major General Clarence R.
Huebner's 1st Division would assault one half of Omaha Beach,
the 116th of Major General Charles H. Gerhardt's 29th Division
the other.* Those zones had been subdivided into sectors, each

---

* Although the 1st and 29th Divisions' combat teams shared the assault,
the actual landings were technically under the command of the 1st Division in this opening phase.

with a code name. Men of the 1st Division would land on Easy Red, Fox Green and Fox Red, the 29th on Charlie, Dog Green, Dog White, Dog Red and Easy Green.

The landing schedules for both Omaha and Utah beaches were planned on an almost minute-by-minute timetable. In the 29th Division's half of Omaha Beach at H Hour minus five minutes—6:25 A.M.—thirty-two amphibious tanks were to swim onto Dog White and Dog Green and take up firing positions at the water's edge to cover the first phase of the assault. At H Hour itself—6:30 A.M.—eight LCTs would bring in more tanks, landing them directly from the sea on Easy Green and Dog Red. One minute later—6:31 A.M.—the assault troops would swarm across the beach on all sectors. Two minutes after that—6:33 A.M.—the underwater demolition engineers were due; they had the tough job of clearing sixteen 50-yard paths through the mines and obstacles. They had just twenty-seven minutes to finish this ticklish job. At six-minute intervals from 7 A.M. on, five assault waves, the main body of troops, would begin landing.

This was the basic landing plan for both beaches. The build-up was so carefully timed that heavy equipment like artillery was expected to be landed on Omaha Beach within an hour and a half and even cranes, half-tracks and tank recovery vehicles were scheduled to come in by 10:30 A.M. It was an involved, elaborate timetable which looked as if it could not possibly hold up—and in all probability the planners had taken this into consideration, too.

The first-wave assault troops could not yet see the misty shores of Normandy. They were still more than nine miles away. Some warships were already dueling with German naval coastal batteries, but the action as yet was remote and impersonal for the soldiers in the boats—nobody was firing directly at them. Seasickness was still their biggest enemy. Few were immune. The assault boats, each loaded with about thirty men and all their weighty equipment, rode so low in the water that waves rolled over the side and out again. With each wave the boats pitched and tossed, and Colonel Eugene Caffey of the 1st Engineers Special Brigade remembers that some of the men in his boat "just lay there with the water sloshing back and forth over them, not caring whether they lived or died." But for those among them not yet incapacitated by seasickness, the sight of the great invasion fleet looming up all about them was awesome and wonderful. In Corporal Gerald Burt's boatload of demolition engineers, one man wistfully remarked that he wished he'd brought his camera.

Thirty miles away Lieutenant Commander Heinrich Hoffmann, in the lead E-boat of his 5th Flotilla, saw a strange, unreal fog blanketing the sea ahead. As Hoffmann watched, a single plane flew out of the whiteness. That confirmed his suspicion—it must be a smoke screen. Hoffmann, followed by the other two E-boats, plunged into the haze to investigate—and got the shock of his life. On the other side he found himself face to face with a staggering array of warships—almost the entire British fleet. Everywhere he looked there were battleships, cruisers and destroyers towering over him. "I felt as though I were sitting in a rowboat," Hoffmann says. Almost instantly shells began to fall around his dodging, twisting boats. Without a moment's hesitation, the cocky Hoffmann, unbelievably outnumbered, ordered the attack. Seconds later, in the only German naval offensive of D Day, eighteen torpedoes knifed through the water toward the Allied fleet.

On the bridge of the Norwegian destroyer *Svenner*, the Royal Navy's Lieutenant Desmond Lloyd saw them coming. So did officers on the bridges of *Warspite, Ramillies* and *Largs. Largs* promptly slammed her engines to full speed astern. Two torpedoes sliced between *Warspite* and *Ramillies. Svenner* couldn't get out of the way. Her captain yelled, "Hard aport! Full ahead

195

starboard! Full astern port!" in a vain effort to swing the destroyer so that the torpedoes would pass parallel to the ship. Lieutenant Lloyd, watching through his binoculars, saw that the torpedoes were going to hit directly beneath the bridge. All he could think of was, "How high will I fly?" With agonizing slowness *Svenner* turned to port and for a moment Lloyd thought they might escape. But the maneuver failed. A torpedo slammed into the boiler room. *Svenner* seemed to lift from the water, shuddered and broke in two. Nearby, Leading Stoker Robert Dowie, on the mine sweeper H.M.S. *Dunbar,* was amazed to see the destroyer slide beneath the water with "her bow and stern sticking up to form a perfect V." There were thirty casualties. Lieutenant Lloyd, unhurt, swam about for nearly twenty minutes, keeping a sailor with a broken leg afloat, until they were both picked up by the destroyer *Swift.*

To Hoffmann, safely back again on the other side of the smoke screen, the important thing now was to raise the alarm. He flashed the news to Le Havre, serenely unaware that his radio had been knocked out of commission in the brief battle that had just taken place.

On the flagship *Augusta* lying off the American beaches, Lieutenant General Omar N. Bradley plugged his ears with cotton and then trained his binoculars on the landing craft speeding toward the beaches. His troops, the men of the U.S. First Army, were moving steadily in. Bradley was deeply concerned. Up to a few hours before he had believed that an inferior and overextended German "static" division, the 716th, was holding the coastal area, roughly from Omaha Beach all the way east to the British zone. But just before he left England, Allied intelligence had passed on the information that an additional German division had moved into the invasion area. The news had arrived too late for Bradley to inform his already briefed and "sealed" troops. Now the men of the 1st and 29th divisions were heading for Omaha Beach, unaware that the tough, battle-tested 352nd Division manned the defenses.*

The naval bombardment which Bradley prayed would make their job easier was about to begin. A few miles away Contre-Amiral Jaujard, on the French light cruiser *Montcalm*, spoke to his officers and men. *"C'est une chose terrible et monstrueuse que d'être obligé de tirer sur notre propre patrie,"* he said, his voice heavy with emotion, *"mais je vous demande de le faire aujourd'hui* [It is a terrible and monstrous thing to have to fire on our homeland, but I want you to do it this day]." And four miles off Omaha Beach on the destroyer U.S.S. *Carmick*, Commander Robert O. Beer pressed a button on the ship's intercom and said, "Now hear this! This is probably going to be the biggest party you boys will ever go to—so let's all get out on the floor and dance!"

The time was 5:50 A.M. The British warships had been firing off their beaches for more than twenty minutes. Now the bombardment in the American zone began. The entire invasion area erupted with a roaring storm of fire. The maelstrom of sound thundered back and forth along the Normandy coast as the big ships slammed steadily away at their preselected targets. The gray sky brightened with the hot flash of their guns and along the beaches great clouds of black smoke began to bunch up into the air.

Off Sword, Juno and Gold the battleships *Warspite* and *Ramillies* lobbed tons of steel from their 15-inch guns toward powerful German gun batteries at Le Havre and around the

---

* Allied intelligence was under the impression that the 352nd had only recently taken up these positions and then only for "a defense exercise." Actually units had been in the coastal zone and overlooking Omaha Beach for more than two months—and some even longer. Pluskat and his guns, for example, had been there since March. But up to June 4 Allied intelligence had still placed the 352nd around St.-Lô, more than twenty miles away.

mouth of the Orne. Maneuvering cruisers and destroyers poured streams of shells into pillboxes, concrete bunkers and redoubts. With incredible accuracy, the sharpshooting H.M.S. *Ajax* of River Plate fame knocked out a battery of four 6-inch guns from six miles offshore. Off Omaha, the big battleships *Texas* and *Arkansas,* mounting between them a total of ten 14-inch, twelve 12-inch and twelve 5-inch guns, pumped six hundred shells onto the coastal battery position atop Pointe du Hoc in an all-out attempt to ease the way for the Ranger battalions even now heading for the 100-foot-high sheer cliffs. Off Utah the battleship *Nevada* and the cruisers *Tuscaloosa, Quincy* and *Black Prince* seemed to lean back as they hurled salvo after salvo at the shore batteries. While the big ships blasted away from five to six miles offshore, the small destroyers pressed in to a mile or two off the beaches and, line astern, sent a saturating fire into targets all over the network of coastal fortifications.

The fearsome salvos of the naval bombardment made deep impressions on the men who saw and heard them. Sub-Lieutenant Richard Ryland of the Royal Navy felt immense pride in "the majestic appearance of the battleships," and wondered "whether this would be the last occasion such a sight would be seen." On the U.S.S. *Nevada,* Yeoman Third Class Charles Langley was almost frightened by the massive fire power of the fleet. He did not see "how any army could possibly withstand the bombardment" and believed that "the fleet would be able to pull out in two or three hours." And in the speeding assault boats, as this roaring canopy of steel flashed over their heads, the sodden, miserable, seasick men, bailing with their helmets, looked up and cheered.

Now a new sound throbbed over the fleet. Slowly at first, like the mumbling of some giant bee, and then building to a great crescendo of noise, the bombers and fighters appeared. They flew straight in over the massive fleet, flying wing tip to wing tip, formation after formation—nine thousand planes. Spitfires,

Thunderbolts and Mustangs whistled in over the heads of the men. With apparent disregard for the rain of shells from the fleet, they strafed the invasion beaches and headlands, zoomed up, swept around and came in again. Above them, crisscrossing at every altitude, were the 9th Air Force's B-26 medium bombers, and above these, out of sight in the heavy cloud layer, droned the heavies—the R.A.F. and 8th Air Force Lancasters, Fortresses and Liberators. It seemed as though the sky could not possibly hold them all. Men looked up and stared, eyes damp, faces contorted with a sudden emotion almost too great to bear. It was going to be all right now, they thought. There was the air cover —the enemy would be pinned down, the guns knocked out, the beaches would be cratered with foxholes. But, unable to see through the cloud layers, and unwilling to risk bombing their own troops, 329 bombers assigned to the Omaha area were already unloading thirteen thousand bombs up to three miles inland from their targets, the deadly guns* of Omaha Beach.

The last explosion was very near. Major Werner Pluskat thought the bunker was shaking itself apart. Another shell hit the cliff face at the very base of the hidden position. The shock of it spun Pluskat around and hurled him backward. He fell heavily to the ground. Dust, dirt and concrete splinters showered about him. He couldn't see through the clouds of white dust, but he could hear his men shouting. Again and again shells smashed into the cliff. Pluskat was so dazed by the concussion that he could hardly speak.

The phone was ringing. It was the 352nd Division headquarters. "What's the situation?" a voice asked.

* There were 8 concrete bunkers with guns of 75 millimeters or larger caliber; 35 pillboxes with artillery pieces of various sizes and/or automatic weapons; 4 batteries of artillery; 18 antitank guns; 6 mortar pits; 35 rocket-launching sites, each with four 38-millimeter rocket tubes; and no less than 85 machine gun nests.

"We're being shelled," Pluskat managed to say, "heavily shelled."

Somewhere far behind his position he now heard bombs exploding. Another salvo of shells landed on the cliff top, sending an avalanche of earth and stones in through the bunker's apertures. The phone rang again. This time Pluskat couldn't find it. He let it ring. He noticed that he was covered from head to foot with a fine white dust and his uniform was ripped.

For a moment the shelling lifted and through the thick haze of dust Pluskat saw Theen and Wilkening on the concrete floor. He yelled to Wilkening, "Better get to your position while you have a chance." Wilkening looked glumly at Pluskat—his observation post was in the next bunker, some distance away. Pluskat took advantage of the lull to phone his batteries. To his amazement not one of his twenty guns—all brand-new Krupps of various calibers—had been hit. He could not see how the batteries, only half a mile or so from the coast, had escaped; there were not even any casualties among the crews. Pluskat began to wonder if observation posts along the coast were being mistaken for gun positions. The damage around his own post seemed to indicate it.

The phone rang just as the shelling began again. The same voice he had heard earlier demanded to know "the exact location of the shelling."

"For God's sake," Pluskat yelled, "they're falling all over. What do you want me to do—go out and measure the holes with a ruler?" He banged down the phone and looked around him. Nobody in the bunker seemed to be hurt. Wilkening had already left for his own bunker; Theen was at one of the apertures. Then Pluskat noticed that Harras was gone. But he had little time to bother about the big dog now. He picked up the phone again, walked over to the second aperture and looked out. There seemed to be even more assault boats in the water than when he had last looked, and they were closer now. Soon they would be in range.

He called Colonel Ocker at regimental headquarters. "All my guns are intact," he reported.

"Good," said Ocker, "now you'd better get back to your headquarters immediately."

Pluskat rang his gunnery officers. "I'm going back," he told them. "Remember, no gun must fire until the enemy reaches the water's edge."

The landing craft carrying U.S. 1st Division troops to their sector on Omaha Beach had not far to go now. Behind the bluffs overlooking Easy Red, Fox Green and Fox Red, the gun crews in Pluskat's four batteries waited for the boats to get just a little nearer.

"This is London calling.

"I bring you an urgent instruction from the Supreme Commander. The lives of many of you depend upon the speed and thoroughness with which you obey it. It is particularly addressed to all who live within thirty-five kilometers of any part of the coast."

Michel Hardelay stood at the window of his mother's house in Vierville at the western end of Omaha Beach and watched the invasion fleet maneuver. The guns were still firing, and Hardelay could feel the concussion through the soles of his shoes. The whole family—Hardelay's mother, his brother, his niece and the maid—had gathered in the living room. There seemed no doubt about it now, they all agreed: the invasion was going to take place right at Vierville. Hardelay was philosophical about his own seaside villa; now it would most certainly come down. In the background the BBC message, which had been repeated over and over for more than an hour, continued.

201

"Leave your towns at once, informing, as you go, any neighbors who may not be aware of the warning. . . . Stay off frequented roads. . . . Go on foot and take nothing with you which you cannot easily carry. . . . Get as quickly as possible into the open country. . . . Do not gather in large groups which may be mistaken for troop concentrations. . . ."

Hardelay wondered if the German on horseback would make his usual trip down to the gun crews with the morning coffee. He looked at his watch; if the soldier was coming, it was nearly time. Then Hardelay saw him on the same big-rumped horse, with the same bouncing coffee cans that he always carried. The man rode calmly down the road, turned the bend—and saw the fleet. For a second or two he sat motionless. Then he jumped off the horse, stumbled and fell, picked himself up and ran for cover. The horse continued slowly on down the road to the village. The time was 6:15 A.M.

★ 2 ★

B<small>Y</small> NOW the long, bobbing lines of assault craft were less than a mile from Omaha and Utah beaches. For the three thousand Americans in the first wave H Hour was just fifteen minutes away.

The noise was deafening as the boats, long white wakes

streaming out behind them, churned steadily for the shore. In the slopping, bouncing craft the men had to shout to be heard over the roar of the diesels. Overhead, like a great steel umbrella, the shells of the fleet still thundered. And rolling out from the coast came the booming explosions of the Allied air forces' carpet bombing. Strangely, the guns of the Atlantic Wall were silent. Troops saw the coastline stretching ahead and wondered about the absence of enemy fire. Maybe, many thought, it would be an easy landing after all.

The great square-faced ramps of the assault craft butted into every wave, and chilling, frothing green water sloshed over everyone. There were no heroes in these boats—just cold, miserable, anxious men, so jam-packed together, so weighed down by equipment that often there was no place to be seasick except over one another. *Newsweek*'s Kenneth Crawford, in the first Utah wave, saw a young 4th Division soldier, covered in his own vomit, slowly shaking his head in abject misery and disgust. "That guy Higgins," he said, "ain't got nothin' to be proud of about inventin' this goddamned boat."

Some men had no time to think about their miseries—they were bailing for their lives. Almost from the moment the assault craft left the mother ships, many boats had begun to fill with water. At first men had paid little attention to the sea slopping about their legs; it was just another misery to be endured. Lieutenant George Kerchner of the Rangers watched the water slowly rise in his craft and wondered if it was serious. He had been told that the LCA was unsinkable. But then over the radio Kerchner's soldiers heard a call for help: "This is LCA 860! . . . LCA 860! . . . We're sinking! . . . We're sinking!" There was a final exclamation: "My God, we're sunk!" Immediately Kerchner and his men began bailing.

Directly behind Kerchner's boat, Sergeant Regis McCloskey, also of the Rangers, had his own troubles. McCloskey and his men had been bailing for more than an hour. Their boat carried ammunition for the Pointe du Hoc attack and all of the Rangers' packs. The boat was so waterlogged McCloskey was sure it would sink. His only hope lay in lightening the wallowing craft. McCloskey ordered his men to toss all unnecessary equipment overboard. Rations, extra clothing and packs went over the side. McCloskey heaved them all into the swells. In one pack was $1,200 which Private Chuck Vella had won in a crap game; in another was First Sergeant Charles Frederick's false teeth.

Landing craft began to sink in both the Omaha and Utah areas—ten off Omaha, seven off Utah. Some men were picked up by rescue boats coming up behind, others would float around for hours before being rescued. And some soldiers, their yells and screams unheard, were dragged down by their equipment and ammunition. They drowned within sight of the beaches, without having fired a shot.

In an instant the war had become personal. Troops heading for Utah Beach saw a control boat leading one of the waves suddenly rear up out of the water and explode. Seconds later heads bobbed up and survivors tried to save themselves by clinging to the wreckage. Another explosion followed almost immediately. The crew of a landing barge trying to launch four of the thirty-two amphibious tanks bound for Utah had dropped the ramp right onto a submerged sea mine. The front of the craft shot up and Sergeant Orris Johnson on a nearby LCT watched in frozen horror as a tank "soared more than a hundred feet into the air, tumbled slowly end over end, plunged back into the water and disappeared." Among the many dead, Johnson learned later, was his buddy, Tanker Don Neill.

Scores of Utah-bound men saw the dead bodies and heard the yells and screams of the drowning. One man, Lieutenant (j.g.) Francis X. Riley of the Coast Guard, remembers the scene vividly. The twenty-four-year-old officer, commanding an LCI, could only listen "to the anguished cries for help from wounded and shocked soldiers and sailors as they pleaded with us to pull them out of the water." But Riley's orders were to "disembark the troops on time regardless of casualties." Trying to close his mind to the screams, Riley ordered his craft on past the drowning men. There was nothing else he could do. The assault waves sped by, and as one boat carrying Lieutenant Colonel James Batte and the 4th Division's 8th Infantry Regiment troops threaded its way through the dead bodies, Batte heard one of his gray-faced men say, "Them lucky bastards—they ain't seasick no more."

The sight of the bodies in the water, the strain of the long trip in from the transport ships and now the ominous nearness of the flat sands and the dunes of Utah Beach jerked men out of their lethargy. Corporal Lee Cason, who had just turned twenty, suddenly found himself "cursing to high heaven against Hitler and Mussolini for getting us into this mess." His companions were startled at his vehemence—Cason had never before been known to swear. In many boats now soldiers nervously checked and rechecked their weapons. Men became so possessive of their ammunition that Colonel Eugene Caffey could not get a single man in his boat to give him a clip of bullets for his rifle. Caffey, who was not supposed to land until 9 A.M., had smuggled himself aboard an 8th Infantry craft in an effort to catch up with his veteran 1st Engineer Brigade. He had no equipment and although all the men in the boat were overloaded with ammunition, they were "hanging onto it for dear life." Caffey was finally able to load the rifle by taking up a collection of one bullet from each of eight men.

In the waters off Omaha Beach there had been a disaster. Nearly half of the amphibious tank force scheduled to support the assault troops had foundered. The plan was for sixty-four of these tanks to be launched two to three miles offshore. From there they were to swim in to the beach. Thirty-two of them had been allotted to the 1st Division's area—Easy Red, Fox Green and Fox Red. The landing barges carrying them reached their positions, the ramps were dropped and twenty-nine tanks were launched into the heaving swells. The weird-looking amphibious vehicles, their great balloonlike canvas skirts supporting them in the water, began breasting the waves, driving toward the shore. Then tragedy overtook the men of the 741st Tank Battalion. Under the pounding of the waves the canvas water wings ripped, supports broke, engines were flooded—and, one after another, twenty-seven tanks foundered and sank. Men came clawing up out of the hatches, inflating their life belts, plunging into the sea. Some succeeded in launching survival rafts. Others went down in the steel coffins.

Two tanks, battered and almost awash, were still heading for the shore. The crews of three others had the good fortune to be on a landing barge whose ramp jammed. They were put ashore later. The remaining thirty-two tanks—for the 29th Division's half of the beach—were safe. Officers in charge of the craft carrying them, overwhelmed by the disaster they had seen, wisely decided to take their force directly onto the beach. But the loss of the 1st Division tanks would cost hundreds of casualties within the next few minutes.

From two miles out the assault troops began to see the living and the dead in the water. The dead floated gently, moving with the tide toward the beach, as though determined to join their fellow Americans. The living bobbed up and down in the swells, savagely pleading for the help the assault boats could not tender. Sergeant Regis McCloskey, his ammunition boat again safely under way, saw the screaming men in the water, "yelling for help, begging us to stop—and we couldn't. Not for anything or anyone." Gritting his teeth, McCloskey looked away as his boat sped past, and then, seconds later, he vomited over the side. Captain Robert Cunningham and his men saw survivors struggling, too. Instinctively their Navy crew swung the boat toward the men in the water. A fast launch cut them off. Over its loud-speaker came the grim words, "You are not a rescue

ship! Get on shore!" In another boat nearby, Sergeant Noel Dube
of an engineer battalion said the Act of Contrition.

Now the deadly martial music of the bombardment seemed
to grow and swell as the thin wavy lines of assault craft closed
in on Omaha Beach. Landing ships lying about one thousand
yards offshore joined in the shelling; and then thousands of
flashing rockets whooshed over the heads of the men. To the
troops it seemed inconceivable that anything could survive the
massive weight of fire power that flayed the German defenses.
The beach was wreathed in haze, and plumes of smoke from
grass fires drifted lazily down from the bluffs. Still the German
guns remained silent. The boats bored in. In the thrashing surf
and running back up the beach men could now see the lethal
jungles of steel-and-concrete obstacles. They were strewn everywhere, draped with barbed wire and capped with mines. They
were as cruel and ugly as the men had expected. Back of the defenses the beach itself was deserted; nothing and no one moved
upon it. Closer and closer the boats pressed in . . . 500 yards
. . . 450 yards. Still no enemy fire. Through waves that were
four to five feet high the assault craft surged forward, and now
the great bombardment began to lift, shifting to targets farther
inland. The first boats were barely 400 yards from the shore
when the German guns—the guns that few believed could have
survived the raging Allied air and sea bombardment—opened
up.

Through the din and clamor one sound was nearer, deadlier
than all the rest—the sound of machine gun bullets clanging
across the steel, snoutlike noses of the boats. Artillery roared.
Mortar shells rained down. All along the four miles of Omaha
Beach German guns flayed the assault craft.

It was H Hour.

They came ashore on Omaha Beach, the slogging, unglamor-
ous men that no one envied. No battle ensigns flew for them, no
horns or bugles sounded. But they had history on their side.

They came from regiments that had bivouacked at places like Valley Forge, Stoney Creek, Antietam, Gettysburg, that had fought in the Argonne. They had crossed the beaches of North Africa, Sicily and Salerno. Now they had one more beach to cross. They would call this one "Bloody Omaha."

The most intense fire came from the cliffs and high bluffs at either end of the crescent-shaped beach—in the 29th Division's Dog Green area to the west and the 1st Division's Fox Green sector to the east. Here the Germans had concentrated their heaviest defenses to hold two of the principal exits leading off the beach at Vierville and toward Colleville. Everywhere along the beach men encountered heavy fire as their boats came in, but the troops landing at Dog Green and Fox Green hadn't a chance. German gunners on the cliffs looked almost directly down on the waterlogged assault craft that heaved and pitched toward these sectors of the beach. Awkward and slow, the assault boats were nearly stationary in the water. They were sitting ducks. Coxswains at the tillers, trying desperately to maneuver their unwieldy craft through the forest of mined obstacles, now had to run the gantlet of fire from the cliffs.

Some boats, unable to find a way through the maze of obstacles and the withering cliff fire, were driven off and wandered aimlessly along the beach seeking a less heavily defended spot to land. Others, doggedly trying to come in at their assigned sectors, were shelled so badly that men plunged over the sides into deep water, where they were immediately picked off by machine gun fire. Some landing craft were blown apart as they came in. Second Lieutenant Edward Gearing's assault boat, filled with thirty men of the 29th Division, disintegrated in one blinding moment three hundred yards from the Vierville exit at Dog Green. Gearing and his men were blown out of the boat and strewn over the water. Shocked and half drowned, the nineteen-year-old lieutenant came to the surface yards away from where his boat had gone down. Other survivors began to bob up,

Minutes before H Hour and Omaha Beach looms ahead. Spray-drenched assault troops crouch down in Coast Guard LCA racing for shore.

[ABOVE] *Waves of assault boats thrash past cruiser U.S.S. Augusta. On bridge* [TOP, LEFT] *bespectacled Lt. Gen. Omar N. Bradley, U.S. 1st Army Commander, watches landing craft heading in for Omaha Beach. Next to him is Rear Admiral Alan Kirk, Overlord Western Task Force Commander. Landing craft* [MIDDLE, LEFT] *receives direct hit and bursts into flame off Omaha. Survivors of another damaged craft struggle ashore from life raft* [BOTTOM, LEFT].

211

[TOP, LEFT] *H Hour on Omaha Beach. Assault troops struggling through obstacles and heavy surf while under fire. This photo, taken by the late Bob Capa of* Life, *is probably the best remembered picture of D Day.*

WIDE WORLD

[MIDDLE, LEFT] *H Hour plus 15 minutes. Pinned down by enemy fire, troops take cover behind obstacles.* Courtesy Col. John T. O'Neill

[BOTTOM, LEFT] *H Hour plus 25 minutes. Engineers of Assault Team 10 move in. Note troops behind obstacles and taking cover back of engineers' tankdozer.* Courtesy Col. John T. O'Neill

[BELOW] *Omaha Beach wounded sheltering behind sea wall, waiting to be evacuated.*

From 0001B

Date; 6 June 1944

Time:

To.: 2400B

CP Location: USS ANCON, ENGLISH CHANNEL
off Coast of France

Time	No.	From	Synopsis	Rec'd Via	Disposition #
0230	1		Arrived in Transport Area at 0230.		
0251	2		Dropped Anchor at 0251.		
0630	3	CG	Land CT 115 at H/4 unless otherwise directed.		Comdr CTF 124
0708	4		1st wave landed 0635 2d wave landed 0636	Rad	J
0830	5		16 Inf and 116 Inf touched down 060635.	Rad	J
0630	6	Talley	It 1 DUKW No one waterborne	Rad	V Corps & J
0636	7	Talley	It 3 Dog Dogs Launched Saw empty LCT returning.	Rad	V Corps & J
0655	8	PC552	NK First wave foundered.	Rad	Navy & J
0702	9	Javelin	LCA unit is landing half on DOG GREEN half on CHARLIE.	Rad	Navy & J
0700	10	Talley	Brilliant white flare seen near POINTE DE HOE.	Rad	V Corps & J
0641	11	PC 552	Entire first wave foundered.	Rad	Chase & J
0807	17	Thomas Jefferson	Returning boats report floating mines near beach endangering landings. Many boats have swamped because of them. Many persons in water.	R d	COMTRANSDIV 3 & J
0730	23	DC/S V Corps	LCIL 94 and 493 landed 0740. Firing heavy on beach.	Rad	V Corps & J
0838	24	Control Vessel Dog Red	The obstacles are mined. No chance of destroying mines by demolition yet.	Rad	J
0816	25	LCT 535	There are DUKWS in distress between here and the beach.	Rad	Ancon & J
0710	27	CTG 124.4 (Rngr Co)	Two LCTS knocked out by enemy btry back of center of Beach Dog Green.	Rad	Ancon & J
0809	28	Control Craft	All of DD Tks for Fox Green beach sank between disembarkation point and line of departure.	Rad	CG, G-3, J
0824	29	CTG 124.9	Btrys at MAISY still in commission. Being kept under fire.	Rad	CG, G-3, J
0830	30	50th Div	Request progress of your trs. Progress of 50th Div going according to plan.	Rad	CG, G-3, J
0833	31	LCT 538	Failed to unload due to indirect fire of 88's. Hit. 5 Army casualties.	Rad	PC 617, G-3, J

214

Time	No.	From	Message	Method	To
0843	32	V Corps	Wave Claude & Eric touched down at 0720. Obstacles not breached. Four tks held up by enemy fire, heavy this area. Wave E & C forced to withdraw. Casualties appeared heavy.	Rad	CG V Corps, CG, G-3, J.
0849	34	1st Bn 116Ct	Held up by enemy MG fire. Request fire support.	Rad	Co CT 116, CG, G-3, J
0859	35	Rngr Co	Brit Off reports on Dog Green Beach. Heavy MG fire. Obstacles not cleared.	Rad	CG, G-3, J.
0910	36	Rngr Co	Tide rising rapidly. Obstacles still on beach. Need demolition squad.	Rad	CG, G-3, J.
0909	44	CG	Enemy btry back of center of beach Dog Green. Find and Silence.	Rad	CTG, 124. 9
0930	46	Prince Leopold	Rngrs landed safely. Heavy opposition. Beach not cleared of obstruction. Very dangerous for LCA's.	Rad	Prince Charles, CG, G-3, J.
	48	Control Vessel	Do not know whether firing on beach is friendly or enemy. Keeping LCI'S from landing.	Rad	USS Chase, CG, G-3, J.
0945	49	Div Bat 5	Btrys at MAISY completely destroyed.	Rad	CG, G-3, J.
0946	50	CG	Firing on Beach Easy Red is keeping LCI's from landing.	Rad	CTG 124.8, J.
0950	52	ACG	Beach too many vehs. Send combat trs.	Rad	CG, G-3, J.
0955	63	CTG 124.8	Control vessel reports many wounded at DOG RED beach needing immediate evacuation. Many LCTS standing by bouy but cannot unload because of heavy shell fire on beach.	Rad	CTF 124 + V Corps & J.
1040	75	CG 1st Div	Reinforce 2d Bn 16th Inf at once.	Rad	Co. CT 18, & J
	76	Beachmaster Easy Red	Send in H Plus 195 wave at once.	Rad	Ancon & J
1115	93	Comdesron 18	Inf advancing send reinforcements. Also Dog Green needs inf.	Rad	CG & CTG 124.9, G-3 & J
1137	99	Thomas Jefferson	Fire support on Easy Green beach reported excellent. Germans reported leaving positions and surrendering to American soldiers.	Rad	Comtransdiv 3, CG, G-3, J.
1320	154	CG	16th Inf at COLLEVILLE SUR MER 687882. Other units progressing slowly- Beaches not yet clear of fire 061315.	Rad	50 Div & J.
1341	155	Navy	Beaches DOG GREEN WHITE RED are entirely clear of opposition and ready for landing trs. No opposition on beach. EASY GREEN AND RED trs ashore apparently waiting infantry reinforcements. All fire support ships are waiting on Army for target assignments. Request you get this info to Army ashore.	Rad	CG & J.

These excerpts from U.S. 1st Division's operations journal give almost minute-by-minute account of the seven-hour crisis on Omaha Beach up to time troops began to move inland shortly after 1 P.M. Note that in first twenty-five minutes after H Hour, Patrol Craft 552, in messages number 8 and 11, reported entire first wave had foundered. AUTHOR'S COLLECTION

[ABOVE] *Men of U.S. 4th Division wade ashore on Utah Beach. First-wave casualties were light, but heavy artillery fire flayed beach later in morning.* [BELOW] *4th Division medics tend wounded on sands.*

"Now listen, there's just the two of us. We can't afford to break up. For God's sake, do exactly as I do. Fly behind me and follow every move. We're going in alone—and I don't think we're coming back." These were the instructions Wing Commander Josef Priller [LEFT] gave his wingman, Sergeant Heinz Wodarczyk, just before they took off in the only Luftwaffe air attack made during the initial Allied landings.

German 88 shell explodes among assault troops on Utah Beach. In foreground, right, men crouch for safety by sea wall.

Rangers march German POWs down cliff face after Colonel Rudder's force had been relieved on D + 2. The American flag is protection against these troops being shelled by their own men.

4th Division's commanding officer, Maj. Gen. Raymond O. Barton (center), holds conference at first command post, 300 yards in from Utah Beach. On his right, wearing woolen cap, Brig. Gen. Theodore Roosevelt, Assistant Division Commander, who landed with first wave. Left: Lt. Col. Clarence G. Hupfer, Commander, 746th Tank Battalion.   Courtesy Maj. Gen. Barton

The heroic Brig. Gen. Norman Cota, 29th Division Asst. Commander, who, completely oblivious of the rain of enemy fire, calmly walked up and down Omaha beach and sparked the move of 29th Div. troops inland.

Major Werner Pluskat, Omaha beach battery commander who spotted the huge invasion fleet from his forward observation post, a coastal bunker almost in the dead center of the Normandy beachhead.

AUTHOR'S COLLECTION

British troops land under fire. Beach is unidentified, but it is probably Gold. Note, at left, wounded men lying in water and others falling, while at right trooper strides calmly along beach. This is one of the most human of all D Day photos, for it shows what every invasion veteran remembers—sudden death in one place, false security in another. WIDE WORLD

[TOP, RIGHT] *Canadian troops jam LCI as it heads for Juno. Note collapsible bicycles at left.* [BOTTOM, RIGHT] *Led by amphibious tanks, their balloonlike canvas "water wings" now deflated, British troops assault unidentified beach —possibly the western half of Sword.*

Picture above is historic and a rarity—it has never appeared before. It shows Col. R. Ernest Dupuy, Eisenhower's press officer, rising to broadcast the news the free world had been waiting for—that Allied troops had landed in Europe. The time was 9:33 A.M.   *Courtesy Col. Ernest Dupuy*

[RIGHT] *Greatest American success on D Day was Utah Beach assault. Fourth Division troops moved inland faster than anyone had anticipated. At right, troops slosh through inundated area heading for link-up with paratroopers. By roadside is sight that was to become all too common as Normandy battle progressed—bodies of Germans and Americans alike.*

At dusk on D Day, troops on Utah watch glider trains fly over to reinforce still-beleaguered airborne troops.

The beginning of the end for Hitler's Third Reich. German prisoners trudge down Omaha Beach.

too. Their weapons, helmets and equipment were gone. The coxswain had disappeared and nearby one of Gearing's men, struggling beneath the weight of a heavy radio set strapped to his back, screamed out, "For God's sake, I'm drowning!" Nobody could get to the radioman before he went under. For Gearing and the remnants of his section the ordeal was just beginning. It would be three hours before they got on the beach. Then Gearing would learn that he was the only surviving officer of his company. The others were dead or seriously wounded.

All along Omaha Beach the dropping of the ramps seemed to be the signal for renewed, more concentrated machine gun fire, and again the most murderous fire was in the Dog Green and Fox Green sectors. Boats of the 29th Division, coming into Dog Green, grounded on the sand bars. The ramps came down and men stepped out into water three to six feet deep. They had but one object in mind—to get through the water, cross two hundred yards of the obstacle-strewn sand, climb the gradually rising shingle and then take cover in the doubtful shelter of a sea wall. But, weighed down by their equipment, unable to run in the deep water and without cover of any kind, men were caught in crisscrossing machine gun and small-arms fire.

Seasick men, already exhausted by the long hours spent on the transports and in the assault boats, found themselves fighting for their lives in water which was often over their heads. Private David Silva saw the men in front of him being mowed down as they stepped off the ramp. When his turn came, he jumped into chest-high water and, bogged down by his equipment, watched spellbound as bullets flicked the surface all around him. Within seconds machine gun fire had riddled his pack, his clothing and his canteen. Silva felt like a "pigeon at a trap shoot." He thought he spotted the German machine gunner who was firing at him, but he could not fire back. His rifle was clogged with sand. Silva waded on, determined to make the sands ahead. He finally pulled himself up on the beach and dashed for the shelter of the sea wall, completely unaware that he had been wounded twice—once in the back, and once in the right leg.

Men fell all along the water's edge. Some were killed instantly, others called pitifully for the medics as the incoming tide slowly engulfed them. Among the dead was Captain Sherman Burroughs. His friend, Captain Charles Cawthon, saw the body washing back and forth in the surf. Cawthon wondered if Burroughs had recited "The Shooting of Dan McGrew" to his men on the run-in as he had planned. And when Captain Carroll Smith passed by, he could not help but think that Burroughs "would no longer suffer from his constant migraine headaches." Burroughs had been shot through the head.

Within the first few minutes of the carnage at Dog Green one entire company was put out of action. Less than a third of the men survived the bloody walk from the boats to the edge of the beach. Their officers were killed, severely wounded or missing, and the men, weaponless and shocked, huddled at the base of the cliffs all day. Another company in the same sector suffered even higher casualties. Company C of the 2nd Ranger Battalion had been ordered to knock out enemy strongpoints at Pointe de la Percée, slightly west of Vierville. The Rangers landed in two assault craft with the first wave on Dog Green. They were decimated. The lead craft was sunk almost immediately by artillery fire, and twelve men were killed outright. The moment the ramp of the second craft dropped down machine gun fire sprayed the debarking Rangers, killing and wounding fifteen. The remainder set out for the cliffs. Men fell one after another. P.F.C. Nelson Noyes, staggering under the weight of a bazooka, made a hundred yards before he was forced to hit the ground. A few moments later he got up and ran forward again. When he reached the shingle he was machine-gunned in the leg. As he lay there Noyes saw the two Germans who had fired looking down on him from the cliff. Propping himself on his elbows he opened up with his Tommy gun and brought both of them down. By the time Captain Ralph E. Goranson, the company commander, reached the base of the cliff, he had only thirty-five Rangers left out of his seventy-man team. By nightfall these thirty-five would be cut down to twelve.

Misfortune piled upon misfortune for the men of Omaha Beach. Soldiers now discovered that they had been landed in the wrong sectors. Some came in almost two miles away from their original landing areas. Boat sections from the 29th Division found themselves intermingled with men of the 1st Division. For example, units scheduled to land on Easy Green and fight toward an exit at Les Moulins discovered themselves at the eastern end of the beach in the hell of Fox Green. Nearly all the landing craft came in slightly east of their touch-down points. A control boat drifting off station, a strong current running eastward along the beach, the haze and smoke from grass fires which obscured landmarks—all these contributed to the mislandings. Companies that had been trained to capture certain objectives never got near them. Small groups found themselves pinned down by German fire and isolated in unrecognizable terrain, often without officers or communications.

The special Army-Navy demolition engineers who had the job of blowing paths through the beach obstacles were not only widely scattered, they were brought in crucial minutes behind schedule. These frustrated men set to work wherever they found themselves. But they fought a losing battle. In the few minutes they had before the following waves of troops bore down on the beaches, the engineers cleared only five and a half paths instead of the sixteen planned. Working with desperate haste, the demolition parties were impeded at every turn—infantrymen waded in among them, soldiers took shelter behind the obstacles they were about to blow, and landing craft, buffeted by the swells, came in almost on top of them. Sergeant Barton A. Davis of the 299th Engineer Combat Battalion saw an assault boat bearing down on him. It was filled with 1st Division men and was coming straight in through the obstacles. There was a tremendous explosion and the boat disintegrated. It seemed to Davis that everyone in it was thrown into the air all at once. Bodies and parts of bodies landed all around the flaming wreckage. "I saw black dots of men trying to swim through the gasoline that had spread on the water and as we wondered what to do a headless torso flew a good fifty feet through the air and landed with a sickening thud near us." Davis did not see how anyone could have lived through the explosion, but two men did. They were pulled out of the water, badly burned but alive.

But the disaster that Davis had seen was no greater than that which had overtaken the heroic men of his own unit, the Army-Navy Special Engineer Task Force. The landing boats carrying their explosives had been shelled, and the hulks of these craft lay blazing at the edge of the beach. Engineers with small rubber boats loaded with plastic charges and detonators were blown apart in the water when enemy fire touched off the explosives. The Germans, seeing the engineers working among the obstacles, seemed to single them out for special attention. As the teams tied on their charges, snipers took careful aim at the mines on the obstacles. At other times they seemed to wait until the engineers had prepared whole lines of steel trestles and tetrahedra obstacles for blowing. Then the Germans themselves would detonate the obstacles with mortar fire—before the engineers could get out of the area. By the end of the day casualties would be almost fifty per cent. Sergeant Davis himself would be one. Nightfall would find him aboard a hospital ship with a wounded leg, heading back for England.

It was 7 A.M. The second wave of troops arrived on the shambles that was Omaha Beach. Men splashed ashore under the saturating fire of the enemy. Landing craft joined the ever growing graveyard of wrecked, blazing hulks. Each wave of boats gave up its own bloody contribution to the incoming tide, and all along the crescent-shaped strip of beach dead Americans gently nudged each other in the water.

Piling up along the shore was the flotsam and jetsam of the invasion. Heavy equipment and supplies, boxes of ammunition, smashed radios, field telephones, gas masks, entrenching tools, canteens, steel helmets and life preservers were strewn everywhere. Great reels of wire, ropes, ration boxes, mine detectors and scores of weapons, from broken rifles to stove-in bazookas, littered the sand. The twisted wrecks of landing craft canted up crazily out of the water. Burning tanks threw great spirals of black smoke into the air. Bulldozers lay on their sides among the obstacles. Off Easy Red, floating in and out among all the cast-off materials of war, men saw a guitar.

Small islands of wounded men dotted the sand. Passing troops noticed that those who could sat bolt upright as though now immune to any further hurt. They were quiet men, seemingly oblivious to the sights and sounds around them. Staff Sergeant Alfred Eigenberg, a medic attached to the 6th Engineers Special Brigade, remembers "a terrible politeness among the more seriously injured." In his first few minutes on the beach, Eigenberg found so many wounded that he did not know "where to start or with whom." On Dog Red he came across a young soldier sitting in the sand with his leg "laid open from the knee to the pelvis as neatly as though a surgeon had done it with a scalpel." The wound was so deep that Eigenberg could clearly see the femoral artery pulsing. The soldier was in deep shock. Calmly he informed Eigenberg, "I've taken my sulfa pills and I've shaken all my sulfa powder into the wound. I'll be all right, won't I?" The nineteen-year-old Eigenberg didn't quite know what to say. He gave the soldier a shot of morphine and told him, "Sure, you'll be all right." Then, folding the neatly sliced halves of the man's leg together, Eigenberg did the only thing he could think of— he carefully closed the wound with safety pins.

Into the chaos, confusion and death on the beach poured the

men of the third wave—and stopped. Minutes later the fourth
wave came in—and they stopped. Men lay shoulder to shoulder
on the sands, stones and shale. They crouched down behind
obstacles; they sheltered among the bodies of the dead. Pinned
down by the enemy fire which they had expected to be neutral-
ized, confused by their landings in the wrong sectors, bewildered by the absence of the sheltering craters they had expected
from the air force bombing, and shocked by the devastation and
death all around them, the men froze on the beaches. They
seemed in the grip of a strange paralysis. Overwhelmed by it
all, some men believed the day was lost. Technical Sergeant
William McClintock of the 741st Tank Battalion came upon a
man sitting at the edge of the water, seemingly unaware of the
machine gun fire which rippled all over the area. He sat there
"throwing stones into the water and softly crying as if his heart
would break."

The shock would not last long. Even now a few men here and
there, realizing that to stay on the beach meant certain death,
were on their feet and moving.

Ten miles away on Utah Beach the men of the 4th Division
were swarming ashore and driving inland fast. The third wave
of assault boats was coming in and still there was virtually no opposition. A few shells fell on the beach, some scattered machine gun and rifle fire rattled along it, but there was none of the
fierce infighting that the tense, keyed-up men of the 4th had expected. To many of the men the landing was almost routine.
P.F.C. Donald N. Jones in the second wave felt as though it was
"just another practice invasion." Other men thought the assault
was an anticlimax; the long months of training at Slapton Sands
in England had been tougher. P.F.C. Ray Mann felt a little "let
down" because "the landing just wasn't a big deal after all."
Even the obstacles were not as bad as everyone had feared. Only

a few concrete cones and triangles and hedgehogs of steel cluttered the beach. Few of these were mined and all of them were lying exposed, easy for the engineers to get at. Demolition teams were already at work. They had blown one 50-yard gap through the defenses and had breached the sea wall, and within the hour they would have the entire beach cleared.

Strung out along the mile of beach, their canvas skirts hanging limply down, were the amphibious tanks—one of the big reasons why the assault had been so successful. Lumbering out of the water with the first waves, they had given a roaring support to the troops as they dashed across the beach. The tanks and the preassault bombardment seemed to have shattered and demoralized the German troops holding positions back of this beach. Still, the assault had not been without its share of misery and death. Almost as soon as he got ashore, P.F.C. Rudolph Mozgo saw his first dead man. A tank had received a direct hit and Mozgo found "one of the crew lying half in and half out of the hatch." Second Lieutenant Herbert Taylor of the 1st Engineer Special Brigade was numbed by the sight of a man "decapitated by an artillery burst just twenty feet away." And P.F.C. Edward Wolfe passed a dead American "who was sitting on the beach, his back resting against a post, as though asleep." So natural and peaceful did he seem that Wolfe "had an urge to reach over and shake him awake."

Stomping up and down the sands, occasionally massaging his arthritic shoulder, was Brigadier General Theodore Roosevelt. The fifty-seven-year-old officer—the only general to land with first-wave troops—had insisted on this assignment. His first request had been turned down, but Roosevelt had promptly countered with another. In a handwritten note to the 4th's commanding officer, Major General Raymond O. Barton, Roosevelt pleaded his case on the grounds that "it will steady the boys to know I am with them." Barton reluctantly agreed, but the decision preyed on his mind. "When I said goodbye to Ted in England," he recalls, "I never expected to see him alive again." The determined Roosevelt was very much alive. Sergeant Harry Brown of the 8th Infantry saw him "with a cane in one hand, a map in the other, walking around as if he was looking over some real estate." Every now and then a mortar burst on the beach, sending showers of sand into the air. It seemed to annoy Roosevelt; impatiently he would brush himself off.

As the third-wave boats beached and men began to wade ashore, there was the sudden whine of German 88 fire and shells burst among the incoming troops. A dozen men went down. Seconds later, a lone figure emerged from the smoke of the artillery burst. His face was black, his helmet and equipment were gone. He came walking up the beach in complete shock, eyes staring. Yelling for a medic, Roosevelt ran over to the man. He put his arm around the soldier. "Son," he said gently, "I think we'll get you back on a boat."

As yet only Roosevelt and a few of his officers knew that the Utah landings had been made in the wrong place. It had been a fortunate error; heavy batteries that could have decimated the troops were still intact, sited in along the planned assault area. There had been a number of reasons for the mislanding. Confused by smoke from the naval bombardment which had obscured landmarks, caught by a strong current moving down the coast, a solitary control boat had guided the first wave into a landing more than a mile south of the original beach. Instead of invading the beach opposite Exits 3 and 4—two of the vital five causeways toward which the 101st Airborne was driving—the entire beachhead had slipped almost two thousand yards and was now astride Exit 2. Ironically, at this moment Lieutenant Colonel Robert G. Cole and a miscellaneous band of seventy-five 101st and 82nd troopers had just reached the western end of Exit 3. They were the first paratroopers to get to a causeway. Cole and his men concealed themselves in the swamps and settled down to wait; he expected the men of the 4th Division along at any moment.

On the beach, near the approach to Exit 2, Roosevelt was about to make an important decision. Every few minutes from now on wave after wave of men and vehicles were due to land— thirty thousand men and 3,500 vehicles. Roosevelt had to decide whether to bring succeeding waves into this new, relatively quiet area with only one causeway, or to divert all other assault troops and take their equipment to the original Utah Beach with its two causeways. If the single exit could not be opened and held, a nightmarish jumble of men and vehicles would be trapped on the beach. The General huddled with his battalion commanders. The decision was made. Instead of fighting for the planned objectives which lay back of the original beach, the 4th would drive inland on the single causeway and take out German positions when and where they found them. Everything now depended on moving as fast as possible before the enemy recov- ered from the initial shock of the landings. Resistance was light and the men of the 4th were moving off the beach fast. Roosevelt turned to Colonel Eugene Caffey of the 1st Engineer Special Brigade. "I'm going ahead with the troops," he told Caffey. "You get word to the Navy to bring them in. We're going to start the war from here."

Off Utah the U.S.S. *Corry's* guns were red-hot. They were fir- ing so fast that sailors stood on the turrets playing hoses on the barrels. Almost from the moment Lieutenant Commander George Hoffman had maneuvered his destroyer into firing posi- tion and dropped anchor, the *Corry's* guns had been slamming shells inland at the rate of eight 5-inchers a minute. One Ger- man battery would never bother anyone again; the *Corry* had ripped it open with 110 well-placed rounds. The Germans had

The Longest Day   June 6, 1944

been firing back—and hard. The *Corry* was the one destroyer the enemy spotters could see. Smoke-laying planes had been assigned to protect the "inshore close support" bombarding group, but the *Corry*'s plane had been shot down. One battery in particular, on the bluffs overlooking the coast above Utah—the gun flashes located it near the village of St.-Marcouf—seemed to be concentrating all its fury on the exposed destroyer. Hoffman decided to move back before it was too late. "We swung around," recalls Radioman Third Class Bennie Glisson, "and showed them our fantail like an old maid to a Marine."

But the *Corry* was in shallow water, close to a number of knife-edged reefs. Her skipper could not make the dash for safety until he was clear. For a few minutes he was forced to play a tense cat-and-mouse game with the German gunners. Trying to anticipate their salvos, Hoffman put the *Corry* through a series of jolting maneuvers. He shot forward, went astern, swung to port, then to starboard, stopped dead, went forward again. All the while his guns engaged the battery. Nearby, the destroyer U.S.S. *Fitch* saw his predicament and began firing on the St.-Marcouf guns too. But there was no letup from the sharpshooting Germans. Almost bracketed by their shells, Hoffman inched the *Corry* out. Finally, satisfied that he was away from the reefs, he ordered, "Hard right rudder! Full speed ahead!" and the *Corry* leaped forward. Hoffman looked behind him. Salvos were smacking into their wake, throwing up great plumes of spray. He breathed easier; he had made it. It was at that instant that his luck ran out. Tearing through the water at more than twenty-eight knots the *Corry* ran headlong onto a submerged mine.

There was a great rending explosion that seemed to throw the destroyer sideways out of the water. The shock was so great that Hoffman was stunned. It seemed to him "that the ship had been lifted by an earthquake." In his radio shack Bennie Glisson, who had been looking out a porthole, suddenly felt that he had been "dropped into a concrete mixer." Jerked off his feet, he was

234

hurled upward against the ceiling, and then he crashed down and smashed his knee.

The mine had cut the *Corry* almost in half. Running across the main deck was a rip more than one foot in width. The bow and the stern pointed crazily upward; about all that held the destroyer together was the deck superstructure. The fireroom and engine room were flooded. There were few survivors in the number two boiler room—the men there were almost instantly scalded to death when the boiler blew up. The rudder was jammed. There was no power, yet somehow in the steam and fire of her death agonies the *Corry* continued to charge crazily through the water. Hoffman became suddenly aware that some of his guns were still firing—his gunners, without power, continued to load and fire manually.

The twisted pile of steel that had once been the *Corry* thrashed through the sea for more than a thousand yards before finally coming to a halt. Then the German batteries zeroed in. "Abandon ship!" Hoffman ordered. Within the next few minutes at least nine shells plowed into the wreck. One blew up the 40-millimeter ammunition. Another set off the smoke generator on the fantail, almost asphyxiating the crew as they struggled into boats and rafts.

The sea was two feet above the main deck when Hoffman, taking one last look around, dived overboard and swam toward a raft. Behind him the *Corry* settled on the bottom, her masts and part of her superstructure remaining above the waves—the U.S. Navy's only major D-Day loss. Of Hoffman's 294-man crew thirteen were dead or missing and thirty-three injured, more casualties than had been suffered in the Utah Beach landings up to this time.

Hoffman thought he was the last to leave the *Corry*. But he wasn't. Nobody knows now who the last man was, but as the boats and rafts pulled away, men on the other ships saw a sailor climb the *Corry*'s stern. He removed the ensign, which had been shot down, and then, swimming and climbing over the wreckage, he reached the main mast. From the U.S.S. *Butler* Coxswain Dick Scrimshaw watched in amazement and admiration as the sailor, shells still falling about him, calmly tied on the flag and ran it up the mast. Then he swam away. Above the wreck of the *Corry* Scrimshaw saw the flag hang limp for a moment. Then it stretched out and fluttered in the breeze.

Rockets trailing ropes shot up toward the 100-foot-high cliff at Pointe du Hoc. Between Utah and Omaha beaches the third American seaborne attack was going in. Small-arms fire poured down on Lt. Col. James E. Rudder's three Ranger companies as they began the assault to silence the massive coastal batteries which intelligence said menaced the American beaches on either side. The nine LCAs carrying the 225 men of the 2nd Ranger Battalion clustered along the little strip of beach beneath the cliff overhang. It afforded some protection from the machine gun fire and from the grenades that the Germans were now rolling down on them—but not much. Offshore the British destroyer *Talybont* and the U.S. destroyer *Satterlee* lobbed in shell after shell onto the cliff top.

Rudder's Rangers were supposed to touch down at the base of the cliff at H Hour. But the lead boat had strayed and led the little flotilla straight toward Pointe de la Percée, three miles east. Rudder had spotted the mistake, but by the time he got the assault craft back on course, precious time had been lost. The delay would cost him his 500-man support force—the rest of the 2nd Rangers and Lieutenant Colonel Max Schneider's 5th Ranger Battalion. The plan had been for Rudder to fire flares as soon as his men had scaled the cliff, as a signal for the other Rangers waiting in their boats some miles offshore to follow in. If no signal was received by 7 A.M., Colonel Schneider was to assume that the Pointe du Hoc assault had failed and head for

Omaha Beach four miles away. There, following in behind the 29th Division, his Rangers would swing west and drive for the Pointe to take the guns from the rear. It was now 7:10 A.M. No signal had been given, so Schneider's force was already heading for Omaha. Rudder and his 225 Rangers were on their own.

It was a wild, frenzied scene. Again and again the rockets roared, shooting the ropes and rope ladders with grapnels attached. Shells and 40-millimeter machine guns raked the cliff top, shaking down great chunks of earth on the Rangers. Men spurted across the narrow, cratered beach trailing scaling ladders, ropes and hand rockets. Here and there at the cliff top Germans bobbed up, throwing down "potato masher" hand grenades or firing *Schmeissers*. Somehow the Rangers dodged from cover to cover, unloaded their boats and fired up the cliff—all at the same time. And off the Pointe, two DUKWS—amphibious vehicles—with tall, extended ladders, borrowed for the occasion from the London Fire Brigade, tried to maneuver closer in. From the tops of the ladders Rangers blasted the headlands with Browning automatic rifles and Tommy guns.

The assault was furious. Some men didn't wait for the ropes to catch. Weapons slung over their shoulders, they cut handholds with their knives and started up the nine-story-high cliff like flies. Some of the grapnels now began to catch and men swarmed up the ropes. Then there were wild yells as the Germans cut the ropes and Rangers hurtled back down the cliff. P.F.C. Harry Robert's rope was cut twice. On his third try he finally got to a cratered niche just under the edge of the cliff. Sergeant Bill "L-Rod" Petty tried going up hand over hand on a plain rope but, although he was an expert free climber, the rope was so wet and muddy he couldn't make it. Then Petty tried a ladder, got thirty feet up and slid back when it was cut. He started back up again. Sergeant Herman Stein climbing another ladder, was almost pushed off the cliff face when he accidentally inflated his Mae West. He "struggled for an eternity" with the life preserver but there were men ahead and behind him on the ladder. Somehow Stein kept on going.

Now men were scrambling up a score of ropes that twisted and snaked down from the top of the cliff. Suddenly Sergeant Petty, on his way up for the third time, was peppered by chunks of earth flying out all around him. The Germans were leaning out over the edge of the cliff, machine-gunning the Rangers as they climbed. The Germans fought desperately, despite the fire that was still raining on them from the Rangers on the fire ladders and from the destroyers offshore. Petty saw the climber next to him stiffen and swing out from the cliff. Stein saw him, too. So did twenty-year-old P.F.C. Carl Bombardier. As they watched, horrified, the man slid down the rope and fell, bouncing from ledges and rock outcroppings, and it seemed to Petty "a lifetime before his body hit the beach." Petty froze on the rope. He could not make his hand move up to the next rung. He remembers saying to himself, "This is just too hard to climb." But the German machine guns got him going again. As they began to spray the cliff dangerously near him, Petty "unfroze real fast." Desperately he hauled himself up the last few yards.

Everywhere men were throwing themselves over the top and into shell holes. To Sergeant Regis McCloskey, who had successfully brought his half-sinking ammunition boat in to the beach, the high plateau of Pointe du Hoc presented a weird, incredible sight. The ground was so pitted by the shells and bombs of the pre-H-Hour naval and air bombardment that it looked like "the craters of the moon." There was an eerie silence now as men pulled themselves up and into the protective craters. The fire had stopped for the moment, there was not a German to be seen, and everywhere men looked the yawning craters stretched back toward the mainland—a violent, terrible no man's land.

Colonel Rudder had already established his first command post, a niche at the edge of the cliff. From it his signal officer, Lieutenant James Eikner, sent out the message "Praise the

Lord." It meant "All men up cliff." But it was not quite true. At the base of the cliff the Rangers' medical officer, a pediatrician in private practice, was tending the dead and the dying on the beach—perhaps twenty-five men. Minute by minute the valiant Ranger force was being chipped away. By the end of the day there would only be ninety of the original 225 still able to bear arms. Worse, it had been a heroic and futile effort—to silence guns which were not there. The information which Jean Marion, the French underground sector chief, had tried to send to London was true. The battered bunkers atop Pointe du Hoc were empty—the guns had never been mounted.*

In his bomb crater at the top of the cliff, Sergeant Petty and his four-man BAR team sat exhausted after the climb. A little haze drifted over the churned, pitted earth and the smell of cordite was heavy in the air. Petty stared almost dreamily around him. Then on the edge of the crater he saw two sparrows eating worms. "Look," said Petty to the others, "they're having breakfast."

Now on this great and awful morning the last phase of the assault from the sea began. Along the eastern half of the Normandy invasion coast, Lieutenant General M. C. Dempsey's British Second Army was coming ashore, with grimness and gaiety, with pomp and ceremony, with all the studied nonchalance the British traditionally assume in moments of great emotion. They had waited four long years for this day. They were assaulting not just beaches but bitter memories—memories of Munich and Dunkirk, of one hateful and humiliating retreat after another, of countless devastating bombing raids, of dark days when they

---

* Some two hours later a Ranger patrol found a deserted five-gun battery in a camouflaged position more than a mile inland. Stacks of shells surrounded each gun and they were ready to fire, but the Rangers could find no evidence that they had ever been manned. Presumably these were the guns for the Pointe du Hoc emplacements.

had stood alone. With them were the Canadians, with a score of their own to settle for the bloody losses at Dieppe. And with them, too, were the French, fierce and eager on this homecoming morning.

There was a curious jubilance in the air. As the troops headed toward the beaches the loud-speaker in a rescue launch off Sword roared out "Roll Out the Barrel." From a rocket-firing barge off Gold came the strains of "We Don't Know Where We're Going." Canadians going to Juno heard the rasping notes of a bugle blaring across the water. Some men were even singing. Marine Denis Lovell remembers that "the boys were standing up, singing all the usual Army and Navy songs." And Lord Lovat's 1st Special Service Brigade commandos, spruce and resplendent in their green berets (the commandos refused to wear tin helmets), were serenaded into battle by the eerie wailing of the bagpipes. As their landing boats drew abreast of Admiral Vian's flagship H.M.S. *Scylla*, the commandos gave the "thumbs-up" salute. Looking down on them, eighteen-year-old Able Seaman Ronald Northwood thought they were "the finest set of chaps I ever came across."

Even the obstacles and the enemy fire now lacing out at the boats were viewed with a certain detachment by many men. On one LCT, Telegraphist John Webber watched a Royal Marine captain study the maze of mined obstacles clotting the coastline, then remark casually to the skipper, "I say, old man, you really must get my chaps on shore, there's a good fellow." Aboard another landing craft a 50th Division major stared thoughtfully at the round Teller mines clearly visible on top of the obstacles and said to the coxswain, "For Christ's sake, don't knock those bloody coconuts down or we'll all get a free trip to hell." One boatload of 48th Royal Marine commandos were met by heavy machine gun fire off Juno and men dived for cover behind the deck superstructure. Not the adjutant, Captain Daniel Flunder. He tucked his swagger stick under his arm and calmly paraded up and down the foredeck. "I thought," he explained later, "it was the thing to do." (While he was doing it, a bullet plowed through his map case.) And in a landing craft charging for Sword Major C. K. "Banger" King, just as he had promised, was reading *Henry V*. Amid the roar of the diesels, the hissing of the spray and the sound of gunfire, King spoke into the loud-hailer, "And gentlemen in England now a-bed/Shall think themselves accurs'd they were not here . . ."

Some men could hardly wait for the fighting to begin. Two Irish sergeants, James Percival "Paddy" de Lacy, who had toasted De Valera hours before for "keepin' us out of the war," and his side-kick, Paddy McQuaid, stood at the ramps of an LST and, fortified by good Royal Navy rum, solemnly contemplated the troops. "De Lacy," said McQuaid, staring hard at the Englishmen all around them, "don't you think now that some of these boys seem a wee bit timid?" As the beaches neared, De Lacy called out to his men, "All right, now! Here we go! At the run!" The LST ground to a halt. As the men ran out, McQuaid yelled at the shell-smoked shore line, "Come out, ye bastards, and fight us now!" Then he disappeared under water. An instant later he came up spluttering. "Oh, the evil of it!" he bellowed. "Tryin' to drown me before I even get up on the beach!"

Off Sword, Private Hubert Victor Baxter of the British 3rd Division revved up his Bren gun carrier and, peering over the top of the armored plating, plunged into the water. Sitting exposed on the raised seat above him was his bitter enemy, Sergeant "Dinger" Bell, with whom Baxter had been fighting for months. Bell yelled, "Baxter, wind up that seat so you can see where you're going!" Baxter shouted back, "Not bloody likely! I can see!" Then, as they swept up the beach, the sergeant, caught up in the excitement of the moment, resorted to the very thing that had begun the feud in the first place. He slammed down his fist again and again on Baxter's helmet and roared, "Bash on! Bash on!"

As the commandos touched down on Sword, Lord Lovat's piper, William Millin, plunged off his landing craft into water up to his armpits. He could see smoke piling up from the beach ahead and hear the crump of exploding mortar shells. As Millin floundered toward the shore, Lovat shouted at him, "Give us 'Highland Laddie,' man!" Waist-deep in the water, Millin put the mouthpiece to his lips and splashed on through the surf, the pipes keening crazily. At the water's edge, oblivious to the gunfire, he halted and, parading up and down along the beach, piped the commandos ashore. The men streamed past him, and mingling with the whine of bullets and the screams of shells came the wild skirl of the pipes as Millin now played "The Road to the Isles." "That's the stuff, Jock," yelled a commando. Said another, "Get down, you mad bugger."

All along Sword, Juno and Gold—for almost twenty miles, from Ouistreham near the mouth of the Orne to the village of Le Hamel on the west—the British swarmed ashore. The beaches were choked with landing craft disgorging troops, and nearly everywhere along the assault area the high seas and underwater obstacles were causing more trouble than the enemy.

The first men in had been the frogmen—120 underwater demolition experts whose job it was to cut 30-yard gaps through the obstacles. They had only twenty minutes to work before the first waves bore down upon them. The obstacles were formidable —at places more densely sown than in any other part of the Normandy invasion area. Sergeant Peter Henry Jones of the Royal Marines swam into a maze of steel pylons, gates and hedgehogs and concrete cones. In the 30-yard gap Jones had to blow, he found twelve major obstacles, some of them fourteen feet long. When another frogman, Lieutenant John B. Taylor of the Royal Navy, saw the fantastic array of underwater defenses surrounding him, he yelled out to his unit leader that "this bloody job is impossible." But he did not give it up. Working under fire, Taylor, like the other frogmen, methodically set to work.

They blew the obstacles singly, because they were too large to blow in groups. Even as they worked, amphibious tanks came swimming in among them, followed almost immediately by first-wave troops. Frogmen rushing out of the water saw landing craft, turned sideways by the heavy seas, crash into the obstacles. Mines exploded, steel spikes and hedgehogs ripped along the hulls, and up and down the beaches landing craft began to flounder. The waters offshore became a junkyard as boats piled up almost on top of one another. Telegraphist Webber remembers thinking that "the beaching is a tragedy." As his craft came in Webber saw "LCTs stranded and ablaze, twisted masses of metal on the shore, burning tanks and bulldozers." And as one LCT passed them, heading for the open sea, Webber was horrified to see "its well deck engulfed in a terrifying fire."

On Gold Beach, where frogman Jones was now working with the Royal Engineers trying to clear the obstacles, he saw an LCI approach with troops standing on the deck ready to disembark. Caught by a sudden swell, the craft swerved sideways, lifted and crashed down on a series of mined steel triangles. Jones saw it explode with a shattering blast. It reminded him of a "slow-motion cartoon—the men, standing to attention, shot up into the air as though lifted by a water spout . . . at the top of the spout bodies and parts of bodies spread like drops of water."

Boat after boat got hung up on the obstacles. Of the sixteen landing craft carrying the 47th Royal Marine commandos in to Gold Beach, four boats were lost, eleven were damaged and beached and only one made it back to the parent ship. Sergeant Donald Gardner of the 47th and his men were dumped into the water about fifty yards from shore. They lost all of their equipment and had to swim in under machine gun fire. As they struggled in the water, Gardner heard someone say, "Perhaps we're intruding, this seems to be a private beach." Going into Juno the 48th Royal Marine commandos not only ran afoul of the obstacles, they also came under intense mortar fire. Lieutenant

Michael Aldworth and about forty of his men crouched down in the forward hold of their LCI as shells exploded all about them. Aldworth shoved his head up to see what was happening and saw men from the aft hold running along the deck. Aldworth's men yelled out, "How soon do we get out of here?" Aldworth called back, "Wait a minute, chaps. It's not our turn." There was a moment's pause and then someone inquired, "Well, just how long do you think it will be, old man? The ruddy hold is filling full of water."

The men from the sinking LCI were quickly picked up by a variety of craft. There were so many boats around, Aldworth recalls, that "it was rather like hailing a taxi in Bond Street." Some men were delivered safely onto the beaches; others were taken out to a Canadian destroyer, but fifty commandos discovered themselves on an LCT which had unloaded its tanks and was under instructions to proceed directly back to England. Nothing the infuriated men could say or do would persuade the skipper to change his course. One officer, Major de Stackpoole, had been wounded in the thighs on the run-in, but on hearing the LCT's destination he roared, "Nonsense! You're all bloody well mad!" With that he dived overboard and swam for shore.

For most men the obstacles proved to be the toughest part of the assault. Once they were through these defenses, troops found the enemy opposition along the three beaches spotty— fierce in some sectors, light and even nonexistent in others. On the western half of Gold men of the 1st Hampshire Regiment were almost decimated as they waded through water that was at places three to six feet deep. Struggling through the heaving sea line abreast, they were caught by heavy mortar bursts and crisscrossing machine gun fire that poured out from the village of Le Hamel, a stronghold occupied by the tough German 352nd Division. Men went down one after another. Private Charles Wilson heard a surprised voice say, "I've bought it, mates!" Turning, Wilson saw the man, a strange look of disbelief on his face, slide beneath the water without another word. Wilson plowed on. He had been machine-gunned in the water before—except that at Dunkirk he had been going the other way. Private George Stunell saw men going down all around him too. He came across a Bren gun carrier standing in about three feet of water, its motor running and the driver "frozen at the wheel, too terrified to drive the machine onto the shore." Stunell pushed him to one side and with machine gun bullets whipping all around drove up onto the beach. Stunell was elated to have made it. Then he suddenly pitched headlong to the ground; a bullet had slammed into a can of cigarettes in his tunic pocket with terrific impact. Minutes later he discovered that he was bleeding from wounds in his back and ribs. The same bullet had passed cleanly through his body.

It would take the Hampshires almost eight hours to knock out the Le Hamel defenses, and at the end of D Day their casualties would total almost two hundred. Strangely, apart from the obstacles, troops landing on either side encountered little trouble. There were casualties, but they were fewer than had been anticipated. On the left of the Hampshires, men of the 1st Dorset Regiment were off the beach in forty minutes. Next to them the Green Howards landed with such dash and determination that they moved inland and captured their first objective in less than an hour. Company Sergeant Major Stanley Hollis, killer of ninety Germans up to now, waded ashore and promptly captured a pillbox singlehanded. The nerveless Hollis, using grenades and his Sten gun, killed two and captured twenty in the start of a day that would see him kill another ten.

On the beach to the right of Le Hamel it was so quiet that some men were disappointed. Medic Geoffrey Leach saw troops and vehicles pouring ashore and found that there was nothing "for the medics to do but help unload ammunition." To Marine Denis Lovell, the landing was like "just another exercise back home." His unit, the 47th Royal Marine commandos, moved quickly off the beach, avoided all enemy contact, turned west and set out on a seven-mile forced march to link up with the Americans near Port-en-Bessin. They expected to see the first Yanks from Omaha Beach around noon.

But this was not to be—unlike the Americans on Omaha, who were still pinned down by the rugged German 352nd Division, the British and the Canadians were more than a match for the tired and inferior 716th Division with its impressed Russian and Polish "volunteers." In addition, the British had made the fullest possible use of amphibious tanks and a Rube Goldberg-like collection of armored vehicles. Some, like the "flail" tanks, lashed the ground ahead of them with chains that detonated mines. Other armored vehicles carried small bridges or great reels of steel matting which, when unrolled, made a temporary roadway over soft ground. One group even carried giant bundles of logs for use as steppingstones over walls or to fill in antitank ditches. These inventions, and the extra-long period of bombardment that the British beaches had received, gave the assaulting troops additional protection.

Still some strong pockets of resistance were encountered. On one half of Juno Beach men of the Canadian 3rd Division fought through lines of pillboxes and trenches, through fortified houses, and from street to street in the town of Courseulles before finally breaking through and pushing inland. But all resistance there would be mopped up within two hours. In many places it was being done with quickness and dispatch. Able Seaman Edward Ashworth, off an LCT which had brought troops and tanks in to the Courseulles beach, saw Canadian soldiers march six German prisoners behind a dune some distance away. Ashworth thought that this was his chance to get a German helmet for a souvenir. He ran up the beach and in the dunes discovered the six Germans "all lying crumpled up." Ashworth bent over one of the bodies, still determined to get a helmet. But he found "the man's throat was cut—every one of them had had his throat cut," and Ashworth "turned away, sick as a parrot. I didn't get my tin hat."

Sergeant Paddy de Lacy, also in the Courseulles area, had captured twelve Germans who had come almost eagerly out of a trench, their arms raised high above their heads. De Lacy stood staring at them for a moment; he had lost a brother in North Africa. Then he said to the soldier with him, "Look at the super blokes—just look at them. Here, take them out of my sight." He walked away to make himself a cup of tea to soothe his anger. While he was heating a canteen of water over a Sterno can a young officer "with the down still on his chin" walked over and said sternly, "Now look here, Sergeant, this is no time to be making tea." De Lacy looked up and, as patiently as his twenty-one years of Army service would allow, replied, "Sir, we are not playing at soldiers now—this is real war. Why don't you come back in five minutes and have a nice cup of tea?" The officer did.

Even as the fighting was going on in the Courseulles area, men, guns, tanks, vehicles and supplies were pouring ashore. The movement inland was smoothly and efficiently handled. The beachmaster, Captain Colin Maud, allowed no loiterers on Juno. Most men, like Sub-Lieutenant John Beynon, were a little taken aback at the sight of the tall, bearded officer with the imposing bearing and the booming voice who met each new contingent with the same greeting, "I'm chairman of the reception committee and of this party, so get a move on." Few men cared to argue with the custodian of Juno Beach; Beynon remembers he had a cudgel in one hand and the other held tight to the leash of a fierce-looking Alsatian dog. The effect was all he could have hoped for. INS correspondent Joseph Willicombe recalls a futile argument he had with the beachmaster. Willicombe, who had landed in the first wave of Canadians, had been assured that he would be allowed to send a twenty-five-word message via the beachmaster's two-way radio to the command ship for transmission to the U.S. Apparently no one had bothered to so inform Maud. Staring stonily at Willicombe, he growled, "My dear chap, there's a bit of a war going on here." Willicombe had to admit that the beachmaster had a point.* A few yards away, in the coarse beach grass, lay the mangled bodies of fifteen Canadians who had trod on mines as they dashed ashore.

All along Juno the Canadians suffered. Of the three British beaches theirs was the bloodiest. Rough seas had delayed the landings. Razor-edged reefs on the eastern half of the beach and barricades of obstacles created havoc among the assault craft. Worse, the naval and air bombardment had failed to knock out the coastal defenses or had missed them altogether, and in some sectors troops came ashore without the protection of tanks. Opposite the towns of Bernières and St.-Aubin-sur-Mer men of the Canadian 8th Brigade and the 48th Marine commandos came in under heavy fire. One company lost nearly half its men in the dash up the beach. Artillery fire from St.-Aubin-sur-Mer was so concentrated that it led to one particular horror on the beach. A tank, buttoned up for protection and thrashing wildly up the beach to get out of the line of fire, ran over the dead and the dying. Captain Daniel Flunder of the commandos, looking back from the sand dunes, saw what was happening and oblivious of the bursting shells ran back down the beach shouting at the top of his voice, "They're my men!" The enraged Flunder beat on the tank's hatch with his swagger stick, but the tank kept on going. Pulling the pin on a grenade, Flunder blew one of the

* Correspondents on Juno had no communications until Ronald Clark of United Press came ashore with two baskets of carrier pigeons. The correspondents quickly wrote brief stories, placed them in the plastic capsules attached to the pigeons' legs and released the birds. Unfortunately the pigeons were so overloaded that most of them fell back to earth. Some, however, circled overhead for a few moments—and then headed toward the German lines. Charles Lynch of Reuter's stood on the beach, waved his fist at the pigeons and roared, "Traitors! Damned traitors!" Four pigeons, Willicombe says, "proved loyal." They actually got to the Ministry of Information in London within a few hours.

tank's tracks off. It wasn't until the startled tankers opened the hatch that they realized what had happened.

Although the fighting was bitter while it lasted, the Canadians and the commandos got off the Bernières–St.-Aubin beaches in less than thirty minutes and plunged inland. Follow-up waves experienced little difficulty and within an hour it was so quiet on the beaches that Leading Aircraftsman John Murphy of a barrage balloon unit found that "the worst enemy was the sand lice that drove us crazy as the tide came in." Back of the beaches street fighting would occupy troops for nearly two hours, but this section of Juno, like the western half, was now secure.

The 48th commandos fought their way through St.-Aubin-sur-Mer and, turning east, headed along the coast. They had a particularly tough assignment. Juno lay seven miles away from Sword Beach. To close this gap and link up the two beaches, the 48th was to make a forced march toward Sword. Another commando unit, the 41st, was to land at Lion-sur-Mer on the edge of Sword Beach, swing right and head west. Both forces were expected to join up within a few hours at a point roughly halfway between the two beachheads. That was the plan, but almost simultaneously the commandos ran into trouble. At Langrune, about a mile east of Juno, men of the 48th found themselves in a fortified area of the town that defied penetration. Every house was a strongpoint. Mines, barbed wire and concrete walls—some of them six feet high and five feet thick—sealed off the streets. From these positions heavy fire greeted the invaders. Without tanks or artillery the 48th was stopped cold.

On Sword, six miles away, the 41st after a rough landing turned west and headed through Lion-sur-Mer. They were told by the French that the German garrison had pulled out. The information seemed correct—until the commandos reached the edge of the town. There artillery fire knocked out three supporting tanks. Sniper and machine gun fire came from innocent-looking villas that had been converted into blockhouses, and a rain

249

of mortar shells fell among the commandos. Like the 48th, the 41st came to a standstill.

Now, although no one in the Allied High Command knew about it yet, a vital gap six miles wide existed in the beachhead—a gap through which Rommel's tanks, if they moved fast enough, could reach the coast and, by attacking left and right along the shore, could roll up the British landings.

Lion-sur-Mer was one of the few real trouble spots on Sword. Of the three British beaches, Sword was expected to be the most heavily defended. Troops had been briefed that casualties would be very high. Private John Gale of the 1st South Lancashire Regiment was "cold-bloodedly told that all of us in the first wave would probably be wiped out." The picture was painted in even blacker terms to the commandos. It was drilled into them that "no matter what happens we must get on the beaches, for there will be no evacuation . . . no going back." The 4th commandos expected to be "written off on the beaches," as Corporal James Colley and Private Stanley Stewart remember, for they were told their casualties would run as "high as eighty-four per cent." And the men who were to land ahead of the infantry in amphibious tanks were warned that "even those of you who reach the beach can expect sixty per cent casualties." Private Christopher Smith, driver of an amphibious tank, thought his chances of survival were slim. Rumor had increased the casualty figure to ninety per cent and Smith was inclined to believe it, for as his unit left England men saw canvas screens being set up on Gosport Beach and "it was said that these were being erected to sort out the returned dead."

For a while it looked as though the worst of the predictions might come true. In some sectors first-wave troops were heavily machine-gunned and mortared. In the Ouistreham half of Sword, men of the 2nd East York Regiment lay dead and dying from the water's edge all the way up the beach. Although nobody would ever know how many men were lost in this bloody dash from the boats, it seems likely that the East Yorks suffered most of their two hundred D-Day casualties in these first few minutes. The shock of seeing these crumpled khaki forms seemed to confirm the most dreadful fears of follow-up troops. Some saw "bodies stacked like cordwood" and counted "more than 150 dead." Private John Mason of the 4th commandos, who landed half an hour later, was shocked to find himself "running through piles of dead infantry who had been knocked down like nine pins." And Corporal Fred Mears of Lord Lovat's commandos was "aghast to see the East Yorks lying in bunches. . . . It would probably never have happened had they spread out." As he charged up the beach determined to make "Jesse Owens look like a turtle," he remembers cynically thinking that "they would know better the next time."

Although bloody, the beach fight was brief.* Except for initial losses, the assault on Sword went forward speedily, meeting little sustained opposition. The landings were so successful that many men coming in minutes after the first wave were surprised to find only sniper fire. They saw the beaches shrouded in smoke, medics working among the wounded, flail tanks detonating mines, burning tanks and vehicles littering the shore line, and sand shooting up from occasional shell bursts, but nowhere was there the slaughter they had expected. To these tense troops, primed to expect a holocaust, the beaches were an anticlimax.

In many places along Sword there was even a bank holiday at-

* There will always be differences of opinion about the nature of the fighting on Sword. Men of the East Yorks disagree with their own history, which says that it was "just like a training show, only easier." The troops of the 4th commandos claim that when they landed at H-plus-30 they found the East Yorks still at the water's edge. According to Brigadier E. E. E. Cass, in command of the 8th Brigade that assaulted Sword, the East Yorks were off the beach by the time the 4th commandos landed. It is estimated that the 4th lost thirty men as they came ashore. On the western half of the beach, says Cass, "opposition had been overcome by eight-thirty except for isolated snipers." Men of the 1st South Lancashire Regiment landing there had light casualties and moved inland fast. The 1st Suffolks coming in behind them had just four casualties.

mosphere. Here and there along the seafront little groups of elated French waved to the troops and yelled, *"Vive les Anglais!"* Royal Marine Signalman Leslie Ford noticed a Frenchman "practically on the beach itself who appeared to be giving a running commentary on the battle to a group of townspeople." Ford thought they were crazy, for the beaches and the foreshore were still infested with mines and under occasional fire. But it was happening everywhere. Men were hugged and kissed and embraced by the French, who seemed quite unaware of the dangers around them. Corporal Harry Norfield and Gunner Ronald Allen were astonished to see "a person all dressed up in splendid regalia and wearing a bright brass helmet making his way down to the beaches." He turned out to be the mayor of Colleville-sur-Orne, a small village about a mile inland, who had decided to come down and officially greet the invasion forces.

Some of the Germans seemed no less eager than the French to greet the troops. Sapper Henry Jennings had no sooner disembarked than he was "confronted with a collection of Germans—most of them Russian and Polish 'volunteers'—anxious to surrender." But Captain Gerald Norton of a Royal Artillery unit got the biggest surprise of all: he was met "by four Germans with their suitcases packed, who appeared to be awaiting the first available transportation out of France."

Out of the confusion on Gold, Juno and Sword, the British and the Canadians swarmed inland. The advance was businesslike and efficient and there was a kind of grandeur about it all. As troops fought into towns and villages examples of heroism and courage were all around them. Some remember a Royal Marine commando major, both arms gone, who urged his men along by shouting at them to "get inland, chaps, before Fritz gets wise to this party." Others remember the cocky cheerfulness and bright faith of the wounded as they waited for the medics to catch up with them. Some waved as the troops passed, others yelled, "See you in Berlin, mates!" Gunner Ronald Allen would never forget one soldier who had been badly wounded in the stomach. He was propped up against a wall calmly reading a book.

Now speed was essential. From Gold troops headed for the cathedral town of Bayeux, roughly seven miles inland. From Juno the Canadians drove for the Bayeux-Caen highway and Carpiquet Airport, about ten miles away. And out of Sword the British headed for the city of Caen. They were so sure of capturing this objective that even correspondents, as the London *Daily Mail's* Noel Monks was later to recall, were told that a briefing would be held "at point X in Caen at 4 P.M." Lord Lovat's commandos marching out of the Sword area wasted no time. They were going to the relief of General Gale's embattled 6th Airborne troops holding the Orne and Caen bridges four miles away and "Shimy" Lovat had promised Gale that he would be there "sharp at noon." Behind a tank at the head of the column Lord Lovat's piper Bill Millin played "Blue Bonnets over the Border."

For ten Britishers, the crews of the midget submarines X20 and X23, D Day was over. Off Sword Beach Lieutenant George Honour's X23 threaded through waves of landing craft streaming steadily in toward the shore. In the heavy seas, with her flat superstructure almost awash, all that could be seen of the X23 were her identifying flags whipping in the wind. Coxswain Charles Wilson on an LCT "almost fell overboard with surprise" when he saw what appeared to be "two large flags apparently unsupported" moving steadily toward him through the water. As the X23 passed, Wilson couldn't help wondering "what the devil a midget sub had to do with the invasion." Plowing by, the X23 headed out into the transport area in search of her tow ship, a trawler with the appropriate name of *En Avant*. Operation Gambit was over. Lieutenant Honour and his four-man crew were going home.

The men for whom they had marked the beaches marched into France. Everyone was optimistic. The Atlantic Wall had

253

been breached. Now the big question was, how fast would the Germans recover from the shock?

Berchtesgaden lay quiet and peaceful in the early morning. The day was already warm and sultry, and the clouds hung low on the surrounding mountains. At Hitler's fortress-like mountain retreat on the Obersalzberg, all was still. The Führer was asleep. A few miles away at his headquarters, the *Reichskanzlei*, it was just another routine morning. Colonel General Alfred Jodl, OKW's Chief of Operations, had been up since six. He had eaten his customary light breakfast (one cup of coffee, a soft-boiled egg and a thin slice of toast) and now, in his small soundproofed office, he was leisurely reading the night's reports.

The news from Italy continued to be bad. Rome had fallen twenty-four hours before and Field Marshal Albert Kesselring's troops were being hard pressed as they pulled back. Jodl thought that there might be an Allied breakthrough even before Kesselring disengaged his troops and withdrew to new positions in the north. So concerned was Jodl about the threatened collapse in Italy that he had ordered his deputy, General Walter Warlimont, to proceed to Kesselring's headquarters on a fact-finding trip. Warlimont was to leave by the end of the day.

There was nothing new from Russia. Although Jodl's sphere of authority did not officially include the eastern theater, he had long ago maneuvered himself into a position whereby he "advised" the Führer on the conduct of the Russian war. The Soviet summer offensive would begin any day now, and all along the 2,000-mile front two hundred German divisions—more than 1,500,000 men—were poised, waiting for it. But this morning the Russian front was quiet. Jodl's aide had also passed on several reports from Rundstedt's headquarters about an Allied attack in Normandy. Jodl did not think that the situation there was serious, at least not yet. At the moment his big concern was Italy.

In the barracks at Strub a few miles away, Jodl's deputy, General Warlimont, had been carefully following the Normandy attack since 4 A.M. He had received OB West's teletype message requesting the release of the panzer reserves—the *Panzer Lehr* and 12th S.S. divisions—and he had discussed this by phone with Von Rundstedt's chief of staff, Major General Günther Blumentritt. Now Warlimont rang Jodl.

"Blumentritt has called about the panzer reserves," Warlimont reported. "OB West wants to move them into the invasion areas immediately."

As Warlimont recalls, there was a long silence as Jodl pondered the question. "Are you so sure that this *is* the invasion?" asked Jodl. Before Warlimont could answer, Jodl went on, "According to the reports I have received it could be a diversionary attack . . . part of a deception plan. OB West has sufficient reserves right now. . . . OB West should endeavor to clean up the attack with the forces at their disposal. . . . I do not think that this is the time to release the OKW reserves. . . . We must wait for further clarification of the situation."

Warlimont knew that there was little use in arguing the point, although he thought the Normandy landings were more serious than Jodl seemed to believe. He said to Jodl, "Sir, in view of the Normandy situation, shall I proceed to Italy as planned?" Jodl answered, "Yes, yes, I don't see why not." Then he hung up.

Warlimont put down his phone. Turning to Major General von

Buttlar-Brandenfels, the Army Operations Chief, he told him of Jodl's decision. "I sympathize with Blumentritt," Warlimont said. "This decision is absolutely contrary to my understanding of what the plan was to be in the event of an invasion."

Warlimont was "shocked" by Jodl's literal interpretation of the Hitler edict concerning the control of the panzers. True, they were OKW reserves and therefore they came under Hitler's direct authority. But, like Von Rundstedt, Warlimont had always understood that "in the event of an Allied attack, whether diversionary or not, the panzers would be immediately released —automatically released, in fact." To Warlimont, such a move seemed only logical; the man on the spot, fighting off the invasion, should have all the available forces to use as he saw fit, especially when that man happened to be the last of Germany's "Black Knights," the venerable strategist Von Rundstedt. Jodl could have released the force, but he was taking no chances. As Warlimont was later to recall, "Jodl's decision was the one he thought Hitler would have made." Jodl's attitude, Warlimont felt, was just another example of "the chaos of leadership in the Leader State." But nobody argued with Jodl. Warlimont put through a call to Blumentritt at OB West. Now the decision to release the panzers would depend on the capricious whim of the man whom Jodl considered to be a military genius—Hitler.

The officer who had anticipated just such a situation and who had hoped to discuss it with Hitler was less than a two hour's drive from Berchtesgaden. Field Marshal Erwin Rommel, at his home in Herrlingen, Ulm, seems somehow to have been completely forgotten in all the confusion. There is no record in the meticulously kept Army Group B War Diary that Rommel had even heard as yet about the Normandy landings.

At OB West outside Paris, Jodl's decision produced shock and incredulity. Lieutenant General Bodo Zimmermann, chief of operations, remembers that Von Rundstedt "was fuming with rage, red in the face, and his anger made his speech unintelligible."

Zimmermann couldn't believe it either. During the night, in a phone call to OKW, Zimmermann had informed Jodl's duty officer, Lieutenant Colonel Friedel, that OB West had alerted the two panzer divisions. "No objections whatsoever were made against the movement," Zimmermann bitterly recalls. Now he called OKW again and spoke to the Army Operations Chief, Major General von Buttlar-Brandenfels. He got a frigid reception—Von Buttlar had picked up his cue from Jodl. In an angry outburst Von Buttlar ranted, "These divisions are under the direct control of OKW! You had no right to alert them without our prior approval. You are to halt the panzers immediately—nothing is to be done before the Führer makes his decision!" When Zimmermann tried to argue back, Von Buttlar shut him up by saying sharply, "Do as you are told!"

The next move should have been up to Von Rundstedt. As a field marshal, he could have called Hitler directly, and it is even likely that the panzers might have been immediately released. But Von Rundstedt did not telephone the Führer now or at any time during D Day. Not even the overwhelming importance of the invasion could compel the aristocratic Von Rundstedt to plead with the man he habitually referred to as "that Bohemian corporal."*

But his officers continued to bombard OKW with telephone calls in vain and futile efforts to get the decision reversed. They called Warlimont, Von Buttlar-Brandenfels, and even Hitler's adjutant, Major General Rudolf Schmundt. It was a strange, long-distance struggle that would go on for hours. Zimmermann summed it up this way: "When we warned that if we didn't get the panzers the Normandy landings would succeed and that unforeseeable consequences would follow, we were simply told that *we* were in no position to judge—that the main landing was

---

* According to Von Buttlar-Brandenfels, Hitler was well aware of Von Rundstedt's contempt. "As long as the Field Marshal grumbles," Hitler had once said, "everything is all right."

going to come at an entirely different place anyway." * And Hitler, protected by his inner circle of military sycophants, in the balmy, make-believe world of Berchtesgaden, slept through it all.

At Rommel's headquarters in La Roche-Guyon, the chief of staff, Major General Speidel, knew nothing of Jodl's decision as yet. He was under the impression that the two reserve panzer divisions had been alerted and were already en route. Also Speidel knew the 21st Panzer was moving into an assembly area south of Caen, and although it would be some time before their tanks could move up, some of their reconnaissance forces and infantry were already engaging the enemy. So there was a definite air of optimism at the headquarters. Colonel Leodegard Freyberg recalls that "the general impression was that the Allies would be thrown back into the sea by the end of the day." Vice-Admiral Friedrich Ruge, Rommel's naval aide, shared in the general elation. But Ruge noticed one peculiar thing: The household staff of the Duke and Duchess de La Rochefoucauld was quietly going through the castle taking the priceless Gobelin tapestries down from the walls.

There seemed greater reason for optimism at the headquarters of the Seventh Army, the army that was actually fighting the Allied attack. To staff officers there it looked as though the 352nd Division had thrown the invaders back into the sea in the area between Vierville and Colleville—Omaha Beach. What had happened was that an officer in a bunker overlooking the beach had finally been able to get through to his headquarters with an encouraging report on the progress of the battle. The report was

* Hitler had become so convinced that the "real" invasion would take place in the Pas-de-Calais area that he held Von Salmuth's 15th Army in its positions until July 24. By then it was too late. Ironically Hitler seems to have been the only one who originally believed that the invasion would take place in Normandy. General Blumentritt says that "I well remember a call from Jodl some time in April in which he said 'The Führer has definite information to the effect that a landing in Normandy is not unlikely.'"

considered so important that it was taken down word for word. "At the water's edge," said the observer, "the enemy is in search of cover behind the coastal-zone obstacles. A great many motor vehicles—among them ten tanks—stand burning on the beach. The obstacle demolition squads have given up their activities. Debarkation from the landing boats has ceased . . . the boats keep farther out to sea. The fire of our battle positions and artillery is well placed and has inflicted considerable casualties on the enemy. A great many wounded and dead lie on the beach . . ." *

This was the first good news that the Seventh Army had received. Spirits were so high as a result that when the Fifteenth Army's commanding officer, General von Salmuth, suggested that he send his 346th Infantry Division to help the Seventh out, he was haughtily turned down. "We don't need them," he was told.

Even though everyone was confident, the Seventh Army's chief of staff, General Pemsel, was still trying to piece together an accurate picture of the situation. It was difficult, for he had practically no communications. Wires and cables had been cut or otherwise destroyed by the French underground, by the paratroopers or by the naval and air bombardment. Pemsel told Rommel's headquarters, "I'm fighting the sort of battle that William the Conqueror must have fought—by ear and sight alone." Actually Pemsel did not know how bad his communications really were. He thought that only paratroopers had landed on

* This report was given, sometime between eight and nine, directly to the 352nd's operations chief, Lieutenant Colonel Ziegelmann, by a certain Colonel Goth who commanded the fortifications on Pointe et Raz de la Percée overlooking the Vierville end of Omaha Beach. It caused such elation that Ziegelmann, according to his own account written after the war, considered that he was dealing with "inferior enemy forces." Later reports were even more optimistic and by 11 A.M. General Kraiss, the 352nd's commanding officer, was so convinced that he had rubbed out the Omaha beachhead that he diverted reserves to strengthen the division's right wing in the British sector.

the Cherbourg peninsula. At this time he had no idea that seaborne landings had taken place on the east coast of the peninsula, at Utah Beach.

Difficult as it was for Pemsel to define the exact geographic limits of the attack, he was certain of one thing—the Normandy assault *was* the invasion. He continued to point this out to his superiors at Rommel's and Von Rundstedt's headquarters, but he remained very much in the minority. As both Army Group B and OB West stated in their morning reports, "at the present time, it is still too early to say whether this is a large-scale diversionary attack or the main effort." The generals continued to look for the *Schwerpunkt*. Along the Normandy coast any private could have told them where it was.

Half a mile from Sword Beach Lance Corporal Josef Häger, dazed and trembling, somehow found the trigger of his machine gun and began firing again. The earth seemed to be blowing up all about him. The noise was deafening. His head roared and the eighteen-year-old machine gunner was sick with fear. He had fought well, helping to cover the retreat of his company ever since the 716th Division's line broke back of Sword. How many Tommies he had hit Häger did not know. Fascinated, he had watched them come off the beach and had chopped them down one after another. Often in the past he had wondered what it would be like to kill the enemy. Many times he had talked about it with his friends Huf, Saxler and "Ferdi" Klug. Now Häger had found out: it was terribly easy. Huf hadn't lived long enough to discover how easy it was—he had been killed as they ran back. Häger had left him lying in a hedgerow, his mouth open, a hole where his forehead had been. Häger didn't know where Saxler was, but Ferdi was still beside him, half blind, blood running down his face from a shrapnel burst. And now Häger knew that it was only a question of time before they were all

killed. He and nineteen men—all that remained of the company
—were in a trench before a small bunker. They were being hit
from all sides by machine gun, mortar and rifle fire. They were
surrounded. It was either surrender or be killed. Everyone
knew this—everyone except the captain firing the machine gun
behind them in the bunker. He wouldn't let them in. "We must
hold! We must hold!" he kept yelling.

This was the most terrible time of Häger's life. He no longer
knew what he was firing at. Every time the shelling lifted he automatically pulled the trigger and felt the machine gun pound.
It gave him courage. Then the shelling would begin again and
everyone would yell at the captain, "Let us in! Let us in!"

Perhaps it was the tanks that made the captain change his
mind. They all heard the whirring and clanking. There were two
of them. One stopped a field away. The other ambled slowly
on, crushing its way across a hedge, passing three cows that
munched unconcernedly in a nearby meadow. Then the men in
the trench saw its gun slowly lower, ready to fire at point-blank
range. At that moment the tank suddenly, unbelievably blew
up. A bazooka man in the trench, down to his last bulbous-nosed
rocket projectile, had scored a direct hit. Spellbound, not quite
sure how it had all happened, Häger and his friend Ferdi
saw the hatch of the blazing tank open and through the billow-
ing black smoke a man desperately trying to climb out. Screaming, his clothes on fire, he got halfway through the opening and
then collapsed, his body hanging down the side of the tank.
Häger said to Ferdi, "I hope God gives us a better death."

The second tank, prudently remaining out of bazooka range,
began firing and at last the captain ordered everyone into the
bunker. Häger and the other survivors stumbled inside—into a
fresh nightmare. The bunker, barely the size of a living room,
was filled with dead and dying soldiers. More than thirty other
men in the bunker were so jammed together that they were unable to sit down or even turn about. It was hot and dark and

hideously noisy. The wounded were moaning. Men were talking in several different languages—many of them were Poles or Russians. And all the time, the captain, oblivious to the yells of the wounded to "Surrender! Surrender!" fired his machine gun through the single aperture.

For an instant there was a lull and Häger and the suffocating men in the bunker heard someone outside shout, "All right, Herman—you better come out!" The captain angrily began firing his machine gun. A few minutes later they heard the same voice again. *"You better give up, Fritz!"*

Men were coughing now from the acrid gaseous discharge of the captain's machine gun, which was fouling the already stifling atmosphere. Each time the captain stopped to reload the voice demanded that they surrender. Finally somebody outside called to them in German and Häger would always remember that one of the wounded, apparently using the only two words of English he knew, began chanting back, "Hello, boys! Hello, boys! Hello, boys!"

The firing outside stopped and it seemed to Häger that everyone realized almost at the same moment what was about to happen. There was a small peephole in a cupola over their heads. Häger and several others lifted a man up so that he could see what was happening. Suddenly he yelled, "Flame thrower! They're bringing up a flame thrower!"

Häger knew that the flames could not reach them because the metal air shaft which entered the bunker from the back was built in staggered sections. But the heat could kill them. Suddenly they heard the "woof" of the flame thrower. Now the only way that air could get into the bunker was through the narrow aperture, where the captain continued to blaze away with his machine gun, and through the peephole in the roof.

Gradually the temperature began to rise. Some men panicked. Clawing and pushing and yelling, "We've got to get out!" they tried to drop to the floor and burrow through the legs of the others toward the door. But, pinioned by the press of men around them, they were unable even to reach the floor. Everyone was now begging the captain to surrender. The captain, still firing, didn't even turn from the aperture. The air was getting indescribably foul.

"We'll all breathe in and out on my command," yelled a lieutenant. "*In! . . . Out! . . . In! . . . Out! . . .*" Häger watched the metal fairing of the air shaft go from pink to red and then to a glowing white. "*In! . . . Out! . . . In! . . . Out!*" yelled the officer. "Hello, boys! Hello, boys!" cried the wounded man. And at a radio set in one corner Häger could hear the operator saying over and over, "Come in, Spinach! Come in, Spinach!"

"Sir!" yelled the lieutenant. "The wounded are suffocating—we must surrender!"

"It's out of the question!" roared the captain. "We're going to fight our way out! Count the men and their weapons!"

"No! No!" men yelled from every corner of the bunker.

Ferdi said to Häger, "You're the only one besides the captain with a machine gun. That madman will send you out first, believe me."

By now, many of the men were defiantly pulling the bolts of their rifles and throwing them on the floor. "I won't go," Häger told Ferdi. He pulled the locking pin on his machine gun and threw it away.

Men began to collapse from the heat. Knees buckling, heads lolling, they remained in a partly upright position; they could not fall to the floor. The young lieutenant continued to plead with the captain, but to no avail. No one could get to the door, because the aperture was next to it and the captain was there with his machine gun.

Suddenly the captain stopped firing and turning to the radio operator he said, "Have you made contact?" The operator said, "Nothing, sir." It was then that the captain looked about him as though seeing the jam-packed bunker for the first time. He seemed dazed and bewildered. Then he threw down his machine gun and said resignedly, "Open the door."

Häger saw somebody stick a rifle with a piece of torn white cloth on it through the aperture. From outside a voice said, "All right, Fritz, out you come—one at a time!"

Gasping for air, dazzled by the light, the men reeled out of the dark bunker. If they did not drop their weapons and helmets fast enough, British troops standing on either side of the trench fired into the ground behind them. As they reached the end of the trench their captors cut their belts, laces and tunics and sliced the buttons off the flies of their pants. Then they were made to lie face downward in a field.

Häger and Ferdi ran down the trench, their hands in the air. As Ferdi's belt was cut, a British officer said to him, "In two weeks we'll be seeing your pals in Berlin, Fritz." Ferdi, his face bloody and puffed up from the shrapnel splinters, tried to joke. He said, "By that time we'll be in England." He meant that they would be in a prisoner-of-war camp, but the Britisher misunderstood. "Take these men to the beaches!" he roared. Holding up their pants, they were marched away, passing the still burning tank and the same cows munching quietly in the meadow.

Fifteen minutes later, Häger and the others were working among the obstacles in the surf, removing mines. Ferdi said to Häger, "I bet you never thought when you were putting these things in that one day you'd be taking them up again." *

Private Aloysius Damski had no heart for the fight at all. Damski, a Pole who had been impressed into the 716th Division,

* I was not able to locate the fanatical captain who tried to hold the bunker, but Häger believes that his name was Gundlach and that the junior officer was a Lieutenant Lutke. Later in the day Häger found his missing friend Saxler—he too was working among the obstacles. That night they were taken to England and six days later Häger and 150 other Germans landed in New York en route to a Canadian prisoner-of-war camp.

had long ago decided that if the invasion ever came he would
run up the ramp of the nearest landing craft and surrender. But
Damski didn't get the chance. The British landed under such a
fierce protective bombardment of naval and tank fire that Damski's battery commander, in a position near the western edge of
Gold Beach, promptly ordered a withdrawal. Damski realized
that to run forward would mean certain death—either at the
hands of the Germans behind or at those of the advancing
British ahead. But in the confusion of the withdrawal he struck
out for the village of Tracy, where he was billeted in the home of
an old French lady. If he stayed there, Damski reasoned, he
could surrender when the village was captured.

As he was making his way across the fields he ran into a hard-
bitten Wehrmacht sergeant on horseback. Marching ahead of
the sergeant was another private, a Russian. The sergeant
looked down at Damski and with a broad smile asked, "Now,
just where do you think you're going all by yourself?" They
looked at each other for a moment and Damski knew that the
sergeant had guessed he was running away. Then, still smiling,
the sergeant said, "I think you'd better come with us." Damski
wasn't surprised. As they marched off he bitterly thought that
his luck had never been good and that it certainly wasn't improving.

Ten miles away, roughly in the vicinity of Caen, Private
Wilhelm Voigt of a mobile radio monitoring unit was also wondering how he could surrender. Voigt had lived seventeen
years in Chicago, but he had never taken out naturalization papers. In 1939 his wife, visiting her home in Germany, had been
forced to stay because of an ailing mother. In 1940, against the
advice of friends, Voigt had set out to bring her home. Unable
to reach wartime Germany by regular routes, he had made a
tortuous journey across the Pacific to Japan, then to Vladivostok
and via the Trans-Siberian railway to Moscow. From there he
had traveled to Poland and into Germany. The journey took

nearly four months—and once across the border Voigt could not get out. He and his wife were trapped. Now, for the first time in four years, he could hear American voices in his earphones. For hours he had been planning what he would say when he saw the first U.S. troops. He was going to run up to them yelling, "Hi, you guys, I'm from Chicago!" But his unit was being held too far back. He had made almost a complete circle of the world just to get back to Chicago—and now all he could do was sit in his truck and listen to the voices, only a few short miles away,* that to him spelled home.

Behind Omaha Beach Major Werner Pluskat lay gasping in a ditch. He was almost unrecognizable. He had lost his helmet. His clothes were ripped and torn. His face was scratched and bloody. For more than an hour and a half, ever since he had left his bunker at Ste.-Honorine to return to his headquarters, Pluskat had been crawling through a burning, erupting no man's land. Scores of fighter planes, flying back and forth just behind the bluffs, were strafing everything that moved, and all the while naval gunfire was plowing up the area. His Volkswagen was somewhere behind him, a burning, twisted wreck. Smoke billowed up from burning hedgerows and grass fires. Here and there he had come across trenches filled with dead troops, blasted either by artillery or by the merciless strafing. At first he had tried to run, but he had been pounced on by the planes. Again and again he had been strafed. Now Pluskat crawled. He figured he had made just one mile and he was still three miles from his headquarters at Etreham. Painfully he moved on. Ahead he saw a farmhouse. He decided that when he came abreast of it he would sprint the twenty yards or so from the ditch and ask the occupants for a drink of water. As he drew near, he was amazed

* Voigt never did make it back. He still lives in Germany, where he works for Pan American Airways.

to see two Frenchwomen sitting calmly in the open door, as though immune from the shelling and strafing. They looked across at him and one, laughing spitefully, called out, *"C'est terrible, n'est-ce pas?"* Pluskat crawled past, the laughter still ringing in his ears. At that moment he hated the French, the Normans and the whole rotten stinking war.

Corporal Anton Wuensch of the 6th Parachute Regiment saw the parachute hanging high in the branches of a tree. It was blue and there was a large canvas container swinging below it. In the distance there was a lot of rifle and machine gun fire, but so far Wuensch and his mortar unit had seen nothing of the enemy. They had been marching for almost three hours and now they were in a small wood above Carentan, roughly ten miles southwest of Utah Beach.

Lance Corporal Richter looked at the parachute and said, "It belongs to the Amis [Americans]. Probably contains ammo." Private Fritz "Friedolin" Wendt thought there might be food in it. "God, I'm so hungry," he said. Wuensch told them all to stay in the ditch while he crawled forward. It might be a trick; they might be ambushed when they tried to get the container down, or it could be a booby trap.

Wuensch carefully reconnoitered ahead. Then, satisfied that everything was quiet, he tied two grenades around the tree trunk and pulled the pins. The tree crashed down and with it the parachute container. Wuensch waited, but apparently the explosions had gone unnoticed. He waved his unit in. "Let's see what the Amis have sent us," he yelled.

Friedolin ran forward with his knife and cut through the canvas. He was ecstatic. "Oh, my God," he yelled, "it's food! Food!"

For the next half hour the seven tough paratroopers had the time of their lives. They found cans of pineapple and orange juice, cartons of chocolate and cigarettes, and an assortment of foods the like of which they had not seen in years. Friedolin gorged himself. He even poured powdered Nescafé down his throat and tried to wash it down with condensed milk. "I don't know what it is," he said, "but it tastes wonderful."

Finally, over Friedolin's protest, Wuensch decided that they had better "move on and find the war." Stuffed, their pockets bulging with all the cigarettes they could carry, Wuensch and his men moved out of the wood and headed in single file toward the distant firing. Minutes later the war found them. One of Wuensch's men fell, shot through the temple.

"Sniper!" yelled Wuensch. Everyone dived for cover as shots began to whistle about them.

"Look," yelled one of the men, pointing toward a clump of trees off to the right, "I'm sure I saw him up there."

Wuensch took out his binoculars and, focusing his glasses on the treetops, began a careful search. He thought he saw a slight movement of the branches in one tree, but he wasn't sure. For a long time he held the glasses steady and then he saw the foliage move again. Picking up his rifle, he said, "Now we'll see who's the man and who's the fake." He fired.

At first Wuensch thought he had missed, for as he watched he saw the sniper climbing down the tree. Again Wuensch aimed, this time for a spot on the tree trunk which was clear of branches and foliage. "My boy," he said aloud, "I'm going to get you now." He saw the sniper's legs appear and then his torso. Wuensch fired, again and again. Very slowly the sniper fell backward out of the tree. Wuensch's men cheered and then everybody ran over to the body. They stood looking down at the first American paratrooper they had seen. "He was dark-haired, he was very handsome and very young. There was a trickle of blood at the side of his mouth," Wuensch recalls.

Lance Corporal Richter went through the dead man's pockets and found a wallet with two photographs and a letter. Wuensch remembers that one of them "showed the soldier sitting next to a girl and we all concluded that maybe it was his wife." The other was a snapshot "of the young man and the girl sitting on a veranda with a family, presumably his family." Richter began putting the photographs and the letter into his pocket.

Wuensch said, "What do you want to do that for?"

Richter said, "I thought I'd send this stuff to the address on the envelope after the war."

Wuensch thought he was crazy. "We may be captured by the Amis," he said, "and if they find this stuff on you . . ." He drew his finger across his throat. "Leave it for the medics," said Wuensch, "and let's get out of here."

As his men moved on, Wuensch remained for a moment and stared at the dead American, lying limp and still "like a dog who had been run over." He hurried after his men.

A few miles away a German staff car, its black, white and red pennant flying, raced along the secondary road leading toward the village of Picauville. Major General Wilhelm Falley of the 91st Air Landing Division, together with his aide and a driver, had been in his Horch for almost seven hours, ever since he set out for Rennes and the war games a little before 1 A.M. Sometime between 3 and 4 A.M., the continuous droning of planes and the distant explosions of bombs had caused the concerned Falley to turn back.

They were only a few miles from the headquarters north of Picauville when machine gun bullets ripped across the front of the car. The windshield shattered and Falley's aide, sitting beside the driver, slumped down in his seat. Swaying from side to side, tires screaming, the Horch swerved and smashed into a low wall. The doors flew open with the impact and the driver and Falley were hurled out. Falley's gun slithered out in front of him. He crawled across the road toward it. The driver, shaken and dazed, saw several American soldiers rushing up to the car. Falley was shouting, "Don't kill! Don't kill!" but he continued to crawl toward the gun. There was a shot and Falley collapsed in the road, one hand still stretched out toward the gun.

Lieutenant Malcolm Brannen of the 82nd Airborne looked down at the dead man. Then he stooped and picked up the officer's cap. Stenciled on the sweatband was the name "Falley." The German wore a greenish-gray uniform with red stripes down the seam of the trousers. There were narrow gold epaulets at the shoulders of his tunic and red tabs decorated with gold-braided oak leaves at the collar. An Iron Cross hung from a black ribbon around the man's neck. Brannen wasn't sure, but it looked to him as though he'd killed a general.

On the airfield near Lille, Wing Commander Josef "Pips" Priller and Sergeant Heinz Wodarczyk ran for their two solitary FW-190 fighter planes.

The Luftwaffe's 2nd Fighter Corps headquarters had telephoned. "Priller," the operations officer had said, "the invasion has started. You'd better get up there."

Priller had exploded: "Now you've dropped it! You damned fools! What the hell do you expect me to do with just two planes? Where are my squadrons? Can you call them back?"

The operations officer had remained perfectly cool. "Priller," he had said soothingly, "we don't know yet exactly where your squadrons have landed, but we're going to divert them back to the field at Poix. Move all your ground personnel there immediately. Meanwhile you better get up to the invasion area. Good luck, Priller."

As quietly as his anger would allow Priller had said, "Would you mind telling me where the invasion is?"

The officer, unruffled, had said, "Normandy, Pips—somewhere above Caen."

It had taken Priller the best part of an hour to make the necessary arrangements for the movement of his ground personnel. Now he and Wodarczyk were ready—ready to make the Luftwaffe's only daylight attack against the invasion.*

Just before they got into their planes, Priller went over to his wing man. "Now listen," he said, "there's just the two of us. We can't afford to break up. For God's sake, do exactly as I do. Fly behind me and follow every move." They had been together a long time and Priller felt he must make the situation quite clear. "We're going in alone," he said, "and I don't think we're coming back."

It was 9 A.M. when they took off (8 A.M. to Priller). They flew due west, hugging the ground. Just over Abbeville, high above them, they began to see Allied fighters. Priller noticed that they were not flying in tight formation as they should have been. He remembers thinking that "if I only had some planes, they'd be sitting ducks." As they approached Le Havre, Priller climbed for cover in the clouds. They flew for a few more minutes and then broke through. Below them was a fantastic fleet—hundreds of ships of every size and type, stretching endlessly, it seemed, all the way back across the Channel. There was a steady procession of landing craft carrying men toward shore, and Priller could see the white puffs of explosions on and behind the beaches. The sands were black with troops, and tanks and equipment of all sorts littered the shore line. Priller swept back into the clouds to consider what to do. There were so many planes, so many battleships offshore, so many men on the beaches, that he figured he'd have time for just one pass over the beaches before being shot down.

There was no need for radio silence now. Almost lightheartedly, Priller spoke into his microphone. "What a show! What a show!" he said. "There's everything out here—everywhere you

* In some accounts it has been written that eight JU-88 bombers attacked the beaches during the initial landings. Bombers were over the beachhead on the night of June 6–7, but there is no record that I could find of a D-Day morning raid other than Priller's fighter attack.

look. Believe me, this is the invasion!" Then he said, "Wodar-czyk, we're going in! Good luck!"

They hurtled down toward the British beaches at over 400 m.p.h., coming in at less than 150 feet. Priller had no time to aim. He simply pressed the button on his control stick and felt his guns pounding. Skimming along just over the tops of men's heads, he saw upturned, startled faces.

On Sword, Commander Philippe Kieffer of the French com-mandos saw Priller and Wodarczyk coming. He dived for cover. Six German prisoners took advantage of the confusion and tried to bolt. Kieffer's men promptly mowed them down. On Juno Private Robert Rogge of the Canadian 8th Infantry Brigade heard the scream of the planes and saw them "coming in so low that I could clearly see the pilots' faces." He threw himself flat like everyone else, but he was amazed to see one man "calmly standing up, blazing away with a Sten gun." On the eastern edge of Omaha, Lieutenant (j.g.) William J. Eisemann of the U.S. Navy gasped as the two FW-190s, guns chattering, zoomed down "at less than fifty feet and dodged through the barrage balloons." And on H.M.S. *Dunbar*, Leading Stoker Robert Dowie watched every antiaircraft gun in the fleet open up on Priller and Wodarczyk. The two fighters flew through it all unscathed, then turned inland and streaked up into the clouds. "Jerry or not," said Dowie, unbelievingly, "the best of luck to you. You've got guts."

★ 4 ★

ALL ALONG the Normandy coastline the invasion stormed. For the French, caught up in the battle, these were hours of chaos, elation and terror. Around Ste.-Mère-Église, which was now being heavily shelled, 82nd paratroopers saw farmers calmly working in the fields as though nothing were happening. Every now and then one of them would fall, either wounded or killed. In the town itself paratroopers watched the local barber remove the sign *"Friseur"* from the front of his shop and put up a new one that said "Barber."

A few miles away, in the little coastal hamlet of La Madeleine, Paul Gazengel was bitter and in pain. Not only had the roof of his store and café been blown off, but he had been wounded during the shelling, and now 4th Division troops were taking him and seven other men down to Utah Beach.

"Where are you taking my husband?" demanded his wife of the young lieutenant in charge.

The officer answered in perfect French. "For questioning, madame," he said. "We can't talk to him here, so we're taking him and all the other men to England."

Madame Gazengel couldn't believe her ears. "To England!" she exclaimed. "Why? What has he done?"

The young officer was embarrassed. Patiently he explained that he was simply carrying out instructions.

"What happens if my husband gets killed in the bombing?" asked Madame Gazengel tearfully.

"There's a ninety per cent chance that won't happen, madame," he said.

Gazengel kissed his wife goodbye and was marched off. He had no idea what it was all about—and he never would find out. Two weeks later he would be back in Normandy, with the lame excuse from his American captors that "it was all a mistake."

Jean Marion, French underground sector chief in the seaside town of Grandcamp, was frustrated. He could see the fleet off Utah Beach to his left and Omaha Beach to his right and he knew troops were landing. But it looked to him as though Grandcamp had been forgotten. All morning he had waited in vain for soldiers to come in. But he was heartened when his wife pointed out a destroyer that was slowly maneuvering opposite the town. "The gun!" exclaimed Marion. "The gun I told them about!" A few days earlier he had informed London that a small artillery piece had been mounted on the sea wall, sited so that it would fire only to the left, in the direction of what was now Utah Beach. Now Marion was sure that his message had been received, for he saw the destroyer carefully move into position on the gun's blind side and commence firing. With tears in his eyes Marion jumped up and down each time the destroyer fired. "They got the message!" he cried. "They got the message!" The destroyer—which may have been the *Herndon*—blasted the artillery piece with round after round. Suddenly there was a violent explosion as the gun's ammunition blew up. "*Merveilleux!*" yelled the excited Marion. "*Magnifique!*"

In the cathedral town of Bayeux, roughly fifteen miles away, Guillaume Mercader, the underground intelligence chief for the Omaha Beach area, stood at the window of his living room with his wife Madeleine. Mercader was having a hard time fighting back his tears. After four terrible years, the main body of German troops billeted in the town seemed to be pulling out. He could hear the cannonading in the distance and he knew that heavy fighting must be taking place. Now he had a strong urge to organize his resistance fighters and drive the remainder of the Nazis out. But the radio had warned them to be calm, that there must be no uprising. It was difficult, but Mercader had learned to wait. "We'll be free soon," he told his wife.

Everyone in Bayeux seemed to feel the same way. Although the Germans had posted notices ordering the townspeople to stay indoors, people had gathered quite openly in the cathedral courtyard to hear a running commentary on the invasion from one of the priests. From his vantage point he could clearly see the beaches; hands cupped around his mouth he was yelling down from the belfry of the steeple.

Among those who heard of the invasion from the priest was Anne Marie Broeckx, the nineteen-year-old kindergarten teacher who would find her future husband among the American invaders. At seven she had calmly set out on her bicycle for her father's farm at Colleville, back of Omaha Beach. Pedaling furiously, she had cycled past German machine gun positions and troops marching toward the coast. Some Germans had waved to her and one had warned her to be careful, but nobody stopped her. She had seen planes strafing and Germans diving for cover, but Anne Marie, her tresses flying in the wind and her blue skirt ballooning around her, kept on. She felt perfectly safe; it never dawned on her that her life was in danger.

Now she was less than a mile from Colleville. The roads were deserted. Clouds of smoke drifted inland. Here and there fires were burning. Then she saw the wreckage of several farmhouses. For the first time Anne Marie felt frightened. Frantically she raced on. By the time she reached the crossroads at Colleville she was thoroughly alarmed. The thunder of gunfire rolled all about her and the entire area seemed strangely desolated and uninhabited. Her father's farm lay between Colleville and the beach. Anne Marie decided to continue on foot. Hitching her bicycle over her shoulder, she hiked across the fields. Then, topping a little rise, she saw the farmhouse—still standing. She ran the remainder of the way.

At first Anne Marie thought the farm was deserted, for she could see no movement. Calling to her parents, she dashed into the little farmyard. The windows of the house had been blown out. Part of the roof had disappeared and there was a gaping hole in the door. Suddenly the wrecked door opened and there stood her father and mother. She threw her arms around both of them.

"My daughter," said her father, "this is a great day for France." Anne Marie burst into tears.

Half a mile away, fighting for his life amid the horrors of Omaha Beach, was nineteen-year-old P.F.C. Leo Heroux, the man who would marry Anne Marie.*

While the Allied attack raged in Normandy, one of the region's top underground officials was fuming on a train just outside Paris. Léonard Gille, Normandy's deputy military intelligence chief, had been riding the Paris-bound train for more than twelve hours. The journey seemed interminable. They had crawled through the night, stopping at every station. Now, ironically, the intelligence chief had heard the news from one of the porters. Gille had no idea where in Normandy the assault had taken place, but he could hardly wait to get back to Caen. He was bitter that after all the years of work, his superiors had chosen this of all days to order him to the capital. Worse, there was no way now for him to get off the train. The next stop was Paris.

But back in Caen his fiancée, Janine Boitard, had been busy ever since she had heard the news. At seven she had roused the two R.A.F. pilots she was hiding. "We must hurry," she told

* Anne Marie is one war bride who does not live in the U.S. She and Leo Heroux now live where they first met on June 8—at the Broeckx farm near Colleville back of Omaha Beach. They have three children and Heroux runs an auto-driving school.

them. "I'm taking you to a farm in the village of Gavrus, twelve kilometers from here."

Their destination came as a shock to the two Britishers. Freedom was only ten short miles away, yet they were going to head inland. Gavrus lay southwest of Caen. One of the Britishers, Wing Commander K. T. Lofts, thought they should take a chance and go north to meet the troops.

"Be patient," said Janine. "The area between here and the coast is swarming with Germans. It will be safer to wait."

Shortly after seven they set out on bicycles, the two Britishers dressed in rough farm clothes. The journey was uneventful. Although they were stopped several times by German patrols, their fake identity papers stood the test and they were passed on. At Gavrus, Janine's responsibility ended—two more fliers were a step closer to home. Janine would have liked to have gone farther with them, but she had to return to Caen—to wait for the next downed pilots who would pass along the escape route, and the moment of liberation that she knew was close. Waving goodbye, she jumped on her bicycle and cycled off.

In the prison at Caen, Madame Amélie Lechevalier, expecting to be executed for her part in saving Allied pilots, heard a whisper as the tin plate with her breakfast was slid under the cell door. "Hope, hope," said the voice. "The British have landed." Madame Lechevalier began to pray. She wondered if her husband, Louis, in a cell nearby, had heard the news. All night there had been explosions, but she had thought that it was the usual Allied bombing. Now there was a chance; maybe they would be saved before it was too late.

Suddenly Madame Lechevalier heard a commotion in the corridor. She got down on her knees by the slit beneath the door and listened. She could hear shouting and the word "*Raus! Raus!* [Out! Out!]" repeated over and over. Then there was the tramping of feet, the slamming of cell doors and then silence again. A few minutes later, somewhere outside the prison she heard prolonged machine gun fire.

The Gestapo guards had panicked. Within minutes of the news of the landings, two machine guns had been set up in the prison courtyard. In groups of ten the male prisoners were led out, placed against the wall and executed. They had been picked up on a variety of charges, some true, some false. There were Guy de Saint Pol and René Loslier, farmers; Pierre Audige, a dentist; Maurice Primault, a shop assistant; Colonel Antoine de Touchet, a retired officer; Anatole Lelièvre, the town hall secretary; Georges Thomine, a fisherman; Pierre Menochet, a policeman; Maurice Dutacq, Achille Boutrois, Joseph Picquenot and his son, French railway workers; Albert Anne; Désiré Lemière; Roger Veillat; Robert Boulard—ninety-two in all, of whom only forty were members of the French underground. On this day, the day that began the great liberation, these men, without explanation, without a hearing, without a trial, were slaughtered. Among them was Madame Lechevalier's husband, Louis.

The firing went on for an hour. In her cell Madame Lechevalier wondered what was happening.

★ 5 ★

I_N ENGLAND it was 9:30 A.M. All night General Eisenhower had paced the floor of his trailer, waiting for the reports to come in. He had tried to relax in his usual manner by reading Westerns, but with little success. Then the first messages began to arrive. They were fragmentary, but the news was good. His air and naval commanders were more than satisfied with the progress of the attack and troops were ashore on all five beaches. Overlord was going well. Although the foothold was slight, there would be no need now for him to release the communiqué he had quietly scribbled just twenty-four hours before. In case the attempt to land troops was defeated, he had written: "Our landings in the Cherbourg-Havre area have failed to gain a satisfactory foothold and I have withdrawn the troops. My decision to attack at this time and place was based upon the best information available. The troops, the air and Navy did all that bravery and devotion to duty could do. If there is any blame or fault attached to the attempt, it is mine alone."

Certain that his troops were ashore on the invasion beaches, Eisenhower had authorized the release of a far different communiqué. At 9:33 A.M. his press aide, Colonel Ernest Dupuy, broadcast the news to the world. "Under the command of General Eisenhower," he said, "Allied naval forces, supported by strong air forces, began landing Allied armies this morning on the northern coast of France."

This was the moment the free world had been waiting for— and now that it had come people responded with a curious mixture of relief, exhilaration and anxiety. "At last," said the London *Times* in a D-Day editorial, "the tension has broken."

Most Britons heard the news at work. In some war plants the bulletin was read out over loud-speakers and men and women stood back from their lathes and sang "God Save the King." Village churches threw open their doors. Total strangers talked to one another on commuter trains. On city streets civilians walked up to American soldiers and shook hands. Small crowds gathered on corners to gaze upward at the heaviest air traffic Britons had ever seen.

Wren Lieutenant Naomi Coles Honour, wife of the skipper of

the midget sub X23, heard the news and immediately knew where her husband was. Sometime later she got a call from one of the operations officers at naval headquarters: "George is all right, but you'll never guess what he's been up to." Naomi could hear all that later; the important thing now was that he was safe.

The mother of eighteen-year-old Able Seaman Ronald Northwood of the flagship *Scylla* got so excited she ran across the street to tell her neighbor Mrs. Spurdgeon that "my Ron must be there." Mrs. Spurdgeon wasn't to be outdone. She had "a relative on the *Warspite*" and she was certain he was there too. (With minor variations the same conversation was taking place all over England.)

Grace Gale, wife of Private John Gale, who had landed in the first wave on Sword Beach, was bathing the youngest of their three children when she heard the bulletin. She tried to hold back her tears, but couldn't—she was certain that her husband was in France. "Dear God," she whispered, "bring him back." Then she told her daughter Evelyn to turn off the radio. "We're not going to let your dad down by worrying," she said.

In the cathedral-like atmosphere of the Westminster Bank at Bridgeport in Dorset, Audrey Duckworth was hard at work and didn't hear about the assault until much later in the day. It was just as well. Her American husband, Captain Edmund Duckworth of the 1st Division, had been killed as he stepped onto Omaha Beach. They had been married just five days.

En route to Eisenhower's headquarters at Portsmouth, Lieutenant General Sir Frederick Morgan heard the BBC warn listeners to stand by for a special announcement. Morgan told his driver to stop the car for a moment. He turned up the volume on his radio—and then the author of the original invasion plan heard the news of the attack.

For most of the United States the report came in the middle of the night; on the East Coast it was 3:33 A.M., on the West Coast 12:33 A.M. Most people were asleep, but among the first to hear of D Day were the thousands working on the swing shifts, the men and women who had toiled to produce most of the guns, tanks, ships and planes that were being used in the assault. Everywhere in the great pulsing war plants work stopped for a moment of solemn meditation. In a Brooklyn shipyard, under the harsh glare of arc lamps, hundreds of men and women knelt down on the decks of partially finished Liberty ships and began to say the Lord's Prayer.

Across the nation, in sleeping towns and villages, lights flashed on. Quiet streets suddenly filled with sound as radios were turned up. People woke their neighbors to tell them the news, and so many phoned friends and relatives that telephone switchboards were jammed. In Coffeyville, Kansas, men and women in their night attire knelt on porches and prayed. On a train between Washington and New York a clergyman was asked to hold an impromptu service. In Marietta, Georgia, people thronged into churches at 4 A.M. The Liberty Bell was rung in Philadelphia, and throughout historic Virginia, the home of the 29th Division, church bells tolled in the night just as they had during the Revolution. In little Bedford, Virginia (population 3,800), the news had a special significance. Nearly everyone had a son, brother, sweetheart or husband in the 29th. In Bedford they did not know it yet, but all of their men had landed on Omaha Beach. Out of forty-six Bedford men in the 116th Regiment, only twenty-three would come home again.

Wave Ensign Lois Hoffman, wife of the skipper of the *Corry*, was on duty at the Norfolk, Virginia, naval base when she heard about D Day. From time to time she had kept track of her husband's destroyer through friends in the operations room. The news had no personal significance for her. She still believed her husband was escorting a munitions convoy in the North Atlantic.

In San Francisco, Mrs. Lucille M. Schultz, a nurse at the Veterans Hospital at Fort Miley, was on night duty when the first announcement was made. She wanted to stay by the radio in the hope that the 82nd Airborne would be mentioned; she suspected the division was in the assault. But she was also afraid the radio might excite her cardiac patient, a World War I veteran. He wanted to listen to the reports. "I wish I was there," he said. "You've had your war," said Nurse Schultz as she turned off the radio. Sitting in the darkness, weeping silently, she said the Rosary over and over for her twenty-one-year-old paratrooper son, Arthur, better known to the 505th Regiment as Private Dutch Schultz.

At her home on Long Island, Mrs. Theodore Roosevelt had slept fitfully. About 3 A.M. she awoke and could not get back to sleep. Automatically she turned on the radio—just in time to catch the official D-Day announcement. She knew that it was characteristic of her husband to be somewhere in the thick of the fighting. She did not know that she was probably the only woman in the nation to have a husband on Utah Beach and a son—twenty-five-year-old Captain Quentin Roosevelt of the 1st Division—on Omaha Beach. Sitting up in bed, she closed her eyes and said an old and familiar family prayer: "O Lord support us this day . . . until the shadows lengthen and the evening falls."

In Stalag 17B near Krems, Austria, the news was received with a rejoicing that could hardly be contained. U.S. Air Force enlisted men had picked up the electrifying announcement on tiny handmade crystal sets, some of them built to fit in toothbrush holders, others camouflaged to look like lead pencils. Staff Sergeant James Lang, who had been shot down over Germany more than a year before, was almost afraid to believe the report. The camp's "news monitoring committee" tried to warn the four thousand POWs against overoptimism. "Don't get your hopes up," they cautioned. "Give us time to verify or deny." But in barracks after barracks men were already at work drawing secret maps of the Normandy coast on which they intended to plot the victorious advance of the Allied armies.

At this time the prisoners of war knew more about the invasion than the German people. So far the man in the street had heard nothing officially. It was ironic, because Radio Berlin, beating the Eisenhower communiqué by three hours, had been the first to announce the Allied landings. From six-thirty on, the Germans had showered a somewhat doubting world with a steady stream of newscasts. These short-wave broadcasts could not be heard by the German public. Still, thousands had learned of the landings from other sources. Although listening to foreign broadcasts was forbidden and punishable by a stiff prison term, some Germans had tuned in Swiss, Swedish or Spanish stations. The news had spread swiftly. Many of those who did hear it were skeptical. But there were some, particularly women with husbands in Normandy, who got the report and were deeply concerned. One of these was Frau Werner Pluskat.

She had planned to go to a movie in the afternoon with Frau Sauer, another officer's wife. But when she heard that the Allies were rumored to have landed in Normandy, she became almost hysterical. Immediately she called Frau Sauer, who had also heard something about the attack, and canceled the movie date. "I must know what has happened to Werner," she said. "I may never see him again."

Frau Sauer was very abrupt and very Prussian. "You shouldn't act like this!" snapped Frau Sauer. "You should believe in the Führer and act like a good officer's wife."

Frau Pluskat shot back, "I'll never talk to you again!" Then she slammed down the phone.

In Berchtesgaden it almost seemed as though the men around Hitler had waited for the official Allied communiqué before daring to break the news to him. It was about 10 A.M. (9 A.M. German time) when Hitler's naval aide, Admiral Karl Jesko von Puttkamer, called Jodl's office for the latest report. He was told that there were "definite indications that an important landing has taken place." Gathering all the information he could, Puttkamer and his staff quickly prepared a map. Then Major General Rudolf Schmundt, the Führer's adjutant, awakened Hitler. He was in a dressing gown when he came out of his bedroom. He listened calmly to the report of his aides and then sent for OKW's Chief, Field Marshal Wilhelm Keitel, and Jodl. By the time they arrived Hitler was dressed and waiting—and excited.

The conference that followed was, as Puttkamer recalls, "extremely agitated." Information was scanty, but on the basis of what was known Hitler was convinced that this was not the main invasion, and he kept repeating that over and over again. The conference lasted only a few minutes and ended abruptly, as Jodl was later to remember, when Hitler suddenly thundered at him and Keitel, "Well, is it or isn't it the invasion?" and then turned on his heel and left the room.

The subject of the release of the OKW panzer divisions, which Von Rundstedt so urgently needed, did not even come up.

At ten-fifteen the phone rang in Field Marshal Erwin Rommel's home at Herrlingen. The caller was his chief of staff, Major General Hans Speidel. The purpose: the first complete briefing on the invasion.* Rommel listened, shocked and shaken.

It was not a "Dieppe-type raid." With all the canny instinct that had served him so well for most of his life, Rommel knew that it was the day he had been waiting for—the one he had said would be "the longest day." He waited patiently until

---

* General Speidel has told me that he called Rommel "around 6 A.M. on a private wire." He says the same thing in his own book *Invasion 1944*. But General Speidel had his times confused. For example, his book states that the Field Marshal left La Roche-Guyon on June 5—not on June 4, as Captain Hellmuth Lang and Colonel Hans George von Tempelhof have stated and as the Army Group B War Diary records. On D Day the diary lists only one call to Rommel: the 10:15 A.M. call. The entry reads: "Speidel informs Field Marshal Rommel by phone on the situation. Commander in Chief Army Group B is going to return to his headquarters today."

Speidel had finished the report and then he said quietly, with no tinge of emotion in his voice, "How stupid of me. How stupid of me."

He turned from the phone and Frau Rommel saw that "the call had changed him . . . there was a terrible tension." During the next forty-five minutes, Rommel twice called his aide, Captain Hellmuth Lang, at his home near Strasbourg. Each time he gave Lang a different hour for their return to La Roche-Guyon. That in itself worried Lang; it was unlike the Field Marshal to be so undecisive. "He sounded terribly depressed on the phone," Lang recalls, "and that was not like him, either." The departure time was finally set. "We will leave at one o'clock sharp from Freudenstadt," Rommel told his aide. As Lang hung up the phone he reasoned that Rommel was delaying their departure in order to see Hitler. He did not know that at Berchtesgaden no one but Hitler's adjutant, Major General Schmundt, was even aware that Rommel was in Germany.

★ 6 ★

O N UTAH BEACH the roar of trucks, tanks, half-tracks and jeeps almost drowned out the sporadic whine of German 88s. It was the noise of victory; the 4th Division was moving inland faster than anyone had anticipated.

On Exit 2, the only open causeway running in from the beach, two men stood directing the flood of traffic. Both were generals.

On one side of the road stood Major General Raymond O. Barton, commander of the 4th Division, on the other the boyishly exuberant Brigadier General Teddy Roosevelt. As Major Gerden Johnson of the 12th Infantry Regiment came up he saw Roosevelt "stomping up and down the dusty road, leaning on his cane and smoking his pipe almost as unperturbed as though he were in the middle of Times Square." Roosevelt spotted Johnson and yelled, "Hi, Johnny! Keep right on this road, you're doing fine! It's a great day for hunting, isn't it?" It was a triumphant moment for Roosevelt. His decision to bring the 4th in two thousand yards from the planned touch-down point could have been disastrous. Now he watched the long lines of vehicles and men moving inland and felt an immense personal satisfaction.*

But Barton and Roosevelt, despite their air of unconcern, shared a secret fear: Unless the traffic could be kept constantly moving, the 4th could be stopped dead in its tracks by a determined German counterattack. Again and again the two generals unsnarled traffic jams. Stalled trucks were ruthlessly pushed off the road. Here and there blazing vehicles, victims of enemy shells, threatened to halt the advance. Tanks bulldozed them into the inundated area where troops were sloshing inland. About 11 A.M. Barton got the good news: Exit 3, just one mile away, was open. To ease the pressure Barton immediately sent his tanks rumbling off in the direction of the newly opened exit. The 4th was rolling, rushing toward the link-up with the hard-pressed paratroopers.

When it came, the link-up was unspectacular—lone men meeting one another in unexpected places, often with humorous and emotional results. Corporal Louis Merlano of the 101st may well have been the first airborne soldier to encounter troops of the 4th Division. With two other paratroopers, Merlano, who had

* For his performance on Utah Roosevelt was awarded the Congressional Medal of Honor. On July 12 General Eisenhower confirmed his appointment as the 90th Division's commanding general. Roosevelt never learned of the appointment. He died that same evening of a heart attack.

landed among the beach obstacles just above the original Utah Beach, had fought his way almost two miles down the coast. He was tired, dirty and battered when he met the 4th Division soldiers. He stared at them for a moment and then asked irritably, "Where the hell have you guys been?"

Sergeant Thomas Bruff of the 101st watched a 4th Division scout come off the causeway near Pouppeville, "carrying his rifle like a squirrel gun." The scout looked at the weary Bruff. "Where's the war?" he inquired. Bruff, who had landed eight miles from his drop zone and had fought all night with a small group under the command of General Maxwell Taylor, growled at the soldier, "Anywhere from here on back. Keep going, buddy, you'll find it."

Near Audouville-la-Hubert, Captain Thomas Mulvey of the 101st was hurrying toward the coast along a dirt road when "a soldier with a rifle popped into view from the edge of the bushes, about seventy-five yards ahead." Both men dived for cover. Cautiously they emerged, rifles ready, and in wary silence stared at each other. The other man demanded that Mulvey drop his rifle and advance with arms raised. Mulvey suggested that the stranger do the same. "This," says Mulvey, "went on for several gorounds, with neither of us giving an inch." Finally Mulvey, who could now see that the other man was a U.S. soldier, stood up. The two met in the middle of the road, shook hands and slapped each other on the back.

In Ste.-Marie-du-Mont, Pierre Caldron, the baker, saw paratroopers high in the steeple of the church waving a big orange identification panel. Within a few moments a long line of men, marching in single file, came down the road. As the 4th Division passed through, Caldron lifted his little son high on his shoulders. The boy was not fully recovered from his tonsillectomy of the day before, but this was a sight Caldron did not want his son to miss. Suddenly the baker found himself crying. A stocky U.S. soldier grinned at Caldron and shouted, "*Vive la France!*" Caldron smiled back, nodding his head. He could not trust himself to speak.

Out of the Utah Beach area the 4th Division poured inland. Their D-Day losses were light: 197 casualties, sixty of whom were lost at sea. Terrible fighting lay ahead for the 4th in the next weeks, but this was their day. By evening 22,000 men and 1,800 vehicles would be ashore. With the paratroopers, the 4th Division had secured the first major American beachhead in France.

Savagely, inch by inch, men fought their way off Bloody Omaha. From the sea the beach presented an incredible picture of waste and destruction. The situation was so critical that at noon General Omar Bradley aboard the *Augusta* began to contemplate the possible evacuation of his troops and the diversion of follow-up forces to Utah and the British beaches. But even as Bradley wrestled with the problem, the men in the chaos of Omaha were moving.

Along Dog Green and Dog White, a crusty fifty-one-year-old general named Norman Cota strode up and down in the hail of fire, waving a .45 and yelling at men to get off the beach. Along the shingle, behind the sea wall and in the coarse beach grass at the base of the bluffs, men crouched shoulder to shoulder, peering at the General, unwilling to believe that a man could stand upright and live.

A group of Rangers lay huddled near the Vierville exit. "Lead the way, Rangers!" Cota shouted. Men began to rise to their feet. Farther down the beach was an abandoned bulldozer loaded with TNT. It was just what was needed to blow the antitank wall at the Vierville exit. "Who drives this thing?" he thundered. No one answered. Men seemed still paralyzed by the merciless gunfire that flayed the beach. Cota began to lose his temper.

"Hasn't anyone got guts enough to drive the damn thing?" he roared.

A red-haired soldier got slowly up from the sand and with great deliberation walked over to Cota. "I'll do it," he said.

Cota slapped him on the back. "That's the stuff," the General said. "Now let's get off the beach." He walked away without looking back. Behind him, men began to stir.

This was the pattern. Brigadier General Cota, the 29th Division's assistant commander, had been setting an example almost from the moment he arrived on the beach. He had taken the right half of the 29th's sector; Colonel Charles D. Canham, commanding the 116th, had taken the left. Canham, a bloody handkerchief tied around a wrist wound, moved through the dead, the dying and the shocked, waving groups of men forward. "They're murdering us here!" he said. "Let's move inland and get murdered!" P.F.C. Charles Ferguson looked up in amazement as the Colonel went by. "Who the hell is that son of a bitch?" he asked and then he and the other men with him got up and headed toward the bluffs.

In the 1st Division's half of Omaha Beach, the veterans of Sicily and Salerno came out of the shock faster. Sergeant Raymond Strojny rallied his men and led them up the bluffs through a mine field. On top he knocked out a pillbox with a bazooka. Strojny had become "just a little mad." A hundred yards away Sergeant Philip Streczyk had had his fill of being pinned down, too. Some soldiers remember that Streczyk almost booted men off the beach and up the mined headlands, where he breached the enemy barbed wire. A short while later, Captain Edward Wozenski met Streczyk on a trail running down the bluffs. Horrified, Wozenski saw Streczyk step on a Teller mine. Streczyk said coolly, "It didn't go off when I stepped on it going up, either, Captain."

Ranging up and down the 1st Division sector, oblivious to the artillery and machine gun fire that raked the sands, was the

16th's commanding officer, Colonel George A. Taylor. "Two kinds of people are staying on this beach," he yelled, "the dead and those who are going to die. Now let's get the hell out of here."

Everywhere intrepid leaders, privates and generals alike, were showing the way, getting the men off the beach. Once started, the troops did not stop again. Technical Sergeant William Wiedefeld, Jr., stepped over the dead bodies of a score of his friends and, with face set, went up the hill through the mine fields. Second Lieutenant Donald Anderson, nursing a wound— he had been shot in the back of the neck and the bullet had come out through his mouth—found that he had "the courage to get up, and at that point I changed from a rookie in combat to a veteran." Sergeant Bill Courtney of the 2nd Rangers climbed to the top of a ridge and yelled down to his squad, "Come on up! The s.o.b.s are cleaned out!" Immediately there was a burst of machine gun fire to his left. Courtney wheeled, hurled a couple of grenades and then yelled again, "Come on! Come on! The s.o.b.s are cleaned out *now!*"

Even as the troops began to advance, the first few landing craft began driving right up on the beaches, ramming their way through the obstacles. Coxswains on other boats saw it could be done and followed. Some destroyers, backing up the advance, came so close to the shore that they ran the risk of foundering and, at point-blank range, fired at enemy strong-points all along the bluffs. Under the covering barrage, engineers began to complete the demolition job they had begun almost seven hours earlier. Everywhere along Omaha Beach the deadlock was breaking up.

As the men found it possible to move forward, their fear and frustration gave way to an overpowering anger. Near the top of the Vierville bluff, Ranger P.F.C. Carl Weast and his company commander, Captain George Whittington, spotted a machine gun nest manned by three Germans. As Weast and the captain circled it cautiously, one of the Germans suddenly turned, saw the two Americans and yelled, *"Bitte! Bitte! Bitte!"* Whittington fired, killing all three. Turning to Weast he said, "I wonder what *bitte* means."

Out of the horror that had been Omaha Beach troops pressed inland. At one-thirty General Bradley would receive the message: "Troops formerly pinned down on beaches Easy Red, Easy Green, Fox Red advancing up heights behind beaches." By the end of the day men of the 1st and 29th divisions would be one mile inland. The cost on Omaha: an estimated 2,500 dead, wounded and missing.

★ 7 ★

IT WAS 1 P.M. when Major Werner Pluskat got back to his headquarters at Etreham. The apparition that came through the door bore little resemblance to the commander his officers knew. Pluskat was shivering like a man with the palsy, and all he could say was, "Brandy. Brandy." When it came his hands shook so uncontrollably that he was almost unable to lift the glass.

One of his officers said, "Sir, the Americans have landed." Pluskat glared and waved him away. His staff crowded around him, one problem uppermost in their minds. The batteries, they informed Pluskat, would soon be low on ammunition. The matter had been reported to regiment, he was told, and Lieutenant Colonel Ocker had said that supplies were on the way. But nothing had arrived as yet. Pluskat rang Ocker.

"My dear Plus," came Ocker's airy voice over the wire, "are you still alive?"

Pluskat ignored the question. "What's happening about the ammunition?" he asked bluntly.

"It's on the way," said Ocker.

The colonel's calmness maddened Pluskat. "When?" he shouted. "When will it arrive? You people don't seem to realize what it's like up here."

Ten minutes later Pluskat was summoned to the phone. "I've got bad news," Ocker told him. "I've just learned that the ammunition convoy has been wiped out. It will be nightfall before anything gets up to you."

Pluskat wasn't surprised; he knew from bitter personal experience that nothing could move along the roads. He also knew that at the rate his guns were firing, the batteries would be out of ammunition by nightfall. The question was, which would reach his guns first—the ammunition or the Americans? Pluskat gave orders for his troops to prepare for close combat and then he wandered aimlessly through the château. He felt suddenly useless and alone. He wished he knew where his dog Harras was.

★ 8 ★

By now the British soldiers who had fought D Day's first battle had been holding on to their prize, the bridges over the Orne and the Caen Canal, for more than thirteen hours. Although Major Howard's glider-borne troops had been reinforced at

292

dawn by other 6th Airborne paratroopers, their numbers had been steadily dwindling under fierce mortar and small-arms fire. Howard's men had stopped several small, probing counterattacks. Now the tired, anxious troopers in the captured German positions on either side of the bridge eagerly awaited the link-up from the sea.

In his foxhole near the approaches to the Caen Canal bridge, Private Bill Gray looked at his watch again. Lord Lovat's commandos were almost an hour and a half overdue. He wondered what had happened back up on the beaches. Gray didn't think the fighting could be much worse there than it was at the bridges. He was almost afraid to lift his head; it seemed to him the snipers were becoming more accurate by the minute.

It was during a lull in the firing that Gray's friend, Private John Wilkes, lying beside him, suddenly said, "You know, I think I hear bagpipes." Gray looked at him scornfully. "You're daft," he said. A few seconds later, Wilkes turned to his friend again. "I do hear bagpipes," he insisted. Now Gray could hear them too.

Down the road came Lord Lovat's commandos, cocky in their green berets. Bill Millin marched at the head of the column, his pipes blaring out "Blue Bonnets over the Border." On both sides the firing suddenly ceased, as soldiers gazed at the spectacle. But the shock didn't last long. As the commandos headed across the bridges the Germans began firing again. Bill Millin remembers that he was "just trusting to luck that I did not get hit, as I could not hear very much for the drone of the pipes." Halfway across, Millin turned around to look at Lord Lovat. "He was striding along as if he was out for a walk round his estate," Millin recalls, "and he gave me the signal to carry on."

Disregarding the heavy German fire, the paratroopers rushed out to greet the commandos. Lovat apologized "for being a few minutes late." To the weary 6th Airborne troopers, it was a stirring moment. Although it would be hours before the main body

293

of British troops reached the farthermost points of the defense line held by the paratroopers, the first reinforcements had arrived. As the red and green berets intermingled, there was a sudden, perceptible lightening of the spirits. Nineteen-year-old Bill Gray felt "years younger."

★ 9 ★

Now, on this fateful day for Hitler's Third Reich, as Rommel raced frantically for Normandy, as his commanders on the invasion front tried desperately to halt the storming Allied assault, everything depended on the panzers: the 21st Panzer Division just behind the British beaches, and the 12th S.S. and the *Panzer Lehr* still held back by Hitler.

Field Marshal Rommel watched the white ribbon of road stretching out ahead and urged his driver on. *"Tempo! Tempo! Tempo!"* he said. The car roared as Daniel put his foot down. They had left Freudenstadt just two hours before and Rommel had uttered hardly a word. His aide, Captain Lang, sitting in back, had never seen the Field Marshal so depressed. Lang wanted to talk about the landings, but Rommel showed no inclination for conversation. Suddenly Rommel turned around and looked at Lang. "I was right all along," he said, "all along." Then he stared at the road again.

The 21st Panzer Division couldn't get through Caen. Colonel Hermann von Oppeln-Bronikowski, commanding the division's regiment of tanks, drove up and down the column in a Volkswagen. The city was a shambles. It had been bombed some time earlier and the bombers had done a good job. Streets were piled up with debris, and it seemed to Bronikowski that "everyone in the city was on the move trying to get out." The roads were choked with men and women on bicycles. There was no hope for the panzers. Bronikowski decided to pull back and go around the city. It would take hours, he knew, but there was no other way. And where was the regiment of troops that was supposed to support his attack when he did get through?

Nineteen-year-old Private Walter Hermes of the 21st Panzer Division's 192nd Regiment had never been so happy. It was glorious. He was leading the attack against the British! Hermes sat astride his motorcycle, weaving ahead of the advance company. They were heading toward the coast and soon they would pick up the tanks and then the 21st would drive the British into the sea. Everybody said so. Nearby on other motorcycles were his friends, Tetzlaw, Mattusch and Schard. All of them had expected to be attacked by the British before now, but nothing had happened. It seemed strange that they hadn't caught up with the tanks yet. But Hermes guessed that they must be somewhere ahead, probably attacking already on the coast. Hermes drove happily on, leading the advance company of the regiment up into the eight-mile gap that the British commandos still hadn't closed between Juno and Gold. This was a gap the panzers could have exploited to split the British beaches wide open and menace the entire Allied assault—a gap that Colonel von Oppeln-Bronikowski knew nothing whatever about.

In Paris at OB West, Major General Blumentritt, Rundstedt's chief of staff, called Speidel at Rommel's headquarters. The one-sentence conversation was duly recorded in Army Group B's War Diary. "OKW," said Blumentritt, "has released the 12th S.S. and *Panzer Lehr* divisions." The time was 3:40 P.M. Both generals knew that it was too late. Hitler and his senior officers had held up the two panzer divisions for more than ten hours. There was no hope of either division reaching the invasion area on this vital day. The 12th S.S. would not get to the beachhead until the morning of June 7. The *Panzer Lehr*, almost decimated by continuous air attacks, would not arrive until the ninth. The only chance of catching the Allied assault off balance now lay with the 21st Panzer Division.

Close on 6 P.M., Rommel's Horch pulled up in Rheims. In the city commander's headquarters Lang placed a call to La Roche-Guyon. Rommel spent fifteen minutes on the phone, getting a briefing from his chief of staff. When Rommel came out of the office, Lang saw that the news must have been bad. There was silence in the car as they drove off. Sometime later Rommel drove his gloved fist into the palm of his other hand and said, bitterly, "My friendly enemy, Montgomery." Still later, he said, "My God! If the Twenty-first Panzer can make it, we might just be able to drive them back in three days."

North of Caen, Bronikowski gave the order to attack. He sent thirty-five tanks, under the command of Captain Wilhelm von Gottberg, ahead to take the heights at Périers four miles from the coast. Bronikowski himself would try for the ridge at Biéville two miles away with another twenty-five tanks.

General Edgar Feuchtinger, commander of the 21st Panzer, and General Marcks, the 84th Corps commander, had come to see the attack go in. Marcks came over to Bronikowski. He said, "Oppeln, the future of Germany may very well rest on your shoulders. If you don't push the British back into the sea, we've lost the war."

Bronikowski saluted and replied, "General, I intend to do my best."

As they moved up, the tanks fanning out across the fields, Bronikowski was halted by Major General Wilhelm Richter, commander of the 716th Division. Bronikowski saw that Richter "was almost demented with grief." Tears came to his eyes as he told Bronikowski, "My troops are lost. My whole division is finished."

Bronikowski asked, "What can I do, sir? We'll help as best we can." He got out his map and showed it to Richter. "Where are their positions, sir? Will you point them out?"

Richter just shook his head. "I don't know," he said, "I don't know."

Rommel turned half around on the front seat of the Horch and said to Lang, "I hope there isn't a second landing right now from the Mediterranean." He paused for a moment. "Do you know, Lang," he said thoughtfully, "if I was commander of the Allied forces right now, I could finish off the war in fourteen days." He turned back and stared ahead. Lang watched him, miserable, unable to help. The Horch roared on through the evening.

Bronikowski's tanks rumbled up the rise at Biéville. So far they had encountered no enemy resistance. Then as the first of his Mark IV tanks neared the top, there was the sudden roar of guns opening up somewhere in the distance. He couldn't tell whether he had run headlong onto British tanks or whether the firing was from antitank guns. But it was accurate and fierce. It seemed to be coming from half a dozen places all at once. Suddenly his lead tank blew up without having fired a shot. Two more tanks moved up, their guns firing. But they seemed to make no impression on the British gunners. Bronikowski began to see why: he was being outgunned. The British guns seemed to have a tremendous range. One after the other Bronikowski's tanks were knocked out. In less than fifteen minutes he lost six tanks. He had never seen such shooting. There was nothing Bronikowski could do. He halted the attack and gave the order to pull back.

Private Walter Hermes couldn't understand where the tanks were. The advance company of the 192nd Regiment had reached the coast at Luc-sur-Mer, but there was no sign of the panzers. There was no sign of the British, either, and Hermes was a little disappointed. But the sight of the invasion fleet almost made up for it. On the coast, off to Hermes' left and right, he saw hundreds of ships and craft moving back and forth, and a mile or so offshore were warships of every description. "Beautiful," he said to his friend Schard. "Just like a parade." Hermes and his friends stretched out on the grass and took out their cigarettes. Nothing seemed to be happening and no one had given them any orders.

The British were already in position on the Périers heights. They stopped Captain Wilhelm von Gottberg's thirty-five tanks even before the panzers got into firing range. In a matter of minutes Gottberg lost ten tanks. The delay in orders, the time wasted trying to get around Caen had given the British the opportunity to consolidate fully their positions on the strategic heights. Gottberg roundly cursed everyone he could think of. He pulled back to the edge of a wood near the village of Lebissey. There he ordered his men to dig in their tanks, hulls down, with only the turrets showing. He was sure the British would drive on Caen within a few hours.

But to Gottberg's surprise time passed without an attack. Then, a little after 9 P.M., Gottberg saw a fantastic sight. There was the slowly mounting roar of planes and, off in the distance against the still-bright evening sun, he saw swarms of gliders coming in over the coast. There were scores of them, flying steadily in formation behind their tow planes. Then as he watched, the gliders were cast off and, wheeling and banking, they came soughing down, to land out of sight somewhere between him and the coast. Gottberg swore angrily.

At Biéville Bronikowski had dug in his tanks, too. As he stood by the side of the road, he watched "German officers with twenty to thirty men apiece, marching back from the front—retreating toward Caen." Bronikowski couldn't understand why the British didn't attack. It seemed to him that "Caen and the whole area could be taken within a few hours."* At the end of the procession Bronikowski saw a sergeant, his arms around two hefty German Wacs. They were "as drunk as pigs, their faces were dirty and they swayed from side to side." Reeling by, oblivious to everything, they sang "Deutschland über Alles" at the top of their voices. Bronikowski watched them until they were out of sight. "The war is lost," he said aloud.

Rommel's Horch purred quietly through La Roche-Guyon, moving slowly by the little houses that shouldered each other on either side of the road. The big black car turned off the high-

---

* Although the British made D Day's greatest advances, they failed to capture their principal objective—Caen. Bronikowski was to stay in position with his tanks for more than six weeks—until the city finally fell.

way, passed the sixteen square-cut linden trees and entered the gates of the castle of the Dukes de La Rochefoucauld. As they came to a halt before the door, Lang jumped out and ran ahead to inform Major General Speidel of the Field Marshal's return. In the main corridor he heard the strains of a Wagnerian opera coming from the chief of staff's office. The music welled up as the door suddenly opened and Speidel came out.

Lang was angry and shocked. Forgetting for a moment that he was talking to a general, he snapped, "How can you possibly play opera at a time like this?"

Speidel smiled and said, "My dear Lang, you don't think that my playing a little music is going to stop the invasion, now do you?"

Down the corridor strode Rommel in his long blue-gray field coat, his silver-topped marshal's baton in his right hand. He walked into Speidel's office and, hands clasped behind his back, stood looking at the map. Speidel closed the door, and Lang, knowing that this conference would last some time, made his way to the dining room. Wearily he sat down at one of the long tables and ordered a cup of coffee from the orderly. Nearby another officer was reading a paper. He looked up. "How was the trip?" he asked pleasantly. Lang just stared at him.

On the Cherbourg peninsula near Ste.-Mère-Église, Private Dutch Schultz of the 82nd Airborne leaned against the side of a foxhole and listened to a distant church bell sounding eleven. He could hardly keep his eyes open. He figured he had been awake now almost seventy-two hours—ever since the postponement on the night of June 4 when he had joined in the crap game. It struck him as funny that he had gone to so much trouble to lose all his winnings—nothing at all had happened to him. In fact, Dutch felt a little sheepish. He had not fired a single shot all day.

The Day

Back of Omaha Beach, beneath the bluffs, Medic Staff Sergeant Alfred Eigenberg flopped wearily into a crater. He had lost count of the number of casualties he had treated. He was bone-tired, but there was one thing he wanted to do before he fell asleep. Eigenberg fished a crumpled sheet of V-mail paper out of his pocket and, with the aid of a flashlight, settled down to write home. He scribbled, "Somewhere in France," and then began, "Dear Mom and Dad, I know that by now you've heard of the invasion. Well, I'm all right." Then the nineteen-year-old medic stopped. He couldn't think of anything more to say.

Down on the beach Brigadier General Norman Cota watched the "cat's eyes" blackout lights of trucks and heard the shouts of the MPs and beachmasters as they moved men and vehicles inland. Here and there landing craft still burned, throwing a ruddy glare into the night sky. The surf pounded the shore, and somewhere off in the distance Cota heard the lonely stutter of a machine gun. Suddenly Cota felt very tired. A truck rumbled toward him and Cota flagged it down. He stepped up onto the running board and hooked one arm around the door. For just a moment he looked back at the beach, then he said to the driver, "Run me up the hill, son."

At Rommel's headquarters Lang, like everyone else, had heard the bad news: the 21st Panzer attack had failed. Lang was very depressed. He said to the Field Marshal, "Sir, do you think we can drive them back?"

Rommel shrugged, spread his hands and said, "Lang, I hope we can. I've nearly always succeeded up to now." Then he patted Lang on the shoulder. "You look tired," he said. "Why don't you go to bed? It's been a long day." He turned away and Lang watched him walk down the corridor to his office. The door closed softly behind him.

Outside, nothing stirred in the two great cobbled courtyards.

La Roche-Guyon was silent. Soon this most occupied of all French villages would be free—as would the whole of Hitler's Europe. From this day on the Third Reich had less than one year to live. Beyond the castle gates the main road stretched broad and empty and the windows of the red-roofed houses were shuttered. In the Church of St. Samson the bell tolled midnight.

A NOTE ON CASUALTIES

OVER THE YEARS *a variety of vague and contradictory figures have been given on the losses sustained by Allied troops during the twenty-four-hour period of the assault. None of them can be said to be accurate. At best they must remain estimates, for by the very nature of the assault it was impossible for anyone to arrive at an exact figure. In general most military historians agree that the total Allied casualties reached 10,000; some even put the figure at 12,000.*

American casualties are put at 6,603. This figure is based on the U.S. First Army's after-action report, which gives the following breakdown: 1,465 killed, 3,184 wounded, 1,928 missing and 26 captured. Included in this compilation are 82nd and 101st Airborne losses, which alone are estimated at 2,499 killed, wounded and missing.

The Canadians had 946 casualties, of which 335 were killed. No British figures have ever been issued, but it is estimated that they had at least 2,500 to 3,000 casualties, of which the 6th Airborne suffered losses of 650 killed, wounded and missing.

What were the German D-Day losses? No one can say. In my interviews with senior German officers I was given estimates ranging from 4,000 to 9,000. But by the end of June, Rommel was to report that his casualties for the month were "28 generals, 354 commanders and approximately 250,000 men."

D-DAY VETERANS:
What They Do Today

In the following lists of contributors, all ranks shown are those as of D Day. Occupations may have changed for some men during the months since the lists were compiled.

AMERICAN

Accardo, Nick J., Lt. [4th Div.] *Orthopedic surgeon, New Orleans, La.*
Adams, Ernest C., Lt. Col. [1st Eng. Sp. Brig.] *Col., U.S. Army*
Adams, Jonathan E., Jr., Capt. [82nd Airborne] *Lt. Col., U.S. Army*
Albanese, Salvatore A., S/Sgt. [1st Div.] *Payroll clerk, Verplanck, N. Y.*
Albrecht, Denver, 2nd Lt. [82nd Airborne] *W/Off., U.S. Army*
Allen, Miles L., Pfc. [101st Airborne] *SFC, U.S. Army*
Allen, Robert M., Pfc. [1st Div.] *High-school teacher, athletic coach, Oelwein, Iowa*
Allen, Walter K., T/S [467th AAA (AW) Bn.] *Farmer, Monmouth, Iowa.*
Allison, Jack L., Pvt. [237th Eng.] *Accountant, Chester, W. Va.*
Alpaugh, Stanley H., 2nd Lt. [4th Div.] *Maj., U.S. Army*
Anderson, C. W., Pfc. [4th Div.] *Sgt., Military Police supervisor, U.S. Army*
Anderson, Donald C., Lt. [29th Div.] *Flight test engineer,* General Dynamics, *Edwards, Cal.*
Anderson, Donald D., Sgt. [4th Div.] *Dealer, timber products, Effie, Minn.*
Anderson, Martin H., Stm 1/c [11th & 12th Amphibious Force, USN] *A/2c, U.S.A.F.*
Apel, Joel H., 1st Lt. [457th Bomb Group] *Squadron Cdr., U.S.A.F.*
Apostolas, George N., T/4 [397th AAA Bn.] *Service officer,* Illinois Veterans Commission
Appleby, Sam, Jr., Cpl. [82nd Airborne] *Attorney, Ozark, Mo.*
Araiza, Joe L., Sgt. [446th Bomb Group] *M/Sgt., U.S.A.F.*
Arman, Robert C., Lt. [2nd Rangers] *Capt., Disability retirement, Lafayette, Ind.*
Armellino, John R., Capt. [1st Div.] *Mayor, West New York, N. J.*
Armstrong, Louis M., T/Sgt. [29th Div.] *Post-office clerk, Staunton, Va.*
Arnold, Edgar L., Capt. [2nd Rangers] *Lt. Col., U.S. Army*
Asay, Charles V., Sgt. [101st Airborne] *Linotype operator,* Placer Herald, *Auburn, Cal.*
Ashby, Carroll A., S/Sgt. [29th Div.] *Lt.; Advisor, Army reserve unit, Arlington, Va.*
Azbill, Boyce, Q.M. 2/c [U.S.C.G. LCI (L) 94] *Branch manager,* U.S. Pipe & Supply Co., *Tucson, Ariz.*
Baechle, Joseph W., Sgt. [5th Eng. Spec. Brig.] *Accountant, Cleveland, Ohio*
Bagley, Frank H., Lt. [U.S.S. *Herndon*] *Branch manager,* De Laval Steam Turbine Co., *Milwaukee, Minn.*
Baier, Harold L., Ens. [7th Naval Beach Bn.] *Doctor (Biological research), Frederick, Md.*
Bailey, Edward A., Lt. Col. [65th Armored Field Artillery Bn.] *Col., U.S. Army*

Bailey, Rand S., Lt. Col. [1st Eng. Sp. Brig.] *Ret'd; Part time, Consultant,*
  Rural Electrification Administration, Washington, D.C.
Baker, Richard J., Lt. [344th Bomb Group] *Maj., U.S.A.F.*
Balcer, Charles I., Lt. [HQ VII Corps] *Maj., U.S. Army*
Ball, Sam H., Jr., Capt. [146th Eng.] *Television account executive,* KCMC-TV,
  Texarkana, Tex.
Barber, Alex W., Pfc. [5th Rangers] *Chiropractor, Johnstown, Pa.*
Barber, George R., Capt. (chaplain), [1st Div.] *Minister & investment adviser,*
  Montebello, Cal.
Barrett, Carlton W., Pvt. [1st Div.] *SFC, U.S. Army*
Barton, Raymond O., Maj. Gen. [C.O., 4th Div.] Southern Finance Corp.
  Augusta, Ga.
Bass, Hubert S., Capt. [82nd Airborne] *Maj. (retired), Houston, Tex.*
Bassett, Leroy A., Pvt. [29th Div.] *Claims examiner,* Veterans Administration,
  Fargo, N. Dak.
Batte, James H., Lt. Col. [87th Chem. Mortar Bn.] *Col., U.S. Army*
Bearden, Robert L., Sgt. [82nd Airborne] Bearden's Personal Service,
  Fort Hood, Tex.
Beaver, Neal W., 2nd Lt. [82nd Airborne] *Cost accountant, Toledo, Ohio*
Beck, Carl A., Pvt. [82nd Airborne] *Engineering parts inspector,* IBM,
  Poughkeepsie, N.Y.
Beeks, Edward A., Pfc. [457th AAA AW Bn.] *Foreman mechanic,*
  Scobey, Montana
Beer, Robert O., Comdr. [U.S.S. *Carmick*] *Capt., U.S. Navy*
Belisle, Maurice A., Capt. [1st Div.] *Lt. Col., U.S. Army*
Belmont, Gail H., S/Sgt. [2nd Rangers] *Capt., U.S. Army*
Bengel, Wayne P., Pvt. [101st Airborne] *Senior clerk,* Cunard Steamship Co.,
  Ltd., *Pittsburgh, Pa.*
Billings, Henry J., Cpl. [101st Airborne] *Chief W/Off., U.S. Army*
Billiter, Norman W., Sgt. [101st Airborne] *Chief parachute inspector,*
  Fort Benning, Ga.
Bingham, Sidney V., Maj. [29th Div.] *Col., U.S. Army*
Blackstock, James P., S/Sgt. [4th Div.] *Optician, Philadelphia, Pa.*
Blakeley, Harold W., Brig. Gen., C.O. [4th Div., Artillery] *Maj. Gen.,*
  U.S. Army (retired)
Blanchard, Ernest R., Pfc. [82nd Airborne] *Machinist,* E. Ingraham Clock Co.,
  Bristol, Conn.
Bodet, Alan C., Cpl. [1st Div.] *Assistant cashier,* Guaranty Bank & Trust Co.,
  Jackson, Miss.
Boice, William S., Capt. (chaplain) [4th Div.] *Minister,* First Christian Church,
  Phoenix, Ariz.
Boling, Rufus C., Jr., Pvt. [4th Div.] *Apartment-house superintendent,*
  Brooklyn, New York
Bombardier, Carl E., Pfc. [2nd Rangers] *Tractor Operator, shipper,* Proctor &
  Gamble Mfg. Co., *North Abington, Mass.*
Bour, Lawrence J., Capt. [1st Div.] *Lt. Col., U.S. Army*
Boyd, Dale E., Lt. [1st Div.] *Editor,* Pocahoutas Democrat, *Pocahoutas, Iowa*
Bradley, Omar N., Lieut. Gen. [C.O., U.S. 1st Army] *General of the Army;*
  Chairman, Bulova Watch Co., *New York*
Brandt, Jerome N., Capt. [5th Eng. Sp. Brig.] *Lt. Col., U.S. Army*
Brannen, Malcolm D., Lt. [82nd Airborne] *Maj.;* Stetson University ROTC,
  DeLand, Fla.
Brewer, S. D., Seaman 1/c [U.S.S. *Arkansas*] *Post-office clerk, Hackleburg, Ala.*

Briel, Raymond C., Sgt. [1st Div.] *M/Sgt., U.S.A.F.*
Brinson, William L., Capt. [315th Troop Carrier Group] *Lt. Col., U.S.A.F.*
Broughman, Warner A., Capt. [101st Airborne] *Vocational-education director,*
U.S. Public Health Hospital, *Lexington, Ky.*
Brown, Harry, Sgt. [4th Div.] *Optometrist, Clawson, Mich.*
Bruen, James J., Sgt. [29th Div.] *Police officer, Cleveland, Ohio*
Bruff, Thomas B., Sgt. [101st Airborne] *Capt., U.S. Army*
Bruno, Joseph J., Seamen 1/c [U.S.S. *Texas*] *Freight traffic clerk, U.S. Army,*
Pittsburgh, Pa.
Bryan, Keith, Sgt. [5th Eng. Sp. Brig.] *Veteran's service officer, Columbus, Neb.*
Buckheit, John P., Seaman 1/c [U.S.S. *Herndon*] *Guard,* Olmsted A.F. Base,
Harrisburg, Pa.
Buckley, Walter, Jr., Lt. Comdr. [U.S.S. *Nevada*] *Capt., U.S.Navy*
Buffalo Boy, Herbert J., S/Sgt. [82nd Airborne] *Ranch hand, farmer,*
Fort Yates, N. Dak.
Burke, John L., Cpl. [5th Rangers] *Sales supervisor,* A. H. Robins Inc.,
Delmar, N.Y.
Burlingame, William G., Lt. [355 Fighter Group] *Maj., U.S.A.F.*
Burt, Gerald H., Cpl. [299th Engrs.] *Pipe fitter, Niagara Falls, N.Y.*
Busby, Louis A., Jr., Watertender 1/c [U.S.S. *Carmick*] *Chief boilerman,* U.S.S.
Saratoga
Butler, John C., Jr., Capt. [5th Eng. Sp. Brig.] *Realty officer,* Bureau of Indian
Affairs, *Arlington, Va.*
Byers, John C., T/Sgt. [441st Troop Carrier Group] *Mechanical engineer,*
San Pedro, Cal.
Caffey, Eugene M., Col. [1st Eng. Sp. Brig.] *Maj. Gen. (retired); attorney,*
Darden & Caffey *Las Cruces, N.M.*
Callahan, William R., Capt. [29th Div.] *Maj., U.S. Army*
Canham, Charles D. W., Col. [29th Div.] *Maj. Gen., U.S. Army*
Canoe, Buffalo Boy, T/Sgt. [82nd Airborne] *Judo instructor, Venice, Calif.*
Capobianco, Gaetano, Pfc. [4th Div.] *Butcher, Easton, Pa.*
Carlo, Joseph W., Hosp. Corpsman [LST 288] *Lt. (chaplain), U.S. Navy*
Carden, Fred J., Pfc. [82nd Airborne] *Airborne technician, U.S. Army*
Carey, James R., Jr., Sgt. [8th AF] Carey's West Side Service, *Ossian, Iowa*
Carlstead, Harold C., Ensign [U.S.S. *Herndon*] *accountant; teacher,* North-
western University School of Business, *Chicago, Ill.*
Carpenter, Joseph B., F/O [410th Bomb Group] *M/Sgt., U.S.A.F.*
Carroll, John B., Lt. [1st Div.] *Public relations,* Glass Container & Mfrs. Assn.,
New York, N.Y.
Cassel, Thomas E., Specialist 2/c [Task Force 122-3] *Capt., fire department,*
New York, N.Y.
Cascio, Charles J., Seaman 2/c [LST 312] *Mail carrier, Endicott, N.Y.*
Cason, Lee B., Cpl. [4th Div.] *M/Sgt., U.S. Army*
Cator, Richard D., Pfc. [101st Airborne] *Lt., U.S. Army*
Cawthon, Charles R., Capt. [29th Div.] *Lt. Col., U.S. Army*
Chance, Donald L., S/Sgt. [5th Rangers] *Safety engineer,* Yale & Towne Mfg.
Co., *Philadelphia, Pa.*
Chase, Charles H., Lt. Col. [101st Airborne] *Brig. Gen., U.S. Army*
Chase, Lucius P., Col. [6th Eng. Sp. Brig.] *General counsel & director,*
Kohler Co. *Kohler, Wis.*
Chesnut, Webb W., Lt. [1st Div.] Production Credit Association,
Campbellsville, Ky.
Chontos, Ernest J., Pvt. [1st Div.] *Realtor, Ashtabula, Ohio*

307

Ciarpelli, Frank, Pvt. [1st Div.] *Sanitation inspector*, Health Department, Rochester, N.Y.

Cirinese, Salvatore, Pfc. [4th Div.] *Shoe repairman, Miami, Fla.*

Clark, William R., Capt. [5th Eng. Sp. Brig.] *Postmaster, Loysville, Pa*

Clayton, William J., S/Sgt. [4th Div.] *Clerk*, Railway Express Agency, *Philadelphia, Pa.*

Clements, Edgar, S/Sgt. [4th Div.] *Painter, Dunbar, Pa.*

Cleveland, William H., Col. [HQ 325th Recon. Wing] *Col., U.S.A.F.*

Clifford, Richard W., Capt. [4th Div.] *Dental surgeon, Hudson Falls, N.Y.*

Cochran, Sam L., T/Sgt. [4th Div.] *Capt., U.S. Army*

Coffey, Vernon C., Pvt. [37th Engrs.] *Owner, meat packing, frozen-food-processing firm, Houghton, Iowa*

Coffman, Ralph S., S/Sgt. [29th Div.] *Truck driver*, Southern States Augusta Petroleum Cooperative, *Staunton, Va.*

Coffman, Warren G., Pfc. [1st Div.] *Capt., U.S. Army*

Coleman, Max D., Pfc. [5th Rangers] *Baptist minister, Clarkston, Mo.*

Collins, J. Lawton, Maj. Gen. [C.O., 7th Corps] *Gen. (retired); Chairman*, Charles Pfizer Co., *Washington, D.C.*

Collins, Thomas E., 2nd Lt. [93rd Bomb Group] *Statistician*, Northrop Aircraft Inc., *Gardena, Calif.*

Conley, Richard H., 2nd Lt. [1st Div.] *Capt., U.S. Army*

Conover, Charles M., Lt. [1st Div.] *Lt. Col., U.S. Army*

Cook, William, Ensign [LCT 588] *Comdr., U.S. Navy*

Cook, William S., Signalman 3/c [2nd Beach Bn.] *Manager, grain elevator, Flasher, N. Dak.*

Cooper, John P., Jr., Col. [29th Div.] *Brig. Gen. (retired); executive*, Baltimore Telephone Co. *Baltimore, Maryland*

Copas, Marshall, Sgt. [101st Airborne] *M/Sgt., U.S. Army*

Corky, John T., Lt. Col. [1st Div.] *Col., U.S. Army*

Cota, Norman D., Brig. Gen. [29th Div.] *Maj. Gen. (retired), Civil Defense director, Montgomery Co., Pa.*

Couch, Riley C., Jr., Capt. [90th Div.] *Farmer and rancher, Haskell, Texas*

Cox, John F., Cpl. [434th Troop Carrier Group] *Lt., fire department, Binghamton, N.Y.*

Coyle, James J., 2nd Lt. [82nd Airborne] *Accountant*, American Tobacco Co., *New York, N.Y.*

Crawford, Ralph O., Chief W/Off. [1st Eng. Sp. Brig.] *Postmaster, Dilley, Texas*

Crispen, Frederick J., 2nd Lt. [436th Troop Carrier Group] *M/Sgt., U.S.A.F.*

Cross, Herbert A., 2nd Lt. [4th Div.] *Principal, elementary school, Oneida, Tenn.*

Crowder, Ralph H., Cpl. [4th Div.] *Owner, Mick's Glass Shop, Radford, Va.*

Crowley, Thomas T., Maj. [1st Div.] *General manager*, Division of Crucible Steel Corp., *Pittsburgh, Pa.*

Cryer, William J., Jr., 2nd Lt. [96th Bomb Group] *Partner and General Manager, boat-building and repair yard, Oakland, Calif.*

Cunningham, Robt. E., Capt. [1st Div.] *Photoengraving; author, Stillwater, Okla.*

Dahlen, Johan B., Capt. (chaplain) [1st Div.] *Pastor, Lutheran church, Churchs Ferry, N. Dak.*

Dallas, Thomas S., Maj. [29th Div.] *Lt. Col., U.S. Army*

Danahy, Paul A., Maj. [101st Airborne] *Manufacturer's Representative, Minneapolis, Minn.*

Dance, Eugene A., Lt. [101st Airborne] *Maj., U.S. Army*

Daniel, Derrill M., Lt. Col. [1st Div.] *Maj. Gen., U.S. Army*

D-Day Veterans

Dasher, Benedict J., Capt. [6th Eng. Sp. Brig.] *President,* Universe Life Insurance Co., *Reno, Nev.*

Daughtrey, John E., Lt. (j.g.) [6th Beach Bn.,] *Doctor (general surgery), Lakeland, Fla.*

Davis, Barton A., Sgt. [299th Engrs.] *Assistant treasurer,* Hardinge Brothers, Inc., *Elmira, N.Y.*

Davis, Kenneth S., Comdr. U.S.C.G. [U.S.S. *Bayfield*] *Capt., U.S. Coast Guard*

Dawson, Francis W., Lt. [5th Rangers] *Maj., U.S. Army*

De Benedetto, Russell J., Pfc. [90th Div.] *Realtor, Port Allen, La.*

de Chiara, Albert, Jr., Ens. [U.S.S. *Herndon*] *Manufacturers representative, Passaic, N.J.*

Degnan, Irwin J., 2nd Lt. [HQ V Corps] *Insurance agent, Guttenberg, Iowa*

Deery, Lawrence E., Capt. (chaplain) [1st Div.] *Priest,* St. Joseph's, *Newport, R.I.*

DeMayo, Anthony J., Pfc. [82nd Airborne] *Foreman, electrical construction, New York, N.Y.*

Depace, V. N., Pvt. [29th Div.] *Internal Revenue agent, Pittsburgh, Pa.*

Derda, Fred, Signalman 1/c U.S.C.G. [LCI (L) 90] *Chiropractor, St. Louis, Mo.*

Derickson, Richard B., Lt. Comdr. [U.S.S. *Texas*] *Capt., U.S. Navy*

Desjardins, J. L., CM 3/c [3rd Naval Const. Bn.] *Police Department Custodian, Leominster, Mass.*

Di Benedetto, Angelo, Pfc. [4th Div.] *Letter carrier, Brooklyn, N.Y.*

Dickson, Archie L., Lt. [434th Troop Carrier Group] *Insurance agent, Gulfport, Miss.*

Dokich, Nicholas, Jr., Torpedoman [PT boat] *Torpedoman 3/c, U.S. Navy*

Dolan, John J., Lt. [82nd Airborne] *Attorney, Boston, Mass.*

Donahue, Thomas F., Pfc. [82nd Airborne] *Clerk,* A. and P. Tea Co., *Brooklyn, N.Y.*

Doss, Adrian R. Sr., Pfc. [101st Airborne] *Spec. 1/c U.S. Army*

Doyle, George T., Pfc. [90th Div.] *Printer, Parma Heights, Ohio*

Dube, Noel A., Sgt. [121st Engrs.] *Administrative Assistant, Air Force Commissary, Pease A.F. Base, N.H.*

Dulligan, John F., Capt. [1st Div.] *Veteran's Administration, Boston, Mass.*

Dunn, Edward C., Lt. Col. [4th Cav. Recon.] *Col., U.S. Army*

Duquette, Donald M., Sgt. [254th Engrs.] *M/Sgt., U.S. Army*

Dwyer, Harry A., Chief Signalman [5th Div. Amphibious Force] *Storekeeper, veterans hospital, Sepulveda, Calif.*

Eades, Jerry W., Sgt. [62nd Armored Bn.] *Lead-man, aircraft factory, Arlington, Texas*

East, Charles W., Capt. [29th Div.] *Underwriter, Staunton, Va.*

Eastus, Dalton L., Pvt. [4th Div.] *Meterman,* Indiana and Michigan Electric Co., *Marion, Ind.*

Eaton, Ralph P., Col. [82nd Airborne] *Brig. Gen. (retired), U.S. Army*

Echols, Eugene S., Maj. [5th Eng. Sp. Brig.] *City Engineer, Memphis, Tenn.*

Edelman, Hyman, Pvt. [4th Div.] *Liquor-store owner, Brooklyn, N.Y.*

Edlin, Robert T., Lt. [2nd Rangers] *Insurance agent supervisor,* Universal Life Insurance Co., *Bloomington, Ind.*

Edmond, Emil V. B., Capt. [1st Div.] *Lt. Col., U.S. Army*

Eichelbaum, Arthur, Lt. [29th Div.] *Vice-president, sales, Sands Point, L.I., N.Y.*

Eigenberg, Alfred, S/Sgt. [6th Eng. Sp. Brig.] *Lt., U.S. Army*

Eisemann, William J., Lt. (j.g.) [Rocket Support Div.] *Staff Assistant,* New England Mutual Life Insurance Co., *Bethpage, L.I., N.Y.*

Ekman, William E., Lt. Col. [82nd Airborne] *Col., U.S. Army*

Elinski, John, Pfc. [4th Div.] *Night shipper,* Keebler Biscuit Co.,
Philadelphia, Pa.

Ellery, John B., S/Sgt. [1st Div.] *Professor,* Wayne State University,
Royal Oak, Mich.

Elliott, Robert C., Pvt. [4th Div.] *Disabled, Passaic, N.J.*

Erd, Claude G., Ch. W/Off. [1st Div.] *M/Sgt.,* University of Kentucky, *ROTC,
Lexington, Ky.*

Erwin, Leo F., Pvt. [101st Airborne] *SFC Mess Steward, U.S. Army*

Ewell, Julian J., Lt. Col. [101st Airborne] *Col., U.S. Army*

Fainter, Francis, F., Col. [6th Armored Grp.] *Rep., N. Y. Stock Exchange,*
Westheimer & Co., *Charleston, W. Va.*

Fanning, Arthur E., Lt. U.S.C.G. [LCI (L) 319] *Insurance, Philadelphia, Pa.*

Fanto, James A., Radioman 1/c [6th Beach Bn.] *Chief Radioman, U.S. Navy*

Farr, H. Bartow, Lt. (j.g) [U.S.S. *Herndon*] *Attorney,* IBM, *New York, N.Y.*

Faulk, Willie T., S/Sgt. [409th Bomb Group] *M/Sgt., U.S.A.F.*

Ferguson, Charles A., Pfc. [6th Eng. Sp. Brig.] *Price specialist,* Western Electric
Co., Inc., *New York, N.Y.*

Ferguson, Vernon V., Lt. [452nd Bomb Group] *occupation unknown*

Ferro, Samuel Joseph, Pfc. [299th Engrs.] *Machinist, Binghamton, N.Y.*

Finnigan, William E., Pvt. [4th Div.] *Personnel assistant,* U.S. Military Academy,
West Point, N.Y.

Fish, Lincoln D., Capt. [1st Div.] *President, paper company, Worcester, Mass.*

Fitzsimmons, Robert C., Lt. [2nd Rangers] *Police lieutenant, Niagara Falls, N.Y.*

Flanagan, Larry, Pvt. [4th Div.] *Salesman, Philadelphia, Pa.*

Flora, John L., Jr., Capt. [29th Div.] *Real-estate appraiser,* FHA, *Roanoke, Va.*

Flowers, Melvin L., 2nd Lt. [441st Troop Carrier Grp.] *Capt. U.S.A.F.*

Flynn, Bernard J., 2nd Lt. [1st Div.] *Supervisor, package design,* General Mills
Inc., *Minneapolis, Minn.*

Forgy, Samuel W., Lt. Col. [1st Eng. Sp. Brig.] *President,* The Carabela Trad-
ing Co., Inc., *Manhasset, L.I., N.Y.*

Fowler, Rollin B., F/Off. [435th Troop Carrier Group] *M/Sgt., U.S.A.F.*

Fox, Jack, S/Sgt. [4th Div.] *Capt., U.S. Army*

Francis, Jack L., Cpl. [82nd Airborne] *Roofer, Sacramento, Calif.*

Franco, Robert, Capt. [82nd Airborne] *Surgeon, Richland, Wash.*

French, Gerald M., Lt. [450th Bomb Group] *Capt., U.S.A.F.*

Frey, Leo, Ch. Machinist Mate [LST 16] *W/Off. U.S.C.G.*

Friedman, William, Capt. [1st Div.] *Lt. Col., U.S. Army*

Frisby, Ralph E., 2nd Lt. [29th Div.] *Grocery-store owner, Okmulgee, Okla.*

Frische, William C., Jr., S/Sgt. [4th Div.] *Draftsman,* Gibson Art Co.,
Cincinnati, Ohio

Frohman, Howard J., S/Sgt. [401st Bomb Grp.] *Capt., U.S.A.F.*

Funderburke, Arthur, S/Sgt. [20th Engrs.] *Salesman,* Coca-Cola Bottling Co.,
Macon, Ga.

Gagliardi, Edmund J., SC/3c [LCT 637] *Police officer, Ambridge, Pa.*

Gardner, Edwin E., Pfc. [29th Div.] *Letter carrier, Plainville, Kansas*

Gaskins, Charles Ray, Cpl. [4th Div.] *Owner and operator,* Esso Service Center,
Kannapolis, N.C.

Gavin, James M., Brig. Gen. [82nd Airborne, Ass't Div. Comdr.] *Lt. Gen.*
(retired); vice-president Arthur D. Little Inc., *Wellesley Hills, Mass.*

Gearing, Edward M., 2nd Lt. [29th Div.] *Assistant division comptroller,* NEMS,
Division of Vitro Corp. of America, *Chevy Chase, Md.*

Gee, Ernest L., T/Sgt. [82nd Airborne] *Owner,* Mission Yellow Cab Co.,
San Jose, Calif.

Gerhardt, Charles H., Maj. Gen. [C.O., 29th Div.] *Maj. Gen. (retired); Florida*

Gerow, Leonard T., Maj. Gen. [C.O., 5th Corps] *Gen. (retired); Bank director, Petersburg, Va.*

Gervasi, Frank M., S/Sgt. [1st Div.] *Plant guard, Monroeville, Pa.*

Gibbons, Joseph H., Lt. Comdr. [C.O. Naval Combat Demolition units] *Sales Manager, N. Y. Telephone Co., New York, N.Y.*

Gibbons, Ulrich G., Lt. Col. [4th Div.] *Col., U.S. Army*

Gift, Melvin R., Pvt. [87th Chem. Mortar Bn.] *Dispatch clerk, Chambersburg, Pa.*

Gilhooly, John, Pfc. [2nd Rangers] *Store manager,* A. & P. Tea Co., *Roosevelt, L.I.*

Gill, Dean Dethroe, Sgt. [4th Cav. Recon.] *Cook, Veterans Hosp. Lincoln, Nebraska*

Gillette, John Lewis, Signalman 3/c [2nd Beach Bn.] *Teacher,* Wheatland-Chili Central School, *Scottsville, N.Y.*

Glisson, Bennie W., Radioman 3/c [U.S.S. *Corry*] *Teletype operator*

Goldman, Murray, S/Sgt. [82nd Airborne] *Sales supervisor,* Reddi-Wip Corp., *Monticello, N.Y.*

Goldstein, Joseph I., Pvt. [4th Div.] *Insurance, Sioux City, Iowa*

Goode, Robert Lee, Sgt. [29th Div.] *Mechanic, Bedford, Va.*

Goodmundson, Carl T., Signalman 2/c [U.S.S. *Quincy*] *Telegrapher,* Great Northern Railroad, *Minneapolis, Minn.*

Goranson, Ralph E., Capt. [2nd Rangers] *Director of Overseas Operations,* The E. F. MacDonald Co., *Dayton, Ohio*

Gordon, Fred, SPC [90th Div.] *SP-3, U.S. Army*

Gowdy, George, Lt. [65th Armored Bn.] *Fisherman, St. Petersburg, Fla.*

Greco, Joseph J., Pfc. [299th Engrs.] *Manager,* United Whelan Corp., *Syracuse, N.Y.*

Greenstein, Carl R., 2nd Lt. [93rd Bomb Group] *Capt., U.S.A.F.*

Greenstein, Murray, Lt. [95th Bomb Group] *Installment sales, owner, Bradley Beach, N.J.*

Griffiths, William H., Ens. [U.S.S. *Herndon*] *Comdr., U.S. Navy*

Grissinger, John P., 2nd Lt. [29th Div.] *General Agency for* Mutual Trust Life Insurance Co. of Chicago, *Harrisburg, Pa.*

Grogan, Harold M., T/5 [4th Div.] *U.S. Post Office, Vicksburg, Miss.*

Gudehus, Judson, Lt. [389th Bomb Group] *Salesman,* Toledo Optical Laboratory, *Toledo, Ohio*

Hackett, George R., Jr., Signalman 3/c [LCT Flot. 17] *Q/M 2/c, U.S. Navy*

Hahn, William I., Seaman 1/c [Husky Support Boat Crew] *Coal-mine operator, Wilkes-Barre, Pa.*

Hale, Bartley E., 2nd Lt. [82nd Airborne] *Student,* University of Georgia

Haley, James W., Capt. [4th Div.] *Col., U.S. Army*

Hall, Charles G., 1st Sgt. [4th Div.] *Chief W/Off., U.S.A.F.*

Hall, John Leslie, Jr., Rear Admiral [Assault Force O, Comdr.] *Rear Adm. (retired), U.S. Navy*

Hamlin, Paul A., Jr., Pvt. [299th Eng.] *Reclamation analyst,* IBM, *Vestal, N.Y.*

Hamner, Theodore S., Jr., S/Sgt. [82nd Airborne] *Floor foreman,* B. F. Goodrich Co., *Tuscaloosa, Ala.*

Hanson, Howard K., Pvt. [90th Div.] *Postmaster and farmer, Argusville, N. Dak.*

Harken, Delbert C., MoMM 3/c [LST 134] *Acting postmaster, Ackley, Iowa*

Harker, George S., Lt. [5th Eng. Sp. Brig.] *Research psychologist, Fort Knox, Ky.*

Harrington, James C., Lt. [355th Fighter Group] *Maj., U.S.A.F.*

Harrison, Thomas C., Capt. [4th Div.] *Sales manager*, Henry I. Christal Co., *Chappaqua, N.Y.*

Harrisson, Charles B., Pfc. [1st Eng. Sp. Brig.] *Insurance, Lansdowne, Pa.*

Harwood, Jonathan H., Jr., Capt. [2nd Rangers] *Deceased*

Hass, William R., Jr., Fl/Off. [441st Troop Carrier Group] *Capt., U.S.A.F.*

Hatch, James J., Capt. [101st Airborne] *Col., U.S. Army*

Havener, John K., Lt. [344th Bomb Group] *Materials controller*, International Harvester Co., *Sterling, Ill.*

Haynie, Ernest W., Sgt. [29th Div.] *Store clerk, marine engine supplies, Warsaw, Va.*

Heefner, Mervin C., Pfc. [29th Div.] *occupation unknown*

Heikkila, Frank E., Lt. Col. [6th Eng. Sp. Brig.] *Customer relations*, Westinghouse Electric Corp., *Pittsburgh, Pa.*

Henley, Clifford M., Capt. [4th Div.] *Road contracting, Summerville, S.C.*

Hennon, Robert M., Capt. (chaplain) [82nd Airborne] *Minister, Supervisor*, Evangelical Childrens' Home, *Brentwood, Miss.*

Herlihy, Raymond M., Sgt. [5th Rangers] *Tax Representative*, Prentice-Hall publishers, *Bronx, N.Y.*

Hermann, LeRoy W., Pfc. [1st Div.] *Parcel-post carrier, Akron, Ohio*

Hern, Earlston E., Pfc. [146th Engrs.] *Agent telegrapher*, Atchison, Topeka & Santa Fe Railway Co., *Medford, Okla.*

Herron, Beryl A., Pfc. [4th Div.] *Farmer, Coon Rapids, Iowa*

Hicks, Herbert C., Jr., Lt. Col. [1st Div.] *Col., U.S. Army*

Hicks, Joseph A., Capt. [531st Eng. Shore Regt.] *Board chairman*, Commonwealth Fertilizer Co., *Russellville, Ky.*

Hill, Joel G., T/4 [102nd Cavalry Recon.] *Sawmill and Logging operation, Lookout, Pa.*

Hodgson, John C., Sgt. [5th Rangers] *Post-office worker, Silver Spring, Md.*

Hoffmann, Arthur F., Capt. [1st Div.] *Landscaping, Simsbury, Conn.*

Hoffman, George D., Lt. Comdr. [U.S.S. *Corry*] *Capt., U.S. Navy*

Hogue, Clyde E., Cpl. [743rd Tank Bn.] *Letter carrier, Diagonal, Iowa*

Holland, Harrison H., Lt. [29th Div.] *Coach, U.S. Army pistol team*

Holman, John N., Jr., Seaman 1/c [U.S.S. *Hobson*] *Boy Scout field executive, Macon, Miss.*

Hooper, Joseph O., Pfc. [1st Div.] *Fire-fighter, Chemical Corps, U.S. Army*

Hoppler, Wendell L., Q/master 3/c [LST 515] *Agency instructor*, N.Y. Life Insurance Co., *Forest Park, Ill.*

House, Francis J. E., Pfc. [90th Div.] *Potter*, Homer Laughlin China Co., *E. Liverpool, Ohio*

Huebner, Clarence R., Maj. Gen. [C.O., 1st Div.] *Lieut. Gen. (retired); Director*, Civil Defense, *New York City*

Hughes, Melvin T., Pfc. [1st Div.] *Salesman*, Adams & Morrow Inc., *Patoka, Ind.*

Huggins, Spencer J., Pfc. [90th Div.] *M/Sgt., U.S. Army*

Hunter, Robert F., Maj. [5th Eng. Sp. Brig.] *Civil engineer, Tulsa, Okla.*

Hupfer, Clarence G., Lt. Col. [746th Tank Bn.] *Col. (retired), U.S. Army*

Imlay, M. H., Capt. [USCG Commdr. LCI (L) Flot. 10] *Rear Adm. (retired), U.S.C.G.*

Infinger, Mark H., S/Sgt. [5th Eng. Sp. Brig.] *SFC, U.S. Army*

Irwin, John T., Pfc. [1st Div.] *Sgt. (retired), mail clerk, U.S. Army*

Isaacs, Jack R., Lt. [82nd Airborne] *Pharmacist, Coffeyville, Kan.*

Jakeway, Donald I., Pfc. [82nd Airborne] *Bookkeeper*, Rice Oil Co., *Johnstown, Ohio*

James, Francis W., Pfc. [87th Chem. Mortar Bn.] *Police officer, Winnetka, Ill.*

D-Day Veterans

James, George D., Jr., Lt. [67th Tactical Recon. Group] *Insurance, Umadilla, N.Y.*
Jancik, Stanley W., S/c [LST 538] *Salesman,* Singer Sewing Machine Co., *Lincoln, Neb.*
Janzen, Harold G., Cpl. [87th Chem. Mortar Bn.] *Electrotyper, Elmhurst, Ill.*
Jarvis, Robert C., Cpl. [743 Tank Bn.] *Pumpman,* Socony Mobil Oil Co., *Brooklyn, N.Y.*
Jewet, Milton A., Maj. [299th Engrs.] *Col., Manager power plant,* New York City Transit Authority, *New York, N.Y.*
Johnson, Fancher B., Pvt. [HQ V Corps] *Timekeeper,* California Packing Corp., *Kingsburg, Calif.*
Johnson, Gerden F., Maj. [4th Div.] *Accountant, Schenectady, N.Y.*
Johnson, Orris H., Sgt. [70th Tank Div.] *Café owner, Leeds, N. Dak.*
Jones, Allen E., Pfc. [4th Div.] *SFC, U.S. Army*
Jones, Delbert F., Pfc. [101st Airborne] *Mushroom grower, Avondale, Pa.*
Jones, Desmond D., Pfc. [101st Airborne] *Metallurgical inspector,* Sun Oil Co., *Greenridge, Pa.*
Jones, Donald N., Pfc. [4th Div.] *Cemetery superintendent, Cadiz, Ohio*
Jones, Henry W., Lt. [743rd Tank Bn.] *Rancher, Cedar City, Utah*
Jones, Raymond E., Lt. [401st Bomb Sqdn.] *Operator,* Petroleum Chemicals Inc., *Lake Charles, La.*
Jones, Stanson R., Sgt. [1st Div.] *Lt., U.S. Army*
Jordan, Harold L., Pfc. [457th AAA AW Bn.] *Tool and die apprentice, Indianapolis, Ind.*
Jordan, Hubert H., M/Sgt. [82nd Airborne] *M/Sgt., U.S. Army*
Jordan, James H., Pvt. [1st Div.] *Maintenance, Pittsburgh, Pa.*
Joseph, William S., Lt. [1st Div.] *Painting contractor, San Jose, Calif.*
Judy, Bruce P., Ships Cook 1/c U.S.C.G. [LCI (L) 319] Bruce Judy Catering Service, *Kirkland, Wash.*
Joyner, Jonathan S., Sgt. [101st Airborne] *Post-office worker, Lawton, Okla.*
Kalisch, Bertram, Lt. Col. [Signal Corps, 1st Army] *Col., U.S. Army*
Kanarek, Paul, Sgt. [29th Div.] *Procedure analyst,* U.S. Steel Corp., *South Gate, Calif.*
Karper, A. Samuel, T/5 [4th Div.] *Judge's clerk, New York, N.Y.*
Kaufman, Joseph, Cpl. [743rd Tank Bn.] *Accounting, Monsey, N.Y.*
Keashen, Francis X., Pvt. [29th Div.] *Medical Division Veterans Administration, Philadelphia, Pa.*
Keck, William S., Tech/Sgt. [5th Eng. Sp. Brig.] *Sgt/Maj., U.S. Army*
Keller, John W., Pvt. [82nd Airborne] *Tool and diemaker, Sea Cliff, N.Y.*
Kelly, John J., Capt. [1st Div.] *Attorney,* DeGraff, Foy, Conway & Hall-Harris, *Albany, N.Y.*
Kelly, Timothy G., Ch. Elec. Mate [81st Naval Const. Bn.] *Telephone company employee, Amityville, L.I., N.Y.*
Kennedy, Harold T., Fl/Off. [437th Troop Carrier Grp.] *M/Sgt., U.S.A.F.*
Kerchner, George F., 2nd Lt. [2nd Rangers] *Supervisor, luncheonette chain, Baltimore, Md.*
Kesler, Robert E., S/Sgt. [29th Div.] *Clerk,* Norfolk & Western Railroad, *Roanoke, Va.*
Kidd, Charles W., 2nd Lt. [87th Chem. Mortar Div.] *Executive vice-president,* First Bank of Sitka, *Sitka, Alaska*
Kiefer, Norbert L., Sgt. [1st Div.] *Sales representative,* Benrus Watch Co., *E. Providence, R.I.*
Kindig, George, Pfc. [4th Div.] *Disabled, Brook, Indiana*

313

King, Wm. M., Capt. [741st Tank Bn.] *Director of Student Activities,* Clarkson
College of Technology, *Potsdam, N.Y.*
Kinnard, Harry W. O., Lt. Col. [101st Airborne] *Col., U.S. Army*
Kinney, Prentis McLeod, Capt. [37th Engrs.] *Doctor, Bennettsville, S.C.*
Kirk, Alan Goodrich, Rear Admiral [Comdr., Western Naval Task Force] *Admiral
(retired), U.S. Navy*
Kline, Nathan, S/Sgt. [323rd Bomb Grp.] *Partner,* Kline-Auto Supply Co.,
Allentown, Pa.
Kloth, Glenn C., S/Sgt. [112th Engrs.] *Carpenter, Cleveland, Ohio*
Knauss, Niles H., Pfc. [1st Div.] *Test operator-generators, Allentown, Pa.*
Koester, Wilbert J., Pfc. [1st Div.] *Farmer, Watseka, Ill.*
Kolody, Walter J., Capt. [447th Bomb Group] *Maj., U.S.A.F.*
Koluder, Joseph G., S/Sgt. [387th Bomb Grp.] *Quality control inspector*
Koon, Lewis Fulmer, Capt. (Chaplain) [4th Div.] *Supervisory staff,* Shenandoah
County Public Schools, *Woodstock, Va.*
Kraft, Paul C., Pvt. [1st Div.] *Post-office clerk and farmer, Canton, Miss.*
Kratzel, Siegfried F., S/Sgt. [4th Div.] *Post-office worker, Palmertown, Pa.*
Krause, Edward, Lt. Col. [82nd Airborne] *Col. U.S. Army (retired)*
Krausnick, Clarence E., Sgt. [299th Engrs.] *Carpenter, Syracuse, N.Y.*
Krzyzanowski, Henry S., S/Sgt. [1st Div.] *Sgt. 1/c, U.S. Army*
Kucipak, Harry S., Pfc. [29th Div.] *Electrician, Tupper Lake, N.Y.*
Kuhre, Leland B., Col. [Hqtrs., Eng. Sp. Brig.] *Writer and teacher,
San Antonio, Tex.*
Kurtz, Michael, Cpl. [1st Div.] *Coal miner, New Salem, Pa.*
Lacy, Joseph R., Lt. (chaplain) [2nd & 5th Rangers] *Priest,* St. Michael's Church,
Hartford, Conn.
Lagrassa, Edward, Pfc. [4th Div.] *Power press operator and liquor salesman,
Brooklyn, N.Y.*
Lamar, Kenneth W., Fireman 1/c U.S.C.G. [LST 27] *Chief Engineman,
U.S. Coast Guard*
Lanaro, Americo, T/5 [87th Mortar Bn.] *Painter, Stratford, Conn.*
Lang, James H., S/Sgt. [12th Bomb Grp.] *T/Sgt. U.S.A.F.*
Langley, Charles H., Yeoman 3/c [U.S.S. *Nevada*] *Rural mail carrier,
Loganville, Ga.*
Lapres, Theodore E., Jr., Lt. [2nd Rangers] *Attorney, Margate, N.J.*
Lassen, Donald D., Pvt. [82nd Airborne] *Production Foreman,* Victor Chemical
Works, *Harvey, Ill.*
Law, Robert W., Jr., Lt. [82nd Airborne] *Insurance, Bishopville, S.C.*
Lawton, John III, Cpl. [5th Corps Artillery] *Insurance, Fillmore, Calif.*
Lay, Kenneth E., Maj. [4th Div.] *Col., U.S. Army*
Leary, James E., Jr., Lt. [29th Div.] *Attorney, manager, Personal Health Divi-
sion,* John Hancock Mutual Insurance Co., *Boston, Mass.*
LeBlanc, Joseph L., S/Sgt., [29th Div.] *Social worker, Lynn, Mass.*
Leever, Lawrence C., Comdr. [6th Eng. Sp. Brig.] *Rear Admiral, U.S.N.R.; Chief
Deputy Division Civil Defense, Phoenix, Ariz.*
LeFebvre, Henry E., Lt. [82nd Airborne] *Maj., U.S. Army*
Legere, Lawrence J., Jr., Maj. [101st Airborne] *Lt. Col., U.S. Army*
Leister, Kermit R., Pfc. [29th Div.] *Trainman,* Pennsylvania Railroad,
Philadelphia, Pa.
Lepicier, Leonard R., Lt. [29th Div.] *Maj., U.S. Army*
Lillyman, Frank L., Capt. [101st Airborne] *Lt. Col., U.S. Army*
Lindquist, Roy E., Col. [82nd Airborne] *Maj. Gen., U.S. Army*
Linn, Herschel E., Lt Col. [237th Engrs.] *Lt. Col., U.S. Army*

D-Day Veterans

Littlefield, Gordon A., Comdr. [U.S.S. *Bayfield*] *Rear Adm. (retired)*, U.S.C.G.

Litzler, Frank Henry, Pfc. [4th Div.] *Rancher, Sweeny, Tex.*

Lord, Kenneth P., Maj. [1st Div.] *Assistant to president,* Security Mutual Life Insurance Co., *Binghamton, N.Y.*

Luckett, James S., Lt. Col. [4th Div.] *Col., U.S. Army*

Lund, Melvin C., Pfc. [29th Div.] *Shipping room,* Smith, Follett & Crowl, *Fargo, N.D.*

Luther, Edward S., Capt. [5th Rangers] *Vice-president and sales manager,* Hews Body Co., *Portland, Me.*

MacFadyen, Alexander G., Lt. [U.S.S. *Herndon*] Consolidated Brass Inc., *Charlotte, N.C.*

Mack, William M., Fl/Off. [437 Troop Carrier Command] *Capt., U.S.A.F.*

Magro, Domenick L., Sgt. [4th Div.] *Casting conditioner,* Bethlehem Steel Co., *Buffalo, N.Y.*

Maloney, Arthur A., Lt. Col. [82nd Airborne] *Col. U.S. Army*

Mann, Lawrence S., Capt. [6th Eng. Sp. Brig.] *Assistant Professor of Surgery,* Chicago Medical School, *Chicago, Ill.*

Mann, Ray A., Pfc. [4th Div.] *Feed-mill operator, Laureldale, Pa.*

Marble, Harrison A., Sgt. [299th Engrs.] *Contractor, Syracuse, N.Y.*

Marsden, William M., Lt. [4th Div.] *Civil Defense, coordinator, Richmond, Va.*

Marshall, Leonard S., Capt. [834 Eng. Aviation Bn.] *Lt. Col., U.S.A.F.*

Masny, Otto, Capt. [2nd Rangers] *Salesman,* Oil-Rite Corp., *Manitowoc, Wisc.*

Mason, Charles W., M/Sgt. [82nd Airborne] *Editor,* Airborne Quarterly, *Fayetteville, N.C.*

Matthews, John P., S/Sgt. [1st Div.] *Supervisor, fire-alarm and traffic-signal systems, Hempstead, L.I., N.Y.*

Mazza, Albert, Sgt. [4th Div.] *Police officer, Carbondale, Pa.*

McCabe, Jerome J., Maj. [48th Fighter Group] *Col., U.S.A.F.*

McCain, James W., 2nd Lt. [5th Eng. Sp. Brig.] *Sgt. Maj., U.S. Army*

McCall, Hobby H., Capt. [90th Div.] *Attorney,* McCall, Parkhurst & Crowe, *Dallas, Tex.*

McCardle, Kermit R., Radioman 3/c [U.S.S. *Augusta*] *Terminal Foreman,* Shell Oil Co., *Louisville, Ky.*

McClean, Thomas J., 2nd Lt. [82nd Airborne] *Police officer, New York, N.Y.*

McClintock, William D., T/Sgt. [741st Tank Bn.] *Disabled, N. Hollywood, Cal.*

McCloskey, Regis F., Sgt. [2nd Ranger] *SFC, U.S. Army*

McCormick, Paul O., Pfc. [1st Div.] *Auto Mechanic, Baltimore, Md.*

McDonald, Gordon D., M/Sgt. [29th Div.] *Shipping foreman,* American Viscose Corp., *Roanoke, Va.*

McElyea, Atwood M., 2nd Lt. [1st Div.] *Part-time salesman; Summer Camp Director, Candler, N.C.*

McIlvoy, Daniel B., Jr., Maj. [82nd Airborne] *Pediatrician, Bowling Green, Ky.*

McIntosh, Joseph R., Capt. [29th Div.] *Business and law, Baltimore, Md.*

McKearney, James B., S/Sgt. [101st Airborne] *Air-conditioning and refrigeration, Pennsauken, N.J.*

McKnight, John L., Maj. [5th Eng. Sp. Brig.] *Civil engineer, Vicksburg, Miss.*

McManaway, Fred., Maj. [29th Div.] *Col., U.S. Army*

Meason, Richard P., Lt. [101st Airborne] *Attorney, Phoenix, Ariz.*

Meddaugh, William J., Lt. [82nd Airborne] *Project manager,* IBM, *Hyde Park, N.Y.*

Medeiros, Paul L., Pfc. [2nd Rangers] *Biology teacher,* Father Judge High School, *Philadelphia, Pa.*

315

Merendino, Thomas N., Capt. [1st Div.] Motor vehicle inspector,
    Margate City, N.J.
Mergler, Edward F., W/Off. [5th Eng. Sp. Brig.] *Attorney,* Matson and Mergler,
    Bolivar, N.Y.
Merical, Dillon H., Cpl. [149th Engrs.] *Bank assistant, vice-president,* Dallas
    County State Bank, *Van Meter, Iowa*
Merlano, Louis P., Cpl. [101st Airborne] *District sales manager,* Facit, Inc.,
    New York, N.Y.
Merrick, Robert L., S 1/c [U.S. Coast Guard] *Fire department captain,*
    New Bedford, Mass.
Merrick, Theodore, Sgt. [6th Eng. Sp. Brig.] *Insurance Consultant,*
    Park Forrest, Ill.
Mikula, John, Torpedoman 3/c [U.S.S. *Murphy*] *Reporter, Ford City, Pa.*
Miller, George R., Lt. [5th Rangers] *Part owner, acid plant; farming, Pecos, Tex.*
Miller, Howard G., Pfc. [101st Airborne] *SFC, U.S. Army*
Mills, William L., Jr., Lt. [4th Div.] *Attorney,* Hartsell & Hartsell, *Concord, N.C.*
Milne, Walter J., S/Sgt. [386th Bomb Group] *T/Sgt., U.S.A.F.*
Mockrud, Paul R., Cpl. [4th Div.] *Veterans service officer, Westby, Wisc.*
Moglia, John J., S/Sgt. [1st Div.] *Capt., U.S. Army*
Montgomery, Lester I., Pfc. [1st Div.] *Gas-station operator, Pittsburg, Kans.*
Moody, Lloyd B., Ens. [5th Div. Amphibious Force] *Hardware store operator,*
    Lake View, Iowa
Moore, Elzie K., Lt. Col. [First Eng. Sp. Brig.] *Counselor; teacher,* Culver mili-
    tary academy, *Culver, Ind.*
Mordenga, Christopher J., Pvt. [299th Eng.] *Maintenance,* Treesweet Products,
    Fort Pierce, Fla.
Morecock, Bernard J., Jr., Sgt. [29th Div.] *Administrative supply technician,*
    Virginia National Guard, Glen Allen, Va.
Moreno, John A., Comdr. [U.S.S. *Bayfield*] *Capt., U.S. Navy*
Morrow, George M., Pfc. [1st Div.] *Brick-company employee; Farmer, Rose, Kans.*
Moser, Hyatt W., Cpl. [1st Eng. Sp. Brig.] *Chief W/Off., U.S. Army*
Moulton, Bernard W., Lt. (j.g.) [U.S.S. *Herndon*] *Comdr., U.S. Navy*
Mozgo, Rudolph S., Pfc. [4th Div.] *Capt., U.S. Army*
Mueller, David C., Capt. [435th Troop Carrier Group] *Capt., U.S.A.F.*
Muller, Charles, Jr., Cpl. [237th Engrs.] *Grocery clerk,* A. & P. Tea Co.,
    Newark, N.J.
Mulvey, Thomas P., Capt. [101st Airborne] *Lt. Col., U.S. Army*
Murphy, Robert M., Pvt. [82nd Airborne] *Attorney, Boston, Mass.*
Nagel, Gordon L., Pfc. [82nd Airborne] *Senior mechanic,* American Airlines,
    Tulsa, Okla.
Natalle, E. Keith, Cpl. [101st Airborne] *School administrator, San Francisco, Cal.*
Nederlander, Samuel H., Cpl. [518 Port Bn.] *Scrap Inspector,* Bethlehem Steel
    Co., *Portage, Pa.*
Negro, Frank E., Sgt. [1st Div.] *Post-office clerk, Brooklyn, N.Y.*
Neild, Arthur W., Mach. Mate 1/c [U.S.S. *Augusta*] *Lt., U.S. Navy*
Nelson, Emil Jr., S/Sgt. [5th Rangers] *Auto dealer, assistant service manager,*
    Cedar Lake, Ind.
Nelson, Glen C., Pfc. [4th Div.] *Rural mail carrier, Milboro, S. Dak.*
Nelson, Raider, Pfc. [82nd Airborne] Accro Plastics, *Chicago, Ill.*
Nero, Anthony R., Pvt. [2nd Division] *Disabled; part-time realtor,*
    Cleveland, Ohio
Newcomb, Jesse L., Jr. Cpl. [29th Div.] *Merchant and farmer, Keysville, Va.*

Nickrent, Roy W., S/Sgt. [101st Airborne] *Town marshal and waterworks superintendent, Saybrook, Ill.*

Norgaard, Arnold, Pfc. [29th Div.] *Farming, Arlington, S. Dak.*

Obert, Edward Jules, Jr., Pfc. [747th Tank Bn.] *Supervisor,* Sikorsky Aircraft, *Milford, Conn.*

Olds, Robin, Lt. [8th AF] *Col., U.S.A.F.*

O'Loughlin, Dennis G., Pfc. [82nd Airborne] *Construction, Missoula, Montana*

Olwell, John J., Pvt. [1st Div.] Veterans Administration, *Lyons, N.J.*

O'Mahoney, Michael, Sgt. [6th Eng. Sp. Brig.] *Fabricating plant operator, Mercer, Pa.*

O'Neill, John T., Lt. Col. [C.O. Sp. Eng. Task Force (Prov. Eng. Comb. Grp.)] *Col., U.S. Army*

O'Connell, Thomas C., Capt. [1st Div.] *Maj., U.S. Army*

Orlandi, Mark, S/Sgt. [1st Div.] *Truck driver, Smithport, Pa.*

Owen, Joseph K., Capt. [4th Div.] *Assistant Director of Hospitals, Va., Richmond, Va.*

Owen, Thomas O., 2nd Lt. [2nd Air Div.] *Athletics director and coach, Nashville, Tenn.*

Owens, William D., Sgt. [82nd Airborne] *Office manager, Temple City, Cal.*

Paez, Robert O., Bugler 1/c [U.S.S. *Nevada*] *Film editor,* Atomic Energy Commission, *Eniwetok Atoll, Marshall Islands*

Paige, Edmund M., Cpl. [1st Div.] *Exporter, New Rochelle, N.Y.*

Palmer, Wayne E., S/Sgt. [1st Div.] *Assistant Manager, invoicing and estimating department, Oshkosh, Wis.*

Parker, Donald E., S/Sgt. [1st Div.] *Farmer, Stillwell, Ill.*

Patch, Lloyd E., Capt. [101st Airborne] *Lt. Col., U.S. Army*

Patrick, Glenn, T/5 [4th Div.] *Bulldozer operator, Stockport, Ohio*

Pattillo, Lewis C., Lt. Col. [V Corps] *Civil engineer, Hartselle, Ala.*

Payne, Windrew C., Lt. [90th Div.] *County supervisor,* Farmer's Home Administration, U.S. Dept. of Agriculture, *San Augustine, Tex.*

Pearson, Ben F., Maj. [82nd Airborne] *Paint company vice-president, Savannah, Ga.*

Pence, James L., Capt. [1st Div.] *Supervisor, pharmaceutical laboratories, Elkhart, Ind.*

Perry, Edwin R., Capt. [299th Engrs.] *Lt. Col., U.S. Army*

Perry, John J., Sgt. [5th Rangers] *SFC, U.S. Army*

Peterson, Theodore L., Lt. [82nd Airborne] *occupation unknown, Birmingham, Mich.*

Petty, William L., Sgt. [2nd Rangers] *Boys' camp director, Carmel, N.Y.*

Phillips, Archie C., S/Sgt. [101st Airborne] *Flower grower, Jensen Beach, Fla.*

Phillips, William J., Pvt. [29th Div.] *Electric power company dispatcher, Hyattsville, Md.*

Picchiarini, Ilvo, Motor Mach. Mate 1/c [LST 374] *Steel company employee, Belle Vernon, Pa.*

Pike, Malvin R., T/Sgt. [4th Div.] *Esso Oil company burner and welder, Baker, La.*

Piper, Robert M., Capt. [82nd Airborne] *Lt. Col., U.S. Army*

Plude, Warren M., S/Sgt. [1st Div.] *Sgt., U.S. Army*

Polanin, Joseph J., Cpl. [834th Eng. Aviation Bn.] *Baked-goods distributor, Dickson City, Pa.*

Polezoes, Stanley, 2nd Lt. [1st Air Div.] *Maj., U.S.A.F.*

Polyniak, John, Sgt. [29th Div.] *Accountant, Baltimore, Md.*

Pompei, Romeo T., Sgt. [87th Chemical Mortar Bn.] *Builder, Philadelphia, Pa.*

Potts, Amos P., Jr., Lt. [2nd Rangers] *Materials engineer, Loveland, Ohio*
Powell, Joseph C., Ch. W/Off. [4th Div.] *Ch. W/Off., U.S. Army*
Pratt, Robert H., Lt. Col. [HQ V Corps] *President, manufacturing corporation,*
  Milwaukee, Wis.
Presley, Walter G., Pfc. [101st Airborne] *Appliance repair business, Oddessa, Tex.*
Preston, Albert G., Jr., Capt. [1st Div.] *Tax consultant, Greenwich, Conn.*
Price, Howard P., Lt. [1st Div.] *Sgt., National Guard*
Priesman, Maynard J., T/Sgt. [2nd Rangers] *Fishery proprietor,*
  Oak Harbor, Ohio
Provost, William B., Jr., Lt. (j.g.) [LST 492] *Comdr., university ROTC,*
  Oxford, Ohio
Pruitt, Lanceford B., Lt. Comdr. [LCT Flot. 19] *Comdr., (U.S.N. ret.),*
  San Francisco, Calif.
Pulcinella, Vincent J., T/Sgt. [1st Div.] *M/Sgt., U.S. Army*
Purnell, William C., Lt. Col. [29th Div.] *Gen. (retired); Railway vice-president*
  and general counsel, Baltimore, Md.
Purvis, Clay S., M/Sgt. [29th Div.] *Manager concessions,* Alumni Association,
  University of Virginia, *Charlottesville, Va.*
Putnam, Lyle B., Capt. [82nd Airborne] *Surgeon and general practitioner,*
  Wichita, Kan.
Quinn, Kenneth R., S/Sgt. [1st Div.] *Manager,* Inter-Plan Bank, New Jersey
  Blue Cross, *Hillsdale, N. J.*
Raff, Edson D., Col. [82nd Airborne] *Col., U.S. Army*
Raftery, Patrick H., Jr., 2nd Lt. [440th Troop Carrier Group] *Self-employed, ele-*
  vator construction, Metairie, La.
Rankin, Wayne W., Pfc. [29th Div.] *Teacher, Homes City, Pa.*
Rankins, William F., Jr., Pvt. [518th Port Bn.] *Telephone-company employee,*
  Houston, Tex.
Ranney, Burton E., S/Sgt. [5th Rangers] *Electrician, Decatur, Ill.*
Raudstein, Knut H., Capt. [101st Airborne] *Lt. Col., U.S. Army*
Rayburn, Warren D., Lt. [316th Troop Carrier Group] *Maj., U.S.A.F.*
Read, Wesley J., Cpl. [746th Tank Bn.] *Railroad carman, Du Bois, Pa.*
Reams, Quinton F., Pfc. [1st Div.] *Railroad engineer, Punxsutawney, Pa.*
Reed, Charles D., Capt. (chaplain) [29th Div.] *Methodist minister, Troy, Ohio*
Reeder, Russel P., Jr., Col. [4th Div.] *Col. (retired); Assistant Mgr. Athletics,*
  West Point, N. Y.
Rennison, Francis A., Lt. [U.S. Navy] *Realtor, New York, N. Y.*
Reville, John J., Lt. [5th Rangers] *Police Officer, New York, N. Y.*
Ricci, Joseph J., Sgt. [82nd Airborne] *Pharmacist, Bethalto, Ill.*
Richmond, Alvis, Pvt. [82nd Airborne] *Clerk, Portsmouth, Va.*
Ridgway, Matthew B., Maj. Gen. [C.O., 82nd Airborne] *Gen. (retired); Chairman*
  of the Board, The Mellon Institute, Pittsburgh, Pa.
Riekse, Robert J., Lt. [1st Div.] *Company division manager, Owosso, Mich.*
Riley, Francis X., Lt. (j.g.) U.S.C.G. [LCI (L) 319] *Comdr., U.S. Coast Guard*
Ritter, Leonard C., Cpl. [3807 QM Truck Co.] *Public relations, Chicago, Ill.*
Robb, Robert W., Lt. Col. [HQ VII Corps] *Vice-president, advertising,*
  New York, N. Y.
Roberts, George G., T/Sgt. [306th Bomb Group] *Educational advisor, U.S.A.F.,*
  Belleville, Ill.
Roberts, Milnor, Capt. [HQ Co. V. Corps] *President, advertising company,*
  Pittsburgh, Pa.
Robertson, Francis C., Capt. [365th Fighter Group] *Lt. Col., U.S.A.F.*
Robinson, Robert M., Pfc. [82nd Airborne] *Capt., U.S. Army*
Robison, Charles, Jr., Lt. (j.g.) [U.S.S. *Glennon*] *Comdr., U.S. Navy*

Rocca, Francis A., Pfc. [101st Airborne] *Machine operator, Pittsfield, Mass.*
Rodwell, James S., Col. [4th Div.] *Brig. Gen. (retired), Denver, Colo.*
Rogers, T. DeF., Lt. Col. [1106th Engrs.] *Col. U.S. Army*
Roginski, E. J., S/Sgt. [29th Div.] *Sales manager, Spaulding Bakeries, Inc.,
    Shamokin, Pa.*
Roncalio Teno, 2nd Lt. [1st Div.] *Attorney, Cheyenne, Wyo.*
Rosemond, St. Julien P., Capt. [101st Airborne] *Assistant county attorney,
    Miami, Fla.*
Rosenblatt, Joseph K., Jr., 2nd Lt. [112th Engrs.] *M/Sgt., U.S. Army*
Ross, Robert P., Lt. [37th Engrs.] *Box manufacturer, Waukesha, Wis.*
Ross, Wesley R., 2nd Lt. [146th Engrs.] *Sales engineer, Western XRay Co.,
    Tacoma, Wash.*
Rosson, Walter E., Lt. [389th Bomb Group] *Optometrist, San Antonio, Tex.*
Rountree, Robert E., Lt. U.S.C.G. [U.S.S. Bayfield] *Comdr., U.S. Coast Guard*
Roworth, Wallace H., Radioman 3/c [U.S.S. Joseph T. Dickman] *Engineer,
    Garden City, L. I., N. Y.*
Rubin, Alfred, Lt. [24th Cav. Recon. Sqdn.] *Catering and restaurateur,
    Napierville, Ill.*
Rudder, James E., Lt. Col. [2nd Rangers] *College vice-president,
    College Station, Tex.*
Ruggles, John F., Lt. Col. [4th Div.] *Brig. Gen., U.S. Army*
Runge, William M., Capt. [5th Rangers] *Funeral director, Davenport, Iowa*
Russell, Clyde R., Capt. [82nd Airborne] *Lt. Col., U.S. Army*
Russell, John E., Jr., Sgt. [1st Div.] *Personnel department, steel company,
    New Kensington, Pa.*
Russell, Joseph D., Pvt. [299th Engrs.] *Telephone-company employee,
    Moores Hill, Ind.*
Russell, Kenneth, Pfc. [82nd Airborne] *Bank official, New York, N. Y.*
Ryals, Robert W., T/4 [101st Airborne] *SPF, U.S. Army*
Ryan, Thomas F., S/Sgt. [2nd Rangers] *Police Officer, Chicago, Ill.*
Sammon, Charles E., Lt. [82nd Airborne] *Occupation unknown*
Sampson, Francis L., Capt. (chaplain) [101st Airborne] *Lt. Col., chaplain,
    U.S. Army*
Sanders, Gus L., 2nd Lt. [82nd Airborne] *Credit-bureau operator,
    Springdale, Ark.*
Sands, William H., Brig. Gen. [29th Div.] *Attorney, Norfolk, Va.*
Santarsiero, Charles J., Lt. [101st Airborne] *Occupation unknown*
Saxion, Homer J., Pfc. [4th Div.] *Extrusion press, Titan Metal Mfg. Co.,
    Bellefonte, Pa.*
Scala, Nick A., T/Sgt. [4th Div.] *Order interpreter, engineering service depart-
    ment, Westinghouse Electric Corp., Beaver, Pa.*
Scharfenstein, Charles F., Jr., Lt. U.S.C.G. [LCI (L) 87] *Comdr.,
    U.S. Coast Guard*
Schechter, James H., Cpl. [38th Recon. Sqdn.] *Quarry driller, St. Cloud, Minn.*
Schmid, Earl W., 2nd Lt. [101st Airborne] *Insurance, Fayetteville, N. C.*
Schneider, Max, Lt. Col. [5th Rangers] *Col., U.S. Army (deceased)*
Schoenberg, Julius, T/Sgt. [453rd Bomb Group] *Letter carrier, New York, N. Y.*
Schopp, Dan D., Cpl. [5th Rangers] *M/Sgt., U.S.A.F.*
Schroeder, Leonard T., Jr., Capt. [4th Div.] *Lt. Col., U.S. Army*
Schultz, Arthur B., Pfc. [82nd Airborne] *Security officer, U.S. Army*
Schweiter, Leo H., Capt. [101st Airborne] *Lt. Col., U.S. Army*
Scott, Arthur R., Lt. (j.g.) [U.S.S. Herndon] *Salesman, Arcadia, Calif.*
Scott, Harold A., S/Sgt. [4042 QM Truck Co.] *Post-office employee, Yeadon, Pa.*
Scott, Leslie J., S/Sgt. [1st Div.] *Sgt. Maj., U.S. Army*

Scrimshaw, Richard E., B.M. 3/c [15th Destroyer Sqdn.] *Aircraft mechanic, Washington, D.C.*

Seelye, Irvin W., Pfc. [82nd Airborne] *Teacher, Crete, Ill.*

Settineri, John, Capt. [1st Div.] *Doctor, Jamesville, N. Y.*

Shanley, Thomas J., Lt. Col. [82nd Airborne] *Col., U.S. Army*

Sherman, Herbert A., Jr., Pfc. [1st Div.] *Salesman, South Norwalk, Conn.*

Shindle, Elmer G., T/4 [29th Div.] *Plastics factory worker, Lancaster, Pa.*

Shoemaker, William J., Pvt. [37th Engrs.] *Mechanic, Santa Ana, Calif.*

Shollenberger, Joseph H., Jr., 2nd Lt. [90th Div.] *Maj. U.S. Army*

Shoop, Clarence A., Lt. Col. [CO 7th Recon. Group] *Maj. Gen. (retired); Vice-president, Hughes Aircraft Company, Culver City, Calif.*

Shoop, Dale L., Pvt. [1st Engrs.] *Government-ammunition inspector, Chambersburg, Pa.*

Shorter, Paul R., Sgt. [1st Div.] *SFC, U.S. Army*

Shumway, Hyrum S., 2nd Lt. [1st Div.] *Director, Department of Deaf and Blind, State Department of Education, Cheyenne, Wyo.*

Silva, David E., Pvt. [29th Div.] *Priest, Akron, Ohio*

Simeone, Francis L., Pvt. [29th Div.] *Underwriter, Rocky Hill, Conn.*

Simmons, Stanley R., Gunner's Mate 3/c [Amphibious Unit] *Stone-quarry worker, Swanton, Ohio*

Sink, James D., Capt. [29th Div.] *Superintendent, traffic engineering and communications, Roanoke, Va.*

Sink, Robert F., Col. [101st Airborne] *Maj. Gen., U.S. Army*

Skaggs, Robert N., Lt. Col. [741st Tank Bn.] *Col. (retired); marine sales, Ft. Lauderdale, Fla.*

Slappey, Eugene N., Col. [29th Div.] *Col. (retired), Leesburg, Va.*

Sledge, Edward S. II, Lt. [741st Tank Bn.] *Bank vice-president, Mobile, Ala.*

Smith, Carroll B., Capt. [29th Div.] *Lt. Col., U.S. Army*

Smith, Charles H., Lt. [U.S.S. *Carmick*] *Advertising, Evanston, Ill.*

Smith, Frank R., Pfc. [4th Div.] *Veterans service officer, Waupaca, Wis.*

Smith, Franklin M., Cpl. [4th Div.] *Wholesale electrical distributor, Philadelphia, Pa.*

Smith, Gordon K., Maj. [82nd Airborne] *Lt. Col., U.S. Army*

Smith, Harold H., Maj. [4th Div.] *Attorney, White Oak, Va.*

Smith, Joseph R., Cpl. [81st Chem. Mortar Bn.] *Science teacher, Eagle Pass, Tex.*

Smith, Owen, Pvt. [5th Eng. Sp. Brig.] *Post-office clerk, Los Angeles, Calif.*

Smith, Ralph R., Pvt. [101st Airborne] *Post-office clerk, St. Petersburg, Fla.*

Smith, Raymond, Pvt. [101st Airborne] *Glass-company owner, Whitesburg, Ky.*

Smith, Wilbert L., Pfc. [29th Div.] *Farmer, Woodburn, Iowa*

Snyder, Jack A., Lt. [5th Rangers] *Lt. Col., U.S. Army*

Sorriero, Armand J., Pfc. [4th Div.] *Commercial artist, Philadelphia, Pa.*

Spalding, John M., 2nd Lt. [1st Div.] *Department manager, Interstate Stores Co., Owensboro, Ky.*

Spencer, Lyndon, Capt. U.S.C.G. [U.S.S. *Bayfield*] *Vice Admiral (retired), President, Lake Carrier's Assn., Cleveland, Ohio*

Spiers, James C., Pvt. [82nd Airborne] *Rancher, Picaqune, Miss.*

Spitzer, Arthur D., Cpl. [29th Div.] *Employee, E. I. du Pont Co., Staunton, Va.*

Sproul, Archibald A., Maj. [29th Div.] *Executive vice-president, W. J. Perry Corp.*

Steele, John M., Pvt. [82nd Airborne] *Cost engineer, Hartsville, S. C.*

Stein, Herman E., T/5 [2nd Rangers] *Sheet-metal worker, Ardsley, N. Y.*

Steinhoff, Ralph, Cpl. [467th AAA Bn.] *Butcher, Chicago, Ill.*

Stephenson, William, Lt. [U.S.S. *Herndon*] *Attorney, Sante Fe, N. M.*

Stevens, Roy O., T/Sgt. [29th Div.] *Employee*, Rubatex *division of Bedford, Bedford, Va.*

Stivison, William J., S/Sgt. [2nd Rangers] *Postmaster, Homer City, Pa.*

Strayer, Robert L., Lt. Col. [101st Airborne] *Insurance, Springfield, Pa.*

Street, Thomas F., MoM 1/c U.S.C.G. [LST 16] *Post-office worker, River Edge, N. J.*

Strojny, Raymond F., S/Sgt. [1st Div.] *Sp1, U.S. Army*

Stults, Dallas M., Pfc. [1st Div.] *Coal miner, Monterey, Tenn.*

Stumbaugh, Leo A., 2nd Lt. [1st Div.] *Capt., U.S. Army*

Sturdivant, Hubert N., Lt. Col. [492 Bomb Group] *Col., U.S.A.F.*

Sullivan, Fred P., Lt. [4th Div.] *Salesman*, Mississippi Chemical Corporation, *Winona, Miss.*

Sullivan, Richard P., Maj. [5th Rangers] *Engineering, Dorchester, Mass.*

Swatosh, Robert B., Maj. [4th Div.] *Lt. Col., U.S. Army*

Sweeney, William F., Gunner's Mate 3/c [U.S.C.G. Reserve Flotilla] *Telephone-company employee, East Providence, R. I.*

Swenson, J. Elmore, Maj. [29th Div.] *Lt. Col., U.S. Army*

Tabb, Robert P., Jr., Capt. [237th Eng. Combat Bn.] *Col., U.S. Army*

Tait, John H., Jr., Pharmacist's Mate 1/c U.S.C.G. [LCI (L) 349] *Zanjero*, Salt River Valley Users Association, *Tempe, Ariz.*

Tallerday, Jack, Lt. [82nd Airborne] *Lt. Col., U.S. Army*

Talley, Benjamin B., Col. [HQ V Corps] *Brig. Gen. (retired); vice-president, construction company, New York, N. Y.*

Taylor, Beryl F., Hosp. App. 1/c [LST 338] *Diving instructor, U.S. Navy*

Taylor, Charles A., Ens. [LCT Amphibious Unit] *Assistant director, athletics, Stanford University, Palo Alto, Calif.*

Taylor, Edward G., Ens. [LST 331] *Lt. Comdr., U.S. Coast Guard*

Taylor, H. Afton, 2nd Lt. [1st Eng. Sp. Brig.] Hallmark Cards, Inc., *Independence, Mo.*

Taylor, Ira D., T/Sgt. [4th Div.] *Capt., U.S. Army*

Taylor, Maxwell D., Maj. Gen. [CO 101st Airborne] *General, Chief of Staff (retired); Chairman,* Mexican Light & Power Co.

Taylor, William R., Ens. [U.S. Navy, Liaison Off. communications] *Retailer, building materials, South Hill, Va.*

Telinda, Benjamin E., S/Sgt. [1st Div.] *Locomotive fireman*, Chicago Great Western Railroad, *St. Paul, Minn.*

Thomason, Joel F., Lt. Col. [4th Div.] *Col., U.S. Army*

Thompson, Egbert, W., Jr., Lt. [4th Div.] *County Supervisor*, Farmers Home Administration, USDA, *Bedford, Va.*

Thompson, Melvin, Pvt. [5th Eng. Sp. Brig.] *Mechanic, Yardville, N. J.*

Thompson, Paul W., Col. [6th Eng. Sp. Brig.] *Brig. Gen. (retired); Manager International Editions,* The Reader's Digest, *Pleasantville, N. Y.*

Thornhill, Avery J., Sgt. [5th Rangers] *Chief W/Off., U.S. Army*

Trathen, Robert D., Capt. [87th Chem. Mortar Bn.] *Lt. Col. (retired); Asst. Chief Plans & Training,* U.S. Army Chem. Corps, *Fort McClellan, Ala.*

Tregoning, Wm. H., Lt. (j.g.) U.S.C.G. [Flot. 4] *Manager, service department,* Fairbanks Morse & Co., *East Point, Ga.*

Tribolet, Hervey A., Col. [4th Div.] *Col. (retired), U.S. Army*

Trusty, Lewis, S/Sgt. [8th Air Force] *M/Sgt., U.S.A.F.*

Tucker, William H., Pfc. [82nd Airborne] *Attorney, Athol, Mass.*

Tuminello, Vincent J., Cpl. [1st Div.] *Bricklayer, Massapequa, L. I., N. Y.*

Vandervoort, Benjamin H., Lt. Col. [82nd Airborne] *Col. (retired), U.S. Army, Washington, D.C.*

Vantrease, Glen W., Sgt. [82nd Airborne] *Accountant, Gary, Ind.*

Vaughn, James H., Motor Mach. Mate 1/c [LST 49] *Construction superintendent, McIntyre, Ga.*

Ventrelli, William E., Sgt. [4th Div.] *Foreman,* Department of Sanitation, *New York City, Mount Vernon, N. Y.*

Vickery, Grady M., T/Sgt. [4th Div.] *M/Sgt., U.S. Army*

Viscardi, Peter, Pvt. [4th Div.] *Taxi driver, New York, N. Y.*

Visco, Serafino R., Pvt. [456th AAA AW Bn.] *Post-office worker, Dania, Fla.*

Volponi, Raymond R., Sgt. [29th Div.] *Disabled;* Veterans Administration Hospital, *Altoona, Pa.*

Von Heimburg, Herman E., Capt. [11th Amphibious Force] *Rear Adm., Naval Reserve Training Command*

Wade, James Melvin, 2nd Lt. [82nd Airborne] *Maj., U.S. Army*

Wadham, Lester B., Capt. [1st Eng. Sp. Brig.] Wadham Mutual Investments, *Frankfurt, Germany*

Wadsworth, Loring L., Pfc. [2nd Rangers] Sparrell Funeral Service, *Norwell, Mass.*

Wagner, Clarence D., Radioman 1/c [LST 357] *CPO, U.S. Navy*

Walker, Francis M., Sgt. [6th Eng. Spec. Brig.] *Sgt. 1/c, U.S. Army*

Wall, Charles A., Lt. Col. [Eng. Spec. Brig. Grp.] *President,* Associated Music Publishers, *New York, N. Y.*

Wall, Herman V., Capt. [165 Signal Photo Co.] *Director of photography,* Los Angeles State College Foundation

Wallace, Dale E., Seaman 2/c [SC 1332] *Salesman,* Capitol Tobacco Co., *Jackson, Miss.*

Ward, Charles R., Cpl. [29th Div.] *Investigator,* Ohio Department of Liquor Control, *Ashtabula, Ohio*

Washington, Wm. R., Maj. [1st Div.] *Lt. Col., U.S. Army*

Weast, Carl F., Pfc. [5th Rangers] *Machine operator,* Babcock & Wilcox Co., *Alliance, Ohio*

Weatherley, Marion D., Cpl. [237th Engrs.] *Disabled veteran, Laurel, Del.*

Weintraub, Louis, Cpl. [Photog. Army Pict. Svce., 1st Div.] *Public relations,* Louis Weintraub Associates, Inc., *New York, N. Y.*

Welborn, John C., Lt. Col. [4th Div.] *Col.; president,* U.S. Army Armor Board

Weller, Malcolm R., Maj. [29th Div.] *Chief W/Off., U.S. Army*

Wellner, Herman C., Cpl. [37th Engrs.] *Mason, Boscobel, Wis.*

Welsch, Woodrow J., Cpl. [29th Div.] *Construction engineer, Pittsburgh, Pa.*

Wertz, Raymond J., Cpl. [5th Eng. Spec. Brig.] *Self-employed, construction business, Bassett, Wis.*

Whelan, Thomas J., Cpl. [101st Airborne] *Department-store buyer, Smithtown, L. I., N. Y.*

White, John F., 2nd Lt. [29th Div.] *Prosthetic specialist,* Veterans Administration, *Roanoke, Va.*

White, Maurice C., Sgt. [101st Airborne] *Chief W/Off., U.S. Army*

Wiedefeld, William J., Jr., T/Sgt. [29th Div.] *Postal clerk, Annapolis, Md.*

Walsh, Richard J., Sgt. [452nd Bomb Group] *Sgt., U.S.A.F.*

Wilhelm, Frederick A., Pfc. [101st Airborne] *Painter, Pittsburgh, Pa.*

Wilhoit, William L., Ens. [LCT 540] *Special agent,* Insurance Co. of North America, *Jackson, Miss.*

Willett, John D., Jr., Pfc. [29th Div.] General Electric *employee, Roanoke, Ind.*

Williams, William B., Lt. [29th Div.] *Secretary-treasurer,* Acme Wire Co., *Hamden, Conn.*

Williamson, Jack L., S/Sgt. [101st Airborne] *Post-office clerk, Tyler, Tex.*

Wolf, Edwin J., Lt. Col. [6th Eng. Spec. Brig.] *Attorney, Wolf & Wolf, Baltimore, Md.*

Wolf, Karl E., Lt. [1st Div.] *Assistant professor of law, U.S. Military Academy, West Point, N. Y.*

Wolfe, Edward, Pfc. [4th Div.] *Assistant manager, Singer Sewing Machine Co., Westbury, L. I., N. Y.*

Wood, George B., Capt. (chaplain) [82nd Airborne] *Trinity Episcopal Church, Fort Wayne, Ind.*

Woodward, Robert W., Capt. [1st Div.] *Manufacturer, textiles and textile machines, Rockland, Mass.*

Wordeman, Harold E., Pvt. [5th Eng. Spec. Brig.] *Unemployed—partly disabled, V. A. Hospital, Brooklyn, N. Y.*

Worozbyt, John B., Pfc. [1st Div.] *M/Sgt., U.S. Army*

Wozenski, Edward F., Capt. [1st Div.] *Foreman, Wallace Barnes Co., Bristol, Conn.*

Wylie, James M., Capt. [93rd Bomb Group] *Maj., U.S.A.F.*

Wyman, Willard G., Brig. Gen. [Asst. C.O., 1st Div.] *Gen.; Aeroneutronic Systems, Inc., Santa Anna, Calif.*

Yates, Douglas R., Pfc. [6th Eng. Spec. Brig.] *Farmer, Yoder, Wyo.*

Yeatts, Lynn M., Maj. [746th Tank Bn.] *Operations manager, Commercial Oil Transport Co., Fort Worth, Tex.*

Young, Wallace W., Pfc. [2nd Rangers] *Electrician, Beaver Falls, Pa.*

Young, Willard, Lt. [82nd Airborne] *Lt. Col., U.S. Army*

Zaleski, Roman, Pvt. [4th Div.] *Molder, aluminum foundry, Paterson, N. J.*

Zmudzinski, John J., Pfc. [5th Eng. Spec. Brig.] *Letter carrier, South Bend, Ind.*

Zush, Walter J., T/4 [1st Div.] *Occupation unknown*

BRITISH

Aldworth, Michael, Lt. [48 (Royal Marine) Commando] *Advertising*

Allen, Ronald H. D., Gunner [3rd Div.] *Cashier*

Ashover, Claude G., Coxswain [Royal Navy] *Electrician*

Ashworth, Edward P., Ab/Seaman [Royal Navy] *Furnace man, alloy foundry*

Avis, Cecil, Pvt. [Pioneer Corps] *Landscape gardener*

Baker, Alfred G., Ab/Seaman [Royal Navy] *Chemical worker*

Bagley, Anthony F., Midshipman [Royal Navy] *Banking, office worker*

Bald, Peter W., Pvt. [Pioneer Corp.] *Foreman mechanic, garage*

Batten, Raymond W., Pvt. [6th Airborne] *Male nurse*

Baxter, Hubert V., Pvt. [3rd Div.] *Printer*

Beck, Sidney, J. T., Lt. [50th Div.] *Civil servant*

Beynon, John P., Sub Lt. [R.N.V.R.] *Import manager*

Bicknell, Sidney R., Telegraphist [Royal Navy] *Copy editor*

Bidmead, William H., Pvt. [No. 4 Commando] *Bricklayer*

Blackman, Arthur, John, Leading/Stoker [Royal Navy] *Dock engineer*

Bowley, Eric, F. J., Pvt. [50th Div.] *Inspector, aircraft components*

Brayshaw, Walter, Pvt. [50th Div.] *Factory worker*

Brierley, Denys S. C., Fl/Lt. [Royal Air Force] *Textile manufacturer*

Brookes, John S., Pvt. [50th Div.] *Factory worker*

Cadogan, Roy, Trooper [27th Armoured Brig.] *Surveyor*

Capon, Sidney F., Pvt. [6th Airborne] *Master builder*

Cass, E. E. E., Brigadier [3rd Div.] *Brigadier; British Army (retired)*

Cheesman, Arthur B., Sub. Lt. R.N.V.R. [LCS 254] *Quarry manager*

Cheshire, Jack, Sgt. [No. 6 Beach Grp.] *Printer*

Cloudsley-Thompson, John L., Capt. [7th Armoured Div.] *Lecturer, zoology, University of London*

Cole, Thomas A. W., Gunner [50th Div.] *Inspector, machine tools*

Colley, James S. F., Cpl. [4th Commando] *Occupation unknown*

Collins, Charles L., Cpl. [6th Airborne] *Detective sergeant*

Collinson, Joseph A., Lance/Cpl. [3rd Div.] *Enginering draughtsman*

Cooksey, Frank, Cpl. [No. 9 Beach Grp.] *Aircraft fitter*

Cooper, John B., Ab/Seaman [LCT 597] *Occupation unknown*

Corkill, William A., Signalman ["O" LCT Sqdn.] *Senior clerk, accounting office*

Cowley, Ernest J., Stoker/1c [LCT 7045] *Maintenance engineer*

Cox, Leonard H., Cpl. [6th Airborne] *Engraver*

Cox, Norman V., Lt. R.N.V.R. [4th Flotilla] *Civil servant*

Cullum, Percy E., Petty Officer [Mobile Radio Unit] *Inland Revenue officer*

Cutlack, Edward B., Lt. Comdr. R.N.V.R. [9th Minesweeping Flotilla] *Chief instructor*, East Midland Gas Board

Dale, Reginald G., Cpl. [3rd Div.] *Self-employed*

Deaken, B., Pvt. [6th Airborne] *Shoe repairing*

deLacy, James Percival, Sgt. [8th (Irish) Bn., (att. 3rd Can. Div.)] *Travel agent*

Devereux, Roy P., Trooper [6th Airborne] *Travel agency, branch manager*

Dowie, Robert A., Leading/Stoker [H.M.S. *Dunbar*] *Turbine operator*

Dunn, Arthur H., Maj. [50th Div.] *Retired*

Edgson, Charles L., Capt. [Royal Engrs.] *Schoolteacher*

Ellis, F., Pvt. [50th Div.] *Occupation unknown*

Emery, William H., Pvt. [50th Div.] *Van driver*

Emmett, Frederick W., Lance/Bombardier [50th Div.] *Chemical worker*

Finch, Harold, Pvt. [50th Div.] *Policeman*

Flood, Bernard A., Sapper [3rd Div.] *Post-office supervisor*

Flunder, Daniel J., Capt. [48th (Royal Marine) Commando] *Branch manager, Dunlop Ltd.*

Ford, Leslie W., Royal Marine Signalman 2/c [1st S.S. Brig.] *Occupation unknown*

Fortnam, Stanley, Driver/Mech. [6th Airborne] *Compositor*

Fowler, William R., Lt. [H.M.S. *Halsted*] *Advertising salesman*

Fox, Geoffrey R., Leading/Seaman [48th Landing Craft Flotilla] *Policeman*

Fox, Hubert C., Lt. Comdr. [Naval Assault Grp.] *Dairy Farmer*

Gale, John T. J., Pvt. [3rd Div.] *Post-office worker*

Gardner, Donald H., Sgt. [47th (Royal Marine) Commando] *Civil servant*

Gardner, Thomas H., Maj. [3rd Div.] *Managing director*, Leather Manufacturers

Gibbs, Leslie R., Sgt. [50th Div.] *Charge-hand, steel-works production*

Girling, Donald B., Maj. [50th Div.] *Occupation unknown*

Glew, George W., Gunner [3rd Div.] *Clerk*

Gough, J. G., Maj. [3rd Div.] *Dairy farmer*

Gray, William J., Pvt. [6th Airborne] *Occupation unknown*

Grundy, Ernest, Capt. [50th Div.] *Doctor*

Gunning, Hugh, Capt. [3rd Div.] *Syndication manager*, Daily News Ltd.

Gwinnett, John, Capt. (chaplain) [6th Airborne] *Pastor*, Tower of London

Hammond, William, Cpl. [79th Armoured Div.] *Sqdn. Sgt. Maj., British Army*

Hanneson, Hannes, Capt. [R.A.M.C., LST 21] *Specialist physician*

Hardie, I., Lt. Col. [50th Div.] *British Army, active service*

Hargreaves, Edward R., Maj. [3rd Div.] *Deputy County Medical Officer*

Harris, Harry, Ab/Seaman [H.M.S. *Adventure*] *Coal miner*

Harrison, Roger H., Lt. R.N.V.R. [4th LCT Flot.] *Inspection staff, bank*

Harvey, Adolphus J., Acting Col. [Royal Marine Armoured Support Group] *Market gardener*

D-Day Veterans

Hayden, A. C., Pvt. [3rd Div.] *Laborer*

Hollis, Stanley E. V., Co./Sgt./Maj. [50th Div.] *Sand blaster*

Honour, George B., Lt. R.N.V.R. [Midget Submarine X23] *Area Sales Manager, Schweppes Ltd.*

Horton, Harry, Trooper [No. 3 Commando] *Cpl., H.M. Forces*

Humberstone, Henry F., Pvt. [6th Airborne] *Clothing factory worker*

Hutley, John C., S/Sgt. [Glider Pilot Regt.] *Canteen manager*

Hynes, William, Sgt. [50th Div.] *British Army, active service*

Ingram, Ronald A., Gunner [3rd Div.] *Painter and decorator*

James, Leonard K., Cpl. [3rd Div.] *Advertising*

Jankel, Herbert, Capt. [20th Beach Recovery Section] *Garage proprietor*

Jennings, Henry, Sapper [Royal Engrs.] *Contracting*

John, Frederick R., Trooper [No. 6 Commando] *Senior assistant, accounting office*

Johnson, Frank C., Lance/Bombardier [50th Div.] *Wood machinist*

Jones, Edward, Maj. [3rd Div.] *Classics master*

Jones, Peter H., Sgt. [Royal Marines, Frogman] *Building contractor*

Kendall, Hubert O., Cpl. [6th Airborne] *Shipping and forwarding agent*

Kimber, Donald E., Marine [609 Flotilla LCM] *Machine operator*

King, Gordon W., Lt. [6th Airborne] *Representative, paint firm*

Leach, Geoffrey, J., Pvt. [50th Div.] *Laboratory assistant*

Lee, Arthur W., Ab/Seaman [LCT 564] *Local government officer*

Lee, Norton, Sub. Lt. R.N.V.R. [550 LCA Flotilla] *Painter, interior decorating*

Lloyd, Desmond C., Lt. R.N. [Norwegian destroyer *Svenner*] *Company director*

Lovell, Denis, Marine [4th Commando] *Engineering*

Maddison, Godfrey, Pvt. [6th Airborne] *Miner*

March, Desmond C., Lt. [3rd Div.] *Company director*

Markham, Lewis S., T/O Signalman [R.N. LST 301] *Shipping clerk*

Mason, John T., Pvt. [No. 4 Commando] *Schoolteacher*

Masters, Peter F., Lance/Cpl. [No. 10 Commando] *Art director*, WTOP Television, *Washington, D.C.*

Mathers, George H., Cpl. [Royal Engrs.] *Clerk*

May, John McCallon, Sgt. [6th Airborne] *British Army, active service*

McGowan, Alfred, L/Cpl. [6th Airborne] *Packer, flour mill*

Mears, Frederick G., Cpl. [No. 3 Commando] *Accounting machines factory worker*

Millin, W., Piper [1st S.S. Brig.] *Male nurse*

Minnis, James C., Sub/Lt. R.N.V.R. [LCT 665] *Teacher*

Mitchell, John D., Cpl. [54 Beach Balloon Unit, RAF] *Company director*

Montgomery, Sir Bernard Law, Gen.; *Field Marshal (retired)*

Moore, William J. D., L/Cpl. [3rd Div.] *Male nurse*

Morgan, Vincent H., Pvt. [50th Div.] *Post-office worker*

Morris, Ernest, Cpl. [50th Div.] *occupation unknown*

Morrissey, James F., Pvt. [6th Airborne] *Docker*

Mower, Alan C., Pvt. [6th Airborne] *Security officer, research labs.*

Murphy, John, Leading Aircraftsman [RAF, Balloon Command] *Post-office worker*

Neilsen, Henry R., Capt. [6th Airborne] *Knitwear manufacturer*

Newton, Reginald V., Pvt. [6th Airborne] *Company director*

Nissen, Derek A., Lt. [3rd Div.] *Works manager*

Norfield, Harry T., Cpl. [3rd Div.] *British Admiralty messenger*

Northwood, Ronald J., Ab/Seaman [H.M.S. *Scylla*] *Hairdresser*

Norton, Gerald Ivor D., Capt. [3rd Div.] *Company secretary*

Oliver, Arthur E., L/Cpl. [No. 4 Commando] *Coal miner*

Otway, Terence, Lt. Col. [6th Airborne] *Executive*, Kemsley *newspapers*

Pargeter, George S., Cpl. [Royal Marines] *Production control clerk*
Parker, William, Sapper [50th Div.] *Bus driver*
Paris, Sydney F., Leading Seaman [H.M.S. *Melbreak*] *Police constable*
Peachey, Sidney, Chief P.O. [H.M.S. *Warspite*] *Engineer*
Peskett, Stanley V., Lt. Col. [1st R.M. Armoured Support Regt.] *Royal Marines,
     active service*
Phillips, Sir Farndale, Lt. Col. [47 (Royal Marine) Commando CO] *Maj. Gen.;
     President,* British Trades Federation
Porter, Walter S., Pfc. [53 Pioneer Corps] *Painter, decorator*
Powell, Colin E., Pvt. [6th Airborne] *Sales department, steel company*
Purver, Raymond, Sapper [50th Div.] *Stores foreman*
Purvis, Joseph, Pvt. [5th Div.] *Laborer*
Raphaelli, Cyril, Cpl. [3rd Div.] *British Army, active service*
Ringland, John, Trooper [8th Armoured Brigade] *Post and telegraph officer*
Robertson, D. J., Lt. [27th Armoured Brig.] *Solicitor's managing clerk*
Rolles, John R., Cpl. [3rd Div.] *Lighterman*
Ruthen, Walter S., Pvt. [3rd Div.] *Postman*
Rutter, William I., Pvt. [6th Airborne] *Poultry farmer*
Ryland, Richard A., Sub/Lt. R.N.V.R. [7th Landing Barge Flotilla] *Cultivating
     oysters and writing*
Sawyer, David J., Trooper [79th Armoured Div.] *Power station, foreman*
Scarfe, Norman, Lt. [3rd Div.] *Lecturer, history,* University of Leicester
Scoot, J. E., Marine [48th (Royal Marine) Commando] *Department manager,
     factory*
Sharr, Leonard G., S/Sgt. [6th Airborne] *Partner, textile agency*
Sheard, Edgar T., Trooper [6th Airborne] *Sergeant, British Army*
Sim, John A., Capt. [6th Airborne] *Active service*
Slade, John H., Sapper [50th Div.] *Railway clerk*
Slapp, John A., Cpl. [3rd Div.] *Chief clerk*
Smith, Christopher N., Trooper [27th Armoured Brig.] *Area representative, gas
     board*
Smith, Robert A., Signalman [3rd Div.] *Guard, railways*
Spence, Basil, Capt. [3rd Div.] *Architect,* Coventry Cathedral
Stannard, Ernest W., Dvr/Operator [50th Div.] *Maintenance fitter*
Stevenson, Douglas A., Coder [LCI 100] *Fishmonger*
Stewart, Stanley, Pvt. [4th Commando] *occupation unknown*
Stokes, Albert J., Pvt. [3rd Div.] *Exterminator*
Stott, Frederick, Pvt. [3rd Div.] *Clergyman*
Strevens, George A., Cpl. [3rd Div.] *Inshore fisherman*
Stunell, George C., Pvt. [50th Div.] *occupation unknown*
Sullivan, Bernard J., Lt. R.N.V.R. [553 Assault Flotilla] *Bank clerk*
Swan, Robert M., L/Cpl. [50th Div.] *Bank clerk*
Tait, Harold G., L/Cpl. [6th Airborne] *Grocery manager*
Tappenden, Edward, L/Cpl. [6th Airborne] *Clerk*
Taylor, John B., Lt. [Frogman, Team No. 4] *Tobacconist*
Thomas, William J., Cpl. [50th Div.] *Diesel operator*
Thomson, Roger W. D., Comdr. R.N. [H.M.S. *Sidmouth*] *Manufacturing plant*
Todd, Richard, Lt. [6th Airborne] *Movie actor*
Tomlinson, Percy, W/OP [Mobile Signals Unit R.A.F.] *Plasterer*
Vickers, Francis W., Pvt. [50th Div.] *occupation unknown*
Warburton, Geoffrey A., Signalman [8th Armoured Brig.] *Accounts clerk*
Ward, Percy, CO Sgt/Maj. [50th Div.] *Telephone engineer*

Ward, Patrick, A., Lt. R.N.V.R. [115th Minesweeping Flotilla] *ocupation unknown*
Webber, Dennis J., Lt. [9th Beach Grp.] *Bank clerk*
Webber, John, Telegraphist/O [200 LCT Flotilla] *Opthalmic optician*
Webber, John J., Capt. [6th Airborne] *Accountant*
West, Leonard C., W/O [3rd Div.] *Clerical office, Admiralty*
Weston, Ronald, L/Cpl. [50th Div.] *Chief clerk, Army*
White, Niels W., 2/Lt. [50th Div.] *Fur broker*
Wiggins, John R., Lt. R.N.V.R. [LST 423] *Headmaster*
Wightman, Leslie, Pvt. [3rd Div.] *Chief cinema projectionist*
Wilson, Charles S., Pvt. [50th Div.] *Subway railway clerk*
Wilson, Gordon C., 2nd Lt. [47 (Royal Marine) Commando] *Advertising agency*
Windrum, Anthony W., Maj. [6th Airborne] *Foreign service officer* (retired)
Winter, John E., Stoker/1c [R.N. (Combined Ops)] *Bookmaker*
Wither, Russell J., Sgt. [41 (Royal Marine) Commando] *Wages clerk*
Yelland, Charles H., Sgt. [50th Div.] *foundry worker*

CANADIAN

Anderson, James, Maj. [3rd Can. Div.] *Department minister, social services, New Brunswick*
Arbuckle, Robert, Gunner [19th Can. Field Regt.] *Sectionman, Canadian National Railways*
Axford, Douglas S., Sgt. [3rd Can. Div.] *W/Off., Canadian Army*
Backosti, John, Leading Stoker [H.M.C.S. *Prince Henry*] *A. E. Tech., RCAF*
Bayliss, Gilbert, Fl/Off. [RAF] *Fl/Off., RCAF*
Blackader, K. G., Brigadier [3rd Can. Div.] *Accountant*
Blake, John J., Steward [H.M.C.S. *Prince Henry*] *Ground-Technician, RCAF*
Boon, Arthur, Gunner [3rd Can. Div.] *Employee, Canadian National Railways*
Brebner, Dr. Colin N., Capt. [1st Can. Parachute Bn., 6th Airborne] *Surgeon*
Chalcraft, William R., Fl/Lt. [419 Sqdn.] *Fl/Off., RCAF*
Champoux, Robert A., Cpl. [3rd Can. Div.] *Canadian Army*
Cherrington, Horace D., Sgt. [570th Sqdn.] *Engineer*
Churchill, Henry L., Pvt. [1st Can. Para Bn., 6th Airborne] *occupation unknown*
Cockroft, Gordon, Leading Coder [H.M.C.S. *Lindsay*] *Cpl., Canadian Army, Ordnance Corps*
Couture, George J., Rifleman [3rd Can. Div.] *Recruiting sergeant, Canadian Army*
Cox, Kenneth W., Pvt. [14th Can/Field Ambulance] *Sgt., RCAF*
Cresine, Ellis R., Gunner [3rd Can. Div.] *RCAF, Air Force police*
Davies, Francis J., Lance/Bombardier [3rd Can. Div.] *S/Sgt., Canadian Army*
Dewey, Clarence J., Cpl. [1st TAC Air Force Police] *Fire Fighter, RCAF*
Dunn, Clifford E., Pvt. [3rd Can. Div.] *Dairy business*
Dutton, Eldon R., Signalman [3rd Can. Div.] *Sgt., Canadian Army*
Eldridge, Victor, W./Off. [415 RCAF Sqdn.] *RCAF*
Elmes, William J., Lance/Cpl. [2nd Can. Army] *Canadian Army*
Evans, Cyril, Tpr. [3rd Can. Div.] *Electrician*
Farrell, J. A., Pvt. [3rd Can. Div.] *Broadcaster and writer*
Fitzpatrick, Carl L., Ab/Seaman [H.M.C.S. *Blairmore*] *Lt., Canadian Army*
Forbes, Robert B., Maj. [3rd Can. Div.] *Purchasing manager*
Forth, John W., Maj. [Asst. Sr. Chaplain, 3rd Can. Div.] *Col., director of chaplains, Canadian Army*

Fowler, Donald M., Pvt. [3rd Can. Div.] *Pricing supervisor*
Fuller, Clayton, Maj. [1st Can. Parachute Bn., [6th Airborne] Canadian Brass Company, *Galt, Ont.*
Fraser, George C., Cpl. [3rd Can. Div.] *Clerk*
Gammon, Clinton, C. L., Capt. [3rd Can. Div.] *Papermaker*
Gardiner, George J., Sgt. [3rd Can. Div.] *Cpl., Canadian Army*
Gillan, James D. M., Capt. [3rd Can. Div.] *Canadian Army*
Goeres, Raymond J., F/Lt. [RAF #101 Sqdn.] *F/Lt., RCAF*
Graham, Robert J., Sapper [3rd Can. Div.] *Office Supervisor*
Griffin, Peter, Capt. [1st Can. Parachute Bn. 6th Airborne] *occupation unknown*
Gunnarson, Gunnar H., Rifleman [3rd Can. Div.] *Farming*
Haines, Charles W. R., Pvt. [3rd Can. Div.] *Air Force police, RCAF*
Hall, John T., Fl/Off. [51 Bomber Sqdn.] *Sqdn. Leader, RCAF*
Hamilton, John H., Lance/Cpl. [3rd Can. Div.] *Buyer, wholesale grocery firm*
Hickey, R. M., Capt. (Chaplain) [3rd Can. Div.] *Pastor*
Hilborn, Richard, Lt. [1st Can. Parachute Bn., 6th Airborne] Preston Furniture Co., *Preston, Ont.*
Hillock, Frank W., Wing Comdr. [143 Wing RCAF] *Wing Comdr., RCAF*
Hurtick, Walter J., Fl/Off. [524 Sqdn.] *Sgt., RCAF*
Jeans, Ernest A., Cpl. [1st Can. Parachute Bn., 6th Airborne] *Teacher*
Johnston, Alexand, Sapper [3rd Can. Div.] *Royal Canadian Ordnance Corps*
Johnston, John R., Signalman [3rd Can. Div.] *Telegraph technician, RCAF*
Johnstone, T., Sgt. [2nd Arm. Brig.] *Instructor, Canadian Army*
Labelle, Placide, Capt. [3rd Can. Div.] *Publicity services*
Laing, Gordon K., Pvt. [3rd Can. Div.] *Industrial painter*
Langell, Louis, Pvt. [3rd Can. Div.] *Canadian Army*
LeBlanc, Joseph E. H., Capt. [3rd Can. Div.] *Maj., Canadian Army*
Leroux, Roland A., Sgt. [3rd Can. Div.] *Customs officer*
Liggins, Percival, Pvt. [1st Can. Parachute Bn., 6th Airborne] *Parachute rescue jumper*
Lind, Jack B., Capt. [3rd Can. Div.] *Canadian Army*
Little, Edward T., Lance/Cpl. [1st Can. Parachute Bn., 6th Airborne] *Canadian Army*
Lockhart, Lloyd J., Leading Seaman [H.M.C.S. *Saskatchewan*] *Fire fighter, RCAF*
Lynch, C. Lawrence, Lt. [3rd Can. Div.] *Bank employee*
MacKenzie, Donald L., Pvt. [3rd Can. Div.] *RCAF*
MacLean, Richard O., Sgt. [1st Can. Parachute Bn., 6th Airborne] *Oil and gas distributor*
MacRae, John Lt. [3rd Can. Div.] *Member of Parliament*
Magee, Morris H., Sgt. [3rd Can. Div.] *Cardiographer*
Mandin, Joseph A., Rifleman [3rd Can. Div.] *Airman, RCAF*
Manning, Robert F., C/Petty Off. [Minesweeping Flotilla] *Maintenance superintendent, hydroelectric plant*
Mathieu, Paul, Lt. Col. [3rd Can. Div.] *Assistant Department Minister, Department of National Defence*
McCumber, John M., Cpl. [2nd Armoured Brig.] *Canadian Army*
McDonald, James W., Cpl. [3rd Can. Div.] *Immigration officer on U.S.–Canadian border*
McDougall, Colin C., Capt. [3rd Can. Div.] *Department director, public relations, Canadian Army*
McFeat, William P., Gunner [3rd Can. Div.] *Special placements officer,* Canadian Employment Service

McGechie, William, Fl/Off. [298th Sqdn.] *Assessor, Canadian Department of Mines and Minerals*
McKee, Robert, Fl/Off. [296th Sqdn.] *Sqdn. leader, RCAF*
McLean, Charles W., Maj. [3rd Can. Div.] *General Sales manager, textiles*
McMurray, Robert M., Lance/Cpl. [3rd Can. Div.] *Insurance underwriter*
McNamee, Gordon A., Fl/Off. [405th Sqdn.] *Fl/Lt., RCAF*
McPhatter, Roderick H., Leading Coder [H.M.C.S. *Caraquet*] *Fl/Lt., RCAF*
McTavish, Frank A., Maj. [3rd Can. Div.] *Maj., Canadian Army*
Millar, Ian A. L., Maj. [3rd Can. Div.] *Lt. Col., Canadian Army*
Mitchell, James F., Sqdn. Leader [83rd Sqdn.] *RCAF*
Moffatt, John L., Fl/Off. [575th Sqdn.] *Schoolteacher*
Mosher, Albert B., Pvt. [3rd Can. Div.] *Ground defence instructor, RCAF*
Murch, Hewitt J., Signalman [3rd Can. Div.] *Farmer*
Newin, Harry J., F/Sgt. [625 Sqdn.] *RCAF*
Olmsted, Earl A., Capt. [3rd Can. Div.] *Lt. Col., Canadian Army*
O'Regan, Robert B., Gunner [3rd Can. Div.] *Public relations, Canadian Army*
Osborne, Daniel N., Capt. [3rd Can. Div.] *Maj., Canadian Army*
Paterson, William, Pvt. [6th Airborne] *High-school teacher*
Pearson, Clifford A., Lance/Cpl. [3rd Can. Div.] *Sgt., Canadian Army*
Piers, Desmond W., Lt. Comdr. [H.M.C.S. *Algonquin*] *Commodore, Royal Canadian Navy*
Raich, Jack, Cpl. [3rd Can. Div.] *Sgt., Canadian Army*
Rehill, Cecil, Lt. [3rd Can. Div.] *Canadian Army*
Rogge, Robert E., Pvt. [3rd Can. Div.] *T/Sgt., USAF*
Ruffee, George E. M., Lt. [3rd Can. Div.] *Canadian Army*
Saunders, Frederick T., Lance/Cpl. [3rd Can. Div.] *Foreman supervisor, power station*
Schaupmeyer, John E., Sapper [3rd Can. Div.] *Farming*
Scott, Charles J., Lt. [LCT 926] *Editor*
Stewart, Angus A., Pvt. [3rd Can. Div.] *Farming*
Shawcross, Ronald G., Capt. [3rd Can. Div.] *Manager, envelope company*
Smith, Stanley A. E., Leading Aircadet [2nd T.A.F.] *Cpl., RCAF*
Somerville, Joseph, Pvt. [3rd Can. Div.] *Employee, paper company*
Stanley, Robert W., Pvt. [1st Can. Parachute Bn., 6th Airborne] *Metal worker*
Stothart, Jack G., Capt. [3rd Can. Div.] *Agricultural research*
Thompson, Robert J., Gunner [3rd Can. Div.] *Fire fighter, RCAF*
Thomson, Thomas A., P/Off. [425 Sqdn.] *Fl/Sgt., RCAF*
Todd, Percy A. S., Brig. [3rd Can. Div. (Artillery Comdr.)] *Railway, general manager*
Velux, Gene, Sapper [3rd Can. Div.] *Cpl., Canadian Army*
Vidler, Douglas R., Pvt. [3rd Can. Div.] *Film tester*
Warburton, James A., Lt. [3rd Can. Div.] *Engineer*
Washburn, Arthur S., Lance/Sgt. [3rd Can. Div.] *Civil servant*
Webber, John L., Sgt. [86th Sqdn.] *Flt/Engineer*
White, William B., Pvt. [1st Can. Parachute Bn., 6th Airborne] *Sgt., Canadian Army*
Widenoja, Edwin T., Fl/Off. [433rd Sqdn.] *Pulp and paper tester*
Wilkins, Donald, Maj. [1st Can. Parachute Bn., 6th Airborne] *Investment broker*
Zack, Theodore, Trooper [3rd Can. Div.] *Farmer*

FRENCH

Kieffer, Philippe, Commander [CO French Commandos, Att. No. 4 Commando] *NATO Paris*

French Underground
Auge, Albert—*Caen, French Railways*
Gille, Léonard—*Caen, Normandy Deputy Military Intelligence Chief*
Gille, Louise "Janine" Boitard—*Caen, Allied Pilot Escape Network*
Lechevalier, Amélie—*Caen, Allied Pilot Escape Network*
Marion, Jean—*Grandcamp, Omaha Sector Chief*
Mercader, Guillaume—*Bayeux, Coastal Section Chief*
Picard, Roger—*Southern France, Intelligence*
Rémy, George Jean—*Paris, Radio Communication*

GERMAN

Blumentritt, Gunther, Maj. Gen. [OB West—Rundstedt's Chief of Staff] *Lt. Gen. (retired)*
Bürkner, Leopold, Vice Admiral [Chief of Protocol, Hitler's HQ-OKW] *Airline personnel director*
Damski, Aloysius, Pvt. [716th Div.] *occupation unknown*
Düring, Ernst, Capt. [352nd Div.] *Businessman*
Feuchtinger, Edgar, Lt. Gen. [CO 21st Panzer Div.] *Technical Adviser, German industrial combine*
Freyberg, Leodegard, Col. [Personnel Chief, Army Group B] *Official,* Federation of German Soldiers
Gause, Alfred, Maj. Gen. [Rommel's Chief of Staff (to Mar. 1944)] *U.S. Army Historical Division, Germany*
Häger, Josef, Lance Cpl. [716th Div.] *Machinist*
Halder, Franz, Col. Gen. [Chief of German General Staff (to Sept. 1942)] *U.S. Army Historical Division, Germany*
Hayn, Friedrich, Maj. [Intelligence Officer, 84th Corps] *Author*
Hermes, Walter, Pvt. [192nd Regt., 21st Panzer Div.] *Postman*
Hildebrand, Otto, Lt. [21st Panzer Div.] *Occupation unknown*
Hoffmann, Heinrich, Lt. Comdr. [5th E-boat flotilla] *German Navy, Bonn Defense Ministry*
Hoffner, Hans, Brig. Gen. [Rail Transportation Chief for France, OB West] *German Army*
Hofmann, Rudolf, Maj. Gen. [Chief of Staff, 15th Army] *Retired; consultant to U.S. Army Historical Division, Germany*
Hummerich, Wilhelm, Capt. [709th Div.] *Deputy Commander, German Support Unit, NATO—Allied Forces Central Europe*
Krancke, Theodor, Admiral [Naval Comdr.-in-Chief, West] *Now pensioned and retired. (Until recently employed as laborer)*
Lang, Hellmuth, Capt. [Rommel's Aide] *Storekeeper*
Meyer, Hellmuth, Lt. Col. [Intelligence Officer, 15th Army] *German Army*
Meyer-Detring, Wilhelm, Brig. Gen. [Intelligence Chief, OB West] *Chief, Intelligence, NATO—Allied Forces Central Europe*
Ohmsen, Walter, Capt. [Comdr., Marcouf Battery] *Harbor control officer*
Pemsel, Max, Maj. Gen. [Chief of Staff, 7th Army] *Lt. Gen., German Army*
Pluskat, Werner, Maj. [352nd Div.] *Engineer*

D-Day Veterans

Priller, Josef, Col. [Wing Comdr., 26th Fighter Wing] *Brewery manager*
Reichert, Josef, Maj. Gen. [CO 711th Div.] *Lt. Gen. (retired)*
Richter, Wilhelm, Maj. Gen. [CO 716th Inf. Div.] *Lt. Gen. (retired)*
Ruge, Friedrich, Vice-Admiral [Rommel's Naval Aide] *Inspector of German Naval Forces*
Saul, Carl, Lt. Dr. [709th Inf. Div.] *High-school teacher*
Schenck Zu Schweinsberg, Maj. Baron Hans [21st Panzer Div.] *Private income*
Speidel, Hans, Maj. Gen., Dr. [Rommel's Chief of Staff] *Lt. Gen.; NATO— Commander, Allied Land Forces, Central Europe*
Staubwasser, Anton, Lt. Col. [Intelligence Chief, Army Group B] *German Army*
Stenzel, Willy, Lance/Cpl. [6th Parachute Regiment] *Salesman*
Stöbe, Walter, Prof., Dr. [Chief Meteorologist, Luftwaffe (West)] *Teacher*
Voigt, Wilhelm, Pvt. [Radio Monitoring Group] *Public relations,* Pan American Airways, *Frankfurt, Germany*
von Gottberg, Wilhelm, Capt. [22nd Regt., 21st Panzer] *Manager, automobile agency*
von Kistowski, Werner, Col. [1st Regt., 3rd Flak Corps.] *Lightning-rod salesman*
von Oppeln-Bronikowski, Hermann, Col. [22nd Regt., 21st Panzer Div.] *Gen. (retired); estate steward*
von Puttkamer, Karl Jesko, Adm. [Hitler's Naval Aide] *Personnel director, export firm*
von Salmuth, Hans, Gen. [CO 15th Army] *Gen. (retired)*
von Schramm, Wilhelm, Maj. [Official War Reporter] *Author*
Warlimont, Walter, Gen. [Ass't Chief of Operations, OKW] *Gen. (retired)*
Wuensch, Anton, Cpl. [6th Parachute Regt.] *Occupation unknown*
Zimmermann, Bodo, Lt. Gen. [Chief of Operations, OB West] *Lt. Gen. (retired); magazine and book publisher*

ACKNOWLEDGMENTS

THE PRINCIPAL sources of information for this book came from Allied and German D-Day survivors, French underground workers and civilians—more than 1,000 in all. Freely and unselfishly they gave of their time, and no inconvenience seemed too great. They filled out questionnaires, and after these forms had been collated and cross-checked with those of other veterans they cheerfully provided additional information. They answered my many letters and queries. They supplied me with a wealth of documentation and memorabilia—water-stained maps, tattered diaries, after-action reports, logs, message pads, company rosters, casualty lists, personal letters and photographs—and they made themselves available for interview. I am deeply indebted to these contributors. On preceding pages the reader will find a complete list of all military personnel and French underground workers who helped. To my knowledge this partial list of D-Day participants is the only one of its kind in existence.

Of the total number of survivors located—a task that took the best part of three years—some 700 were interviewed in the U.S., Canada, Great Britain, France and Germany. Some 383 accounts were blended into the text. For a variety of editorial reasons—principally that of repetition—it was impossible to include everyone's account. However, the framework of the book was constructed on the information supplied by all the participants, plus Allied and German after-action reports, war diaries, histories or other official records (such as the magnificent combat interviews conducted during and after the war by Brigadier General S. L. A. Marshall, U.S.A.R., the European Theater Military Historian).

At the onset I wish to thank De Witt Wallace, editor and publisher of *The Reader's Digest*, for underwriting nearly all of the costs and thus making this book possible.

Next I must pay tribute to the U.S. Secretary of Defense; General Maxwell D. Taylor, until recently the U.S. Army's Chief of Staff; Major General H. P. Storke, the Army's Chief of Information; Colonel G. Chesnutt, Lieutenant Colonel John S. Cheseboro and Lieutenant Colonel C. J. Owen of the Army's Magazine and Book branch; Commander Herbert Gimpel of the U.S. Navy's Magazine and Book branch; Major J. Sunderman and Captain W. M. Mack of the U.S. Air Force's Information Division; Mrs. Martha Holler of the Defense Department's Accreditation and Travel Division; and the many public-relations officers in Europe and elsewhere who assisted me at every turn. All of these people aided not only in helping me locate veterans but by opening doors everywhere, granting me permission to

Acknowledgments

examine hitherto classified documents, supplying me with detailed maps, transporting me to and from Europe, and in setting up interviews.

I must also acknowledge the gracious assistance and co-operation of Dr. Kent Roberts Greenfield, until recently Chief Historian, the Office of Chief of Military History, and the members of his staff—Major William F. Heitz, Mr. Israel Wice, Mr. Detmar Finke and Mr. Charles von Luttichau—for giving me permission to draw on official histories and records and for their constant guidance and advice. I would like to mention here the work of Charles von Luttichau, who spent all of his spare time over a period of nearly eight months translating bale loads of German documents and the all important German war diaries.

Among the contributors to the book I would like to thank in particular the following: Sergeant William Petty for meticulously reconstructing the Ranger's action at Pointe du Hoc; Corporal Michael Kurtz of the 1st Division, Second Lieutenant Edward Gearing and Brigadier General Norman Cota of the 29th for their vivid descriptions of Omaha Beach; Colonel Gerden Johnson of the 4th Division for his careful breakdown of the equipment carried by first-wave assault troops; Colonel Eugene Caffey and Sergeant Harry Brown for their portrayals of Brigadier General Theodore Roosevelt on Utah Beach; Major General Raymond O. Barton, the 4th Division's Commanding Officer on D Day, for his guidance and for loaning me his maps and official papers; Brigadier E. E. E. Cass, whose 8th British Brigade led the assault on Sword Beach, for his detailed memorandums and papers and his kind efforts in trying to research the British casualty figures; Mrs. Theodore Roosevelt for her many kindnesses, thoughtful suggestions and criticisms; William Walton, formerly of *Time* and *Life*, the only war correspondent to jump with the 82nd, for digging through his trunks and finding his old notebooks and then over a two-day session re-creating the atmosphere of the assault; Captain Daniel J. Flunder and Lieutenant Michael Aldworth of the 48th Royal Marine Commandos for painting the scene on Juno; and Piper Bill Millin of Lord Lovat's Commandos for his diligent search to find the list of tunes that he played throughout the day.

I would also like to express my appreciation to General Maxwell D. Taylor, who took time out from his grueling schedule to take me step by step through the 101st Airborne's assault and who later read pertinent parts of the manuscript for accuracy. Others who checked for errors and who read two or three versions of the manuscript were Lieutenant General Sir Frederick Morgan, the architect of the original Overlord plan, and Lieutenant General James M. Gavin, who commanded the 82nd's parachute drop into Normandy.

I am also indebted to General Omar N. Bradley, who commanded the U.S. First Army; Lieutenant General Walter B. Smith, who was Chief of Staff to General Dwight D. Eisenhower; Lieutenant General J. T. Crocker, who commanded the 1st British Corps; and General Sir Richard Gale, who commanded the British 6th Airborne. These men kindly answered my queries, or granted me interviews or made available to me their wartime maps and papers.

On the German side I wish to acknowledge the generous co-operation of the Bonn Government and the many service associations who located veterans and set up appointments.

For assistance from the many German contributors I am particularly grateful to Colonel General Franz Halder, former Chief of the German General Staff; Captain Hellmuth Lang, Rommel's aide; Major General Günther Blumentritt, Field Marshal von Rundstedt's Chief of Staff; Lieutenant General Dr. Hans Speidel, Rommel's Chief of Staff; Frau Lucie Maria Rommel and her son, Manfred; Lieutenant General Max Pemsel, the 7th Army's Chief of Staff; General Hans von Salmuth, the 15th Army's commanding officer; General von Oppeln-Bronikowski of the 21st Panzer; Colonel Josef Priller of the Luftwaffe's 26th Fighter Wing; Lieutenant Colonel Hellmuth Meyer of the 15th Army; and Major Werner Pluskat of the 352nd Division. All these and scores of others were kind enough to grant me interviews, spending hours reconstructing various phases of the battle.

In addition to the information collected from D-Day participants, many works by eminent historians and authors were consulted during the research. I would like to express my gratitude to Gordon A. Harrison, author of the official D-Day history, *Cross-Channel Attack*, and Dr. Forest Pogue, author of the U.S. Army's *The Supreme Command*, both of whom gave me guidance and helped me solve many a controversial point. Their books proved invaluable in giving me an over-all picture both politically and militarily of the events leading up to the invasion and in detailing the attack itself. Other books that I found most helpful were *The Invasion of France and Germany* by Samuel E. Morison; *Omaha Beachhead* by Charles H. Taylor; *Utah to Cherbourg* by R. G. Ruppenthal; *Rendezvous with Destiny* by Leonard Rapport and Arthur Norwood, Jr.; *Men Against Fire* by Brigadier General S. L. A. Marshall, U.S.A.R.; and *The Canadian Army: 1939-1945* by Colonel C. P. Stacey. A bibliography of books referred to is appended.

In locating veterans, gathering research and in the final interviewing I was ably assisted by *Reader's Digest* researchers, bureau representatives and editors in the U.S., Canada, Great Britain, France and Germany. In New York Miss Frances Ward and Miss Sally Roberts, under the guidance of Department Editor Gertrude Arundel, waded through piles of documents, questionnaires and correspondence and somehow kept abreast of it all. In London Miss Joan Isaacs did a similar job, including many interviews. With the help of the Canadian War Office, the *Digest's* Shane McKay and Miss Nancy Vail Bashant found and interviewed dozens of Canadian veterans. The European end of the operation was the most difficult, and I must thank Max C. Schreiber, editor of the *Digest's* German edition, for his advice; and especially Associate Editor George Révay, John D. Panitza and Yvonne Fourcade of the *Digest's* European editorial office in Paris for their magnificent work in organizing and researching the project and for their tireless interviewing. My earnest thanks also to the *Digest's* Assistant Managing Editor, Hobart Lewis, for believing in the project in the first place and for holding my hand through the long months of work.

Acknowledgments

There are many, many others to whom I owe debts of gratitude. To mention just a few: Jerry Korn for his thoughtful criticisms and editorial assistance; Don Lassen for his many letters regarding the 82nd Airborne; Don Brice of the Dictaphone Corp., and David Kerr for help in interviewing; Colonel John Virden of the *Army Times*, Kenneth Crouch of the *Bedford Democrat*, Dave Parsons of Pan-American Airways, Ted Rowe of IBM, and Pat Sullivan of General Dynamics—all of whom through their organizations helped me trace survivors; Suzanne Gleaves, Theodore H. White, Peter Schwed, and Phyllis Jackson for their careful readings of each version of the work; Lillian Lang for her secretarial work; Anne Wright, who filed, cross-indexed, handled correspondence and did all the typing; and above all my dear wife, Kathryn, who collated, organized the research, helped in final revision of the manuscript, and contributed more than anyone else—for she had to live through the writing.

C. R.

BIBLIOGRAPHY

Babington-Smith, Constance, *Air Spy*. New York: Harper & Bros., 1957.
Baldwin, Hanson W., *Great Mistakes of the War*. New York: Harper & Bros., 1950.
Baumgartner, Lt. John W.; DePoto, 1st Sgt. Al; Fraccio, Sgt. William; Fuller, Cpl. Sammy, *The 16th Infantry, 1798-1946*. Privately printed.
Bird, Will R., *No Retreating Footsteps*. Nova Scotia: Kentville Publishing Co.
Blond, Georges, *Le Débarquement, 6 Juin 1944*. Paris: Arthème Fayard, 1951.
Bradley, General Omar N., *A Soldier's Story*. New York: Henry Holt, 1951.
Bredin, Lt. Col. A.E.C., *Three Assault Landings*. London: Gale & Polden, 1946.
British First and Sixth Airborne Divisions, the Official Account of, *By Air to Battle*. London: His Majesty's Stationery Office, 1945.
Brown, John Mason, *Many a Watchful Night*. New York: Whittlesey House, 1944.
Butcher, Captain Harry C., *My Three Years with Eisenhower*. New York: Simon and Schuster, 1946.
Canadian Department of National Defence, *Canada's Battle in Normandy*. Ottawa: King's Printer, 1946.
Chaplin, W. W., *The Fifty-Two Days*. Indianapolis and New York: Bobbs-Merrill, 1944.
Churchill, Winston S., *The Second World War* (Vols. I–VI). Boston: Houghton Mifflin, 1948-1953.
Clay, Major Ewart W., *The Path of the 50th*. London: Gale & Polden, 1950.
Colvin, Ian, *Master Spy*. New York: McGraw-Hill, 1951.
Cooper, John P., Jr., *The History of the 110th Field Artillery*. Baltimore: War Records Division, Maryland Historical Society, 1953.
Crankshaw, Edward, *Gestapo*. New York: Viking Press, 1956.
Danckwerts, P. V., *King Red and Co*. Royald Armoured Corps *Journal*, Vol. 1, July 1946.
Dawson, W. Forrest, *Sage of the All American* (82nd Airborne Div.). Privately printed.
Dempsey, Lt. Gen. M. C., *Operations of the 2nd Army in Europe*. London: War Office, 1957.
Edwards, Commander Kenneth, R.N., *Operation Neptune*. London: The Albatross Ltd., 1947.
Eisenhower, Dwight D., *Crusade in Europe*. New York: Doubleday, 1948.
First Infantry Division, with introduction by Hanson Baldwin: H. R. Knickerbocker, Jack Thompson, Jack Belden, Don Whitehead, A. J. Liebling, Mark Watson, Cy Peterman, Iris Carpenter, Col. R. Ernest Dupuy, Drew Middleton and former officers: *Danger Forward*. Atlanta: Albert Love Enterprises, 1947.
First U.S. Army Report of Operations, 20 Oct. '43 to Aug. '44. *Field Artillery Journal*.
Fleming, Peter, *Operation Sea Lion*. New York: Simon and Schuster, 1947.

Bibliography

457 AAA AW Battalion, *From Texas to Teismach*. Nancy, France: Imprimerie A. Humblot, 1945.

Fuller, Major General J. F. C., *The Second World War*. New York: Duell, Sloan and Pearce, 1949.

Gale, Lt. Gen. Sir Richard, *With the 6th Airborne Division in Normandy*. London: Sampson, Lowe, Marston & Co. Ltd., 1948.

Gavin, Lt. Gen. James M., *Airborne Warfare*. Washington, D.C.: Infantry Journal Press, 1947.

Glider Pilot Regimental Association, *The Eagle* (Vol. 2). London, 1954.

Goerlitz, Walter, *The German General Staff* (Introduction by Walter Millis). New York: Frederick A. Praeger, 1953.

Guderian, General Heinz, *Panzer Leader*. New York: E. P. Dutton, 1952.

Gunning, Hugh, *Borderers in Battle*. Berwick-on-Tweed, England: Martin and Co., 1948.

Hansen, Harold A.; Herndon, John G.; Langsdorf, William B., *Fighting for Freedom*. Philadelphia: John C. Winston, 1947.

Harrison, Gordon A., *Cross-Channel Attack*. Washington, D.C.: Office of the Chief of Military History, Department of the Army, 1951.

Hart, B. H. Liddell, *The German Generals Talk*. New York: William Morrow, 1948.

Hart, B. H. Liddell (editor), *The Rommel Papers*. New York: Harcourt, Brace, 1953.

Hayn, Friedrich, *Die Invasion*. Heidelberg: Kurt Vowinckel Verlag, 1954.

Herval, René, *Bataille de Normandie*. Paris: Editions de Notre-Dame.

Hickey, Rev. R. M., *The Scarlet Dawn*. Campbellton, N. B.: Tribune Publishers, Ltd., 1949.

Hollister, Paul, and Strunsky, Robert (editors), *D-Day Through Victory in Europe*. New York: Columbia Broadcasting System, 1945.

Holman, Gordon, *Stand By to Beach!* London: Hodder & Stoughton, 1944.

Jackson, Lt. Col. G. S., *Operations of Eighth Corps*. London: St. Clements Press, 1948.

Johnson, Franklyn A., *One More Hill*. New York: Funk & Wagnalls, 1949.

Karig, Commander Walter, USNR, *Battle Report*. New York: Farrar & Rinehart, 1946.

Lemonnier-Gruhier, François, *La Brèche de Sainte-Marie-du-Mont*. Paris: Editions Spes.

Life (editors of), *Life's Picture History of World War II*.

Lockhart, Robert Bruce, *Comes the Reckoning*. London: Putnam, 1947.

Lockhart, Robert Bruce, *The Marines Were There*. London: Putnam, 1950.

Lowman, Major F. H., *Dropping into Normandy*. Oxfordshire and Bucks Light Infantry Journal, January 1951.

McDougall, Murdoch C., *Swiftly They Struck*. London: Odhams Press, 1954.

Madden, Capt. J. R., *Ex Coelis*. Canadian Army *Journal*, Vol. XI, No. 1.

Marshall, S. L. A., *Men Against Fire*. New York: William Marrow, 1947.

Millar, Ian A. L., *The Story of the Royal Canadian Corps*. Privately printed.

Monks, Noel, *Eye-Witness*. London: Frederick Muller, 1955.

Montgomery, Field Marshal Sir Bernard, *The Memoirs of Field Marshal Montgomery*. Cleveland and New York: The World Publishing Company, 1958.

Morgan, Lt. Gen. Sir Frederick, *Overture to Overlord*. London: Hodder & Stoughton, 1950.

Morison, Samuel Eliot, *The Invasion of France and Germany*. Boston: Little, Brown, 1957.

Moorehead, Alan, *Eclipse*. New York: Coward-McCann, 1945.

Munro, Ross, *Gauntlet to Overlord*. Toronto: The Macmillan Company of Canada, 1945.

Nightingale, Lt. Col. P. R., *A History of the East Yorkshire Regiment*. Privately printed.

North, John, *North-West Europe 1944-5*. London: His Majesty's Stationery Office, 1953.

Norman, Albert, *Operation Overlord*. Harrisburg, Penna.: The Military Service Publishing Co., 1952.

Otway, Col. Terence, *The Second World War, 1939-1945—Airborne Forces*. London: War Office, 1946.

Parachute Field Ambulance (members of 224), *Red Devils*. Privately printed.

Pawle, Gerald, *The Secret War*. New York: William Sloan, 1957.

Pogue, Forrest C., *The Supreme Command*. Washington, D.C.: Office of the Chief of Military History, Department of the Army, 1946.

Pyle, Ernie, *Brave Men*. New York: Henry Holt, 1944.

Rapport, Leonard, and Northwood, Arthur Jr., *Rendezvous with Destiny*. Washington, D.C.: Washington Infantry Journal Press, 1948.

Ridgway, Matthew B., *Soldier: The Memoirs of Matthew B. Ridgway*. New York: Harper & Bros., 1956.

Roberts, Derek Mills, *Clash by Night*. London: Kimber, 1956.

Royal Armoured Corps *Journal*, Vol. IV, *Anti-Invasion*. London: Gale & Polden, 1950.

Ruppenthal, R. G., *Utah to Cherbourg*. Washington, D.C.: Office of the Chief of Military History, Department of the Army, 1946.

Salmond, J. B., *The History of the 51st Highland Division, 1939-1945*. Edinburgh and London: William Blackwood & Sons, Ltd., 1953.

Saunders, Hilary St. George, *The Green Beret*. London: Michael Joseph, 1949.

Saunders, Hilary St. George, *The Red Beret*. London: Michael Joseph, 1950.

Semain, Bryan, *Commando Men*. London: Stevens & Sons, 1948.

Shulman, Milton, *Defeat in the West*. London: Secker and Warburg, 1947.

Smith, Gen. Walter Bedell (with Stewart Beach), *Eisenhower's Six Great Decisions*. New York: Longmans, Green, 1956.

Special Troops of the 4th Infantry Division, *4th Infantry Division*. Baton Rouge, La.: Army & Navy Publishing Co., 1946.

Speidel, Lt. Gen. Dr. Hans, *Invasion 1944*. Chicago: Henry Regnery, 1950.

Stacey, Col. C. P., *The Canadian Army: 1939-1945*. Ottawa: Kings Printers, 1948.

Stanford, Alfred, *Force Mulberry*. New York: William Morrow, 1951.

Story of the 79th Armoured Division, The. Hamburg. Privately printed.

Synge, Capt. W. A. T., *The Story of the Green Howards*. London. Privately printed.

Taylor, Charles H., *Omaha Beachhead*. Washington, D.C.: Office of the Chief of Military History, Department of the Army, 1946.

Von Schweppenburg, General Baron Leo Geyr, "Invasion without Laurels" in *An Cosantoir*, Vol. IX, No. 12, and Vol. X, No. 1. Dublin, 1949-50.

Waldron, Tom, and Gleeson, James, *The Frogmen*. London: Evans Bros., 1950.

Weller, George, *The Story of the Paratroops*. New York: Random House, 1958.

Wertenbaker, Charles Christian, *Invasion!* New York: D. Appleton-Century, 1944.

Wilmot, Chester, *The Struggle for Europe*. New York: Harper & Bros., 1952.

Young, Brig. Gen. Desmond, *Rommel the Desert Fox*. New York: Harper & Bros., 1950.

Bibliography

GERMAN MANUSCRIPTS AND CAPTURED DOCUMENTS

Blumentritt, Lt. Gen. Gunther, *OB West and the Normandy Campaign, 6 June–24 July 1944*, MS. B-284; *A Study in Command*, Vols. I, II, III, MS. B-344.

Dihm, Lt. Gen. Friedrich, *Rommel and the Atlantic Wall* (Dec. '43–Jul. '44), MSS. B-259, B-352, B-353.

Feuchtinger, Lt. Gen. Edgar, *21st Panzer Division in Combat Against American Troops in France and Germany*, MS. A-871.

Guderian, Gen. Heinz, *Panzer Tactics in Normandy*.

Hauser, Gen. Paul, *Seventh Army in Normandy*.

Jodl, General Alfred, *Invasion and Normandy Campaign*, MS. A-913.

Keitel, Field Marshal Wilhelm, and Jodl, General Alfred, *Answers to Questions on Normandy. The Invasion*, MS. A-915.

Pemsel, Lt. Gen. Max, *Seventh Army* (June '42–5 June '44), MS. B-234; *Seventh Army* (June 6–29 July '44), MS. B-763.

Remer, Major General Otto, *The 20 July '44 Plot Against Hitler; The Battle of the 716 Division in Normandy.* (6 June–23 June '44), MS. B-621.

Roge, Commander, *Part Played by the French Forces of the Interior During the Occupation of France, Before and After D-Day*, MS. B-035.

Rommel, Field Marshal Erwin: Captured documents—private papers, photographs and 40 letters to Mrs. Lucia Maria Rommel and son, Manfred (translated by Charles von Luttichau).

Ruge, Admiral Friedrich, *Rommel and the Atlantic Wall* (Dec. '43–July '44), MSS. A-982, B-282.

Scheidt, Wilhelm, *Hitler's Conduct of the War*, MS. ML-864.

Schramm, Major Percy E., *The West* (1 Apr. '44–16 Dec. '44), MS. B-034; *Notes on the Execution of War Diaries*, MS. A-860.

Speidel, Lt. Gen. Dr. Hans, *The Battle in Normandy: Rommel, His Generalship, His Ideas and His End*, MS. C-017; *A Study in Command*, Vols. I, II, III, MS. B-718.

Staubwasser, Lt. Col. Anton, *The Tactical Situation of the Enemy During the Normandy Battle*, MS. B-782; *Army Group B—Intelligence Estimate*, MS. B-675.

Von Buttlar, Maj. Gen. Horst, *A Study in Command*, Vols. I, II, III, MS. B-672.

Von Criegern, Friedrich, *84th Corps* (Jan. 17–June '44), MS. B-784.

Von der Heydte, Lt. Col. Baron Friedrich, *A German Parachute Regiment in Normandy*, MS. B-839.

Von Gersdorff, Maj. Gen., *A Critique of the Defense Against the Invasion*, MS. A-895. *German Defense in the Invasion*, MS. B-122.

Von Rundstedt, Field Marshal Gerd, *A Study in Command*, Vols. I, II, III, MS. B-633

Von Salmuth, General Hans, *15th Army Operations in the Normandy*, MS. B-746.

Von Schlieben, Lt. Col. Karl Wilhelm, *The German 709th Infantry Division During the Fighting in Normandy*, MS. B-845.

Von Schweppenburg, Gen. Baron Leo Geyr, *Panzer Group West* (Mid-'43–5 Jul. '44), MS. B-258.

War Diaries: Army Group B (Rommel's headquarters); OB West (Rundstedt's headquarters); Seventh Army (and Telephone Log); Fifteenth Army. All translated by Charles von Luttichau.

Warlimont, General Walter, *From the Invasion to the Siegfried Line.*

Ziegelman, Lt. Col., *History of the 352 Infantry Division*, MS. B-432.

Zimmermann, Lt. Gen. Bodo, *A Study in Command*, Vols. I, II, III, MS. B-308.

Index

340

Index

Index

Index

Index

Index

Index

Stein, Sgt. Herman, 237-38
Steinber, Pvt. Joseph, 93
Stevens, T/Sgt. Roy, 190
Stewart, Pvt. Stanley, 250
Stöbe, Col. Prof. Walter, 21, 29, 78
Streczyk, Sgt. Philip, 289
Strojny, Sgt. Raymond, 289
Strub, Germany, 255
Stunell, Pvt. George, 245
Supreme Headquarters Allied Expeditionary Force, *see* SHAEF
Svenner (Norwegian destroyer), 91, 195-96
Sweeney, Gunner's Mate 3/c William, 92
Swift (British destroyer), 196
Sword Beach, 44, 67, 90, 120, 126, 160-77, 182-83, 189, 191, 197-198, 240-42, 249-53, 260, 272, 280
Symonds, John Addington, 93

Tait, Lance Cpl. Harold, 122
Tallerday, Lt. Jack, 139
Talybont (British destroyer), 236
Tappenden, Lance Cpl. Edward, 110
Taylor, Col. George A., 290
Taylor, 2nd Lt. Herbert, 231
Taylor, Lt. John B., 242-43
Taylor, Maj. Gen. Maxwell D., 64, 98, 134-35, 138, 141, 181, 287
Tedder, Air Chief Marshal Sir Arthur William, 60-62
Tempelhof, Col. Hans George von, 19, 35, 81, 284*fn.*
Texas (U.S. battleship), 90, 198
"The dice are on the table," 85
Theen, Lt. Fritz, 115-16, 185-86, 200
Thomine, Georges, 278
Thornhill, Sgt. Avery J., 95
Tlapa, Pvt., 133*fn.*
Touchet, Col. Antoine de, 278
Touffréville, 111, 112
Tracy, 265
Tucker, P.F.C. William, 158
Turkey, 49
Tuscaloosa (U.S. cruiser), 91, 198

underground, French, 18, 32, 34, 43, 84-89, 239, 259, 273-78
U.S.S.R., 16, 21, 23, 24, 25, 88, 254-255

United Press, 248*fn.*
U.S. aid to Britain, 24
U.S. Army, Air Forces, 54, 199, 282-283
U.S. Army, historical section, 146*fn.*
U.S. Army, units of:
  Army, First, 196, 303
  battalions:
    2nd Ranger, 68, 93, 95, 133*fn.*, 190, 198, 203-4, 226-27, 236-239, 288, 290
    5th Ranger, 68, 95, 190, 198, 204, 236-39, 288, 290
    112th Engineer, 95
    146th Engineer, 92
    299th Engineer Combat, 227
    741st Tank, 206, 230
  brigades:
    1st Engineer Special, 195, 205, 231, 233
    5th Engineer Special, 69, 95
    6th Engineer Special, 229
  divisions:
    1st Infantry, 68-69, 92, 93, 95, 193, 197, 201, 205, 206, 208, 227, 228, 280, 282, 289-91
    4th Infantry, 38, 67, 69, 77, 92, 134, 135, 192, 193, 203, 205, 230-33, 273, 285-88
    29th Infantry, 70, 92, 94, 95, 190-194, 197, 206, 208, 225, 227, 237, 281, 289, 291
    82nd Airborne, 57, 63, 87, 97, 104, 105, 130-40, 142, 143, 156-57, 232, 270, 273, 282, 300, 303
    90th Infantry, 286*fn.*
    101st Airborne, 57, 64, 87, 98, 105, 106, 130-39, 141, 155-57, 232, 286-87, 303
  regiments:
    8th Infantry, 205, 232
    12th Infantry, 92, 286
    16th Infantry, 93, 193, 290
    116th Infantry, 193, 281, 289
    505th Parachute, 104, 133, 135, 136, 157, 158, 282
    506th Parachute, 130
  squadrons:
    4th Cavalry, 159
    24th Cavalry, 159
U.S. Coast Guard, 70, 90, 92, 204
U.S. Navy, 38, 144, 149, 235

349

Index

ABOUT THE AUTHOR

CORNELIUS RYAN *was born and educated in Dublin, Ireland. He is thirty-eight years old and has been writing for the last eighteen years. He was a senior writer on* Collier's *staff when the magazine went out of business in December 1956. He had been with the magazine for more than six years and handled nearly all of their special projects.*

In 1956 Ryan won the principal Benjamin Franklin Award for his memorable stories on the sinking of the Andrea Doria *("Five Desperate Hours in Cabin 56"—*Reader's Digest *condensation, December 1956) and "One Minute to Ditch," the story of the ditching of a trans-Pacific airliner carrying thirty-six passengers. He also received an Overseas Press Club award for the same stories, and they appeared in book form in 1957 under the title* One Minute to Ditch.

Ryan was trained in London's Fleet Street, first with Reuter's and then the London Daily Telegraph. *As a war correspondent he flew fourteen bombing missions with the Eighth and Ninth U.S. air forces, covered the D-Day landings and General Patton's Third Army in its race across France and Germany. In April of 1945 he was sent to the Far East to cover the end of hostilities there. After the war he covered the Bikini atom-bomb tests, Central America, the Middle East and Europe for the* Telegraph *and as a "stringer" for* Time. *In 1947 he moved permanently to the U.S. and was invited to join Time, Inc. He became a naturalized American in June 1950. He is married to the former Kathryn Ann*

Morgan (she's an associate editor for Time, Inc.'s House & Home*).*

In the eighteen years he has been writing, a flood of material has come out of his typewriter. He has written plays, movie scripts, radio and TV scripts and some seventy major magazine pieces. The Longest Day *is his sixth book.*

He has one brother living in the United States. His mother and three other brothers live in Dublin, Ireland.

DATE DUE

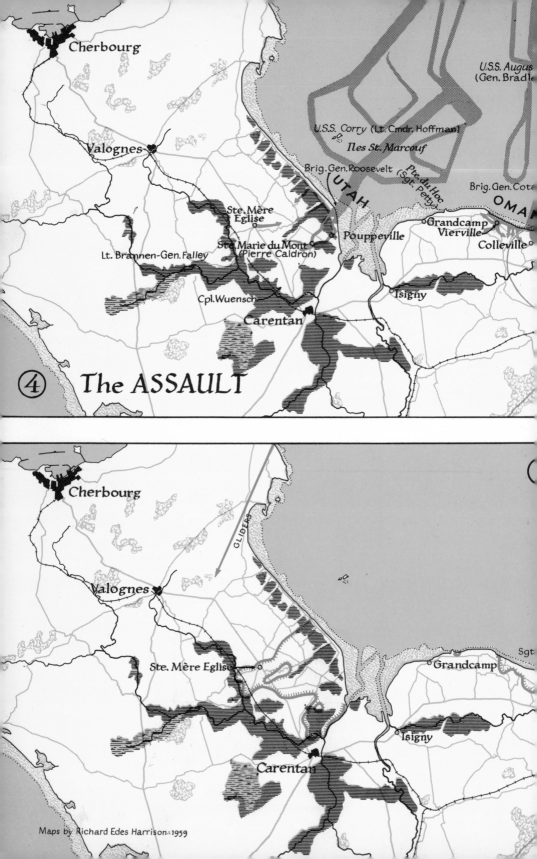

Cherbourg

Valognes

U.S.S. Augus
(Gen. Bradl

U.S.S. Corry (Lt. Cmdr. Hoffman)
Iles St. Marcouf

Brig. Gen. Roosevelt
Pte. du Hoc
(Sgt. Petty)

UTAH

Brig. Gen. Cote

OMA

Ste. Mère
Eglise

Grandcamp
Vierville

Pouppeville

Colleville

Ste. Marie du Mont
(Pierre Caldron)

Lt. Brannen-Gen. Falley

Isigny

Cpl. Wuensch

Carentan

④ The ASSAULT

Cherbourg

GLIDERS

Valognes

Ste. Mère Eglise

Grandcamp

Sgt

Isigny

Carentan

Maps by Richard Edes Harrison·1959